FROM
SURFACES
TO
OBJECTS

FROM SURFACES TO OBJECTS

COMPUTER VISION AND THREE DIMENSIONAL SCENE ANALYSIS

ROBERT B. FISHER

Department of Artificial Intelligence,
University of Edinburgh,
Edinburgh, UK

JOHN WILEY & SONS

Chichester · New York · Brisbane · Toronto · Singapore

John Wiley & Sons Ltd, Baffins Lane, Chichester,
West Sussex PO19 1UD, England

Other Wiley Editorial Offices

John Wiley & Sons, Inc., 605 Third Avenue,
New York, NY 10158-0012, USA

Jacaranda Wiley Ltd, G.P.O. Box 859, Brisbane,
Queensland 4001, Australia

John Wiley & Sons (Canada) Ltd, 22 Worcester Road,
Rexdale, Ontario M9W 1L1, Canada

John Wiley & Sons (SEA) Pte Ltd, 37 Jalan Pemimpin   05-04,
Block B, Union Industrial Building, Singapore 2057

British Library Cataloguing in Publication Data available

ISBN 0 471 92344 3

Printed and bound in Great Britain by Courier International, Tiptree, Essex

CONTENTS

LIST OF FIGURES

PREFACE

Three dimensional scene analysis has reached a turning point. Though researchers have been investigating object recognition and scene understanding since the late 1960's, a new excitement can be felt in the field. I attribute this to four converging activities: (1) the increasing popularity and successes of stereo and active range sensing systems, (2) the set of emerging tools and competences concerned with three dimensional surface shape and its meaningful segmentation and description, (3) Marr's attempt to place three dimensional vision into a more integrated and scientific context and (4) Brooks' demonstration of what a more intelligent three dimensional scene understander might entail. It is the convergence of these that has led to the problem considered in this book: "Assuming that we have easily accessible surface data and can segment it into useful patches, what can we then do with it?". The work presented here takes an integrated view of the problems and demonstrates that recognition can actually be done.

The central message of this book is that surface information can greatly simplify the image understanding process. This is because surfaces are the features that directly link perception to the objects perceived (for normal "camera-like" sensing) and because they make explicit information needed to understand and cope with some visual problems (e.g. obscured features).

Hence, this book is as much about a style of model-based three dimensional scene analysis as about a particular example of that style. That style combines surface patches segmented from the three dimensional scene description, surface patch based object models, a hierarchy of representations, models and recognitions, a distributed network-based model invocation process, and a knowledge-based model matcher. Part of what I have tried to do was show that these elements really do fit together well – they make it easy to extend the competence of current vision systems without extraordinary complications, and don't we all know how fragile complicated computer-based processes are?

This book is an organic entity – the research described started in 1982 and earlier results were reported in a PhD thesis in 1985. Since then, research has continued under the United Kingdom Alvey program, replacing weak results and extending into new areas, and most of the new results are included here. Some of the processes are still fairly simple and need further development, particularly when working with automatically segmented data. Thus, this book is really just a "progress report" and its content will continue to evolve. In a way, I hope that I will be able to rewrite the book in five to ten years, reporting that all problems have been solved by the computer vision community and showing that generic three dimensional object recognition can now be done. Who knows?

The book divides naturally into three parts. Chapters three to six describe the model independent scene analysis. The middle chapters, seven and eight, describe how objects are represented and selected, and thus how one can pass from an iconic to a symbolic scene representation. The final chapters then describe our approach to geometric model-based vision – how to locate, verify and understand a known object given its geometric model.

There are many people I would like to thank for their help with the work and the book. Each year there are a few more people I have had the pleasure of working and sharing ideas with. I feel awkward about ranking people by the amount or the quality of the help given, so I will not do that. I would rather bring them all together for a party (and if enough people buy this book I'll be able to afford it). The people who would be invited to the party are: (for academic advice) Damal Arvind, Jon Aylett, Bob Beattie, Li Dong Cai, Mike Cameron-Jones, Wayne Caplinger, John Hallam, David Hogg, Jim Howe, Howard Hughes, Zi Qing Li, Mark Orr, Ben Paechter, Fritz Seytter, Manuel Trucco, (and for help with the materials) Paul Brna, Douglas Howie, Doug Ramm, David Robertson, Julian Smart, Lincoln Wallen and David Wyse and, of course, Gaynor Redvers-Mutton and the staff at John Wiley & Sons, Ltd. for their confidence and support.

Well, I take it back. I would particularly like to thank Mies for her love, support and assistance. I'd also like to thank the University of Edinburgh, the Alvey Programme, my mother and Jeff Mallory for their financial support, without which this work could not have been completed.

CHAPTER 1

An Introduction to Recognition Using Surfaces

The surface is the boundary between object and non-object and is the usual source and limit of perception. As such, it is the feature that unifies most significant forms of non-invasive sensing, including the optical, sonar, radar and tactile modalities in both active and passive forms. The presence of the surface (including its location) is the primary fact. Perceived intensity is secondary – it informs on the appearance of the surface as seen by the viewer and is affected by the illumination and the composition of the surface.

Grimson, in his celebrated book "From Images to Surfaces: A Computational Study of the Human Early Visual System" [GRI81], described an elegant approach to constructing a surface representation of a scene, starting from a stereo pair of intensity images. The approach, based substantially on Marr's ideas [MAR82], triangulated paired image features (e.g. edge fragments) to produce a sparse depth image, and then reconstructed a complete surface, giving a dense depth image. Though this is not the only way to acquire such a surface description, (e.g. laser ranging and structured light are practical alternatives), there have been only a few attempts at exploiting this rich data for object recognition.

Previous research in object recognition has developed theories for recognizing simple objects completely, or complex objects incompletely. With the knowledge of the "visible" surfaces of the scene, the complete identification and location of more complex objects can be inferred and verified, which is the topic of this book. Starting from a full surface representation, we will look at new approaches to making the transformation from surfaces to objects. The main results, as implemented in the **IMAGINE I** program, are:

- Surface information directly provides three dimensional cues for surface grouping, leading to a volumetric description of the objects in the scene.

- Structural properties can be directly estimated from the three dimensional data, rather than from two dimensional projections.

- These properties plus the generic and structural relationships in the model base can be used to directly invoke models to explain the data.

- Using surfaces as both the model and data primitive allows direct prediction of visibility relationships, surface matching, prediction and analysis of occlusion and verification of identity.

1

- Moderately complex non-rigidly connected structures can be thoroughly recognized, spatially located and verified.

1.1   Object Recognition

The following definition is proposed:

> Three dimensional object recognition is the identification of a model structure with a set of image data, such that geometrically consistent model-to-data correspondences are established and the object's three dimensional scene position is known. All model features should be fully accounted for – by having consistent image evidence either supporting their presence or explaining their absence.

Hence, recognition produces a symbolic assertion about an object, its location and the use of image features as evidence. The matched features must have the correct types, be in the right places and belong to a single, distinct object. Otherwise, though the data might resemble those from the object, the object is improperly assumed and is not at the proposed location.

Traditional object recognition programs satisfy weaker versions of the above definition. The most common simplification comes from the assumption of a small, well-characterized, object domain. There, identification can be achieved via discrimination using simply measured image features, such as object color or two dimensional perimeter or the position of a few linear features. This is identification, but not true recognition (i.e. image understanding).

Recognition based on direct comparison between two dimensional image and model structures – notably through matching boundary sections – has been successful with both grey scale and binary images of flat, isolated, moderately complicated industrial parts. It is simple, allowing geometric predictions and derivations of object location and orientation and tolerating a limited amount of noise. This method is a true recognition of the objects – all features of the model are accounted for and the object's spatial location is determined.

Some research has started on recognizing three dimensional objects, but with less success. Model edges have been matched to image edges (with both two and three dimensional data) while simultaneously extracting the position parameters of the modeled objects. In polyhedral scenes, recognition is generally complete, but otherwise only a few features are found. The limits of the edge-based approach are fourfold:

1. It is hard to get reliable, repeatable and accurate edge information from an intensity image.

2. There is much ambiguity in the interpretation of edge features as shadow, reflectance, orientation, highlight or obscuring edges.

3. The amount of edge information present in a realistic intensity image is overwhelming and largely unorganizable for matching, given current theories.

4. The edge-based model is too simple to deal with scenes involving curved surfaces.

Because of these deficiencies, model-based vision has started to exploit the richer information available in surface data.

Surface Data

In the last decade, low-level vision research has been working towards direct deduction and representation of scene properties – notably surface depth and orientation. The sources include stereo, optical flow, laser or sonar range finding, surface shading, surface or image contours and various forms of structured lighting.

The most well-developed of the surface representations is the $2\frac{1}{2}$D sketch advocated by Marr [MAR82]. The sketch represents local depth and orientation for the surfaces, and labels detected surface boundaries as being from shape or depth discontinuities. The exact details of this representation and its acquisition are still being researched, but its advantages seem clear enough. Results suggest that surface information reduces data complexity and interpretation ambiguity, while increasing the structural matching information.

The richness of the data in a surface representation, as well as its imminent availability, offers hope for real advances beyond the current practical understanding of largely polyhedral scenes. Distance, orientation and image geometry enable a reasonable reconstruction of the three dimensional shape of the object's visible surfaces, and the boundaries lead to a figure/ground separation. Because it is possible to segment and characterize the surfaces, more compact symbolic representations are feasible. These symbolic structures have the same relation to the surface information as edges currently do to intensity information, except that their scene interpretation is unambiguous. If there were:

- reasonable criteria for segmenting both the image surfaces and models,

- simple processes for selecting the models and relating them to the data and

- an understanding of how all these must be modified to account for factors in realistic scenes (including occlusion)

then object recognition could make significant advances.

The Research Undertaken

The goal of object recognition, as defined above, is the complete matching of model to image structures, with the concomitant extraction of position information. Hence, the output of recognition is a set of fully instantiated or explained object hypotheses positioned in three dimensions, which are suitable for reconstructing the object's appearance.

The research described here tried to attain these goals for moderately complex scenes containing multiple self-obscuring objects. To fully recognize the objects, it was necessary to develop criteria and practical methods for:

- piecing together surfaces fragmented by occlusion,

- grouping surfaces into volumes that might be identifiable objects,

- describing properties of three dimensional structures,

- selecting models from a moderately sized model base,

- pairing model features to data features and extracting position estimates and

- predicting and verifying the absence of model features because of variations of viewpoint.

The approach requires object models composed of a set of surfaces geometrically related in three dimensions (either directly or through subcomponents). For each model SURFACE, recognition finds those image surfaces that consistently match it, or evidence for their absence (e.g. obscuring structure). The model and image surfaces must agree in location and orientation, and have about the same shape and size, with variations allowed for partially obscured surfaces. When surfaces are completely obscured, evidence for their existence comes either from predicting self-occlusion from the location and orientation of the model, or from finding closer, unrelated obscuring surfaces.

The object representation requires the complete object surface to be segmentable into what would intuitively be considered distinct surface regions. These are what will now be generally called surfaces (except where there is confusion with the whole object's surface). When considering a cube, the six faces are logical candidates for the surfaces; unfortunately, most natural structures are not so simple. The segmentation assumption presumes that the object can be decomposed into rigid substructures (though possibly non-rigidly joined), and that the rigid substructures can be uniquely segmented into surfaces of roughly constant character, defined by their two principal curvatures. It is also assumed that the image surfaces will segment in correspondence with the model SURFACEs, though if the segmentation criteria is object-based, then the model and data segmentations should be similar. (The SURFACE is the primitive model feature, and represents a surface patch.) Of course, these assumptions are simplistic because surface deformation and object variations lead to alternative segmentations, but a start must be made somewhere.

The three models used in the research are: a trash can, a classroom chair, and portions of a PUMA robot. The major common feature of these objects is the presence of regular distinct surfaces uncluttered by shape texture, when considered at a "human" interpretation scale. The objects were partly chosen for experimental convenience, but also to test most of the theories proposed here. The models are shown in typical views in Chapter 7. Some of the distinctive features of each object and their implications on recognition are:

- trash can:

  * laminar surfaces – surface grouping difficulties

  * rotational symmetry – surface segmentation and multiple recognitions

- chair:

  * convex and concave curved surfaces (seat back) – surface grouping difficulties

  * thin cylindrical surfaces (legs) – data scale incompatible with model scale

- robot:

  * surface blending – non-polyhedral segmentation relationships

  * non-rigidly connected subcomponents – unpredictable reference frame relationships and self-occlusions

These objects were viewed in semi-cluttered laboratory scenes that contained both obscured and unobscured views (example in the next section). Using an intensity image to register all data, nominal depth and surface orientation values were measured by hand at about one hundred points. Values at other nearby points in the images were calculated by interpolation. Obscuring and shape segmentation boundaries were selected by hand to avoid unresolved research problems of segmentation, scale and data errors. No fully developed processes produce these segmentations yet, but several processes are likely to produce them data in the near future and assuming such segmentations were possible to allowed us to concentrate on the primary issues of representation and recognition.

1.2   An Overview of the Research

This section summarizes the work discussed in the rest of the book by presenting an example of **IMAGINE I**'s surface-based object recognition [FIS86b]. The test image discussed in the following example is shown in Figure 1.1. The key features of the scene include:

- variety of surface shapes and curvature classes,

- solids connected with rotational degrees-of-freedom,

- partially and completely self-obscured structure,

- externally obscured structure,

- structure broken up by occlusion and

- intermingled objects.

Recognition is based on comparing observed and deduced properties with those of a prototypical model. This definition immediately introduces five subtasks for the complete recognition process:

- finding the structures that have the properties,

- acquiring the data properties,

- selecting a model for comparison,

- comparing the data with the model structures and properties, and

- discovering or justifying any missing structures.

Figure 1.1: Test Scene

The deduction process needs the location and orientation of the object to predict obscured structures and their properties, so this adds:

- estimating the object's location and orientation.

This, in turn, is based on inverting the geometric relationships between data and model structures, which adds:

- making model-to-data correspondences.

The remainder of this section elaborates on the processes and the data flow dependencies that constrain their mutual relationship in the complete recognition computation context. Figure 1.2 shows the process sequence determined by the constraints, and is discussed in more detail below.

Surface Image Inputs

Recognition starts from surface data, as represented in a structure called a labeled, segmented surface image (Chapter 3). This structure is like Marr's $2\frac{1}{2}$D sketch and includes a pointillistic representation of absolute depth and local surface orientation.

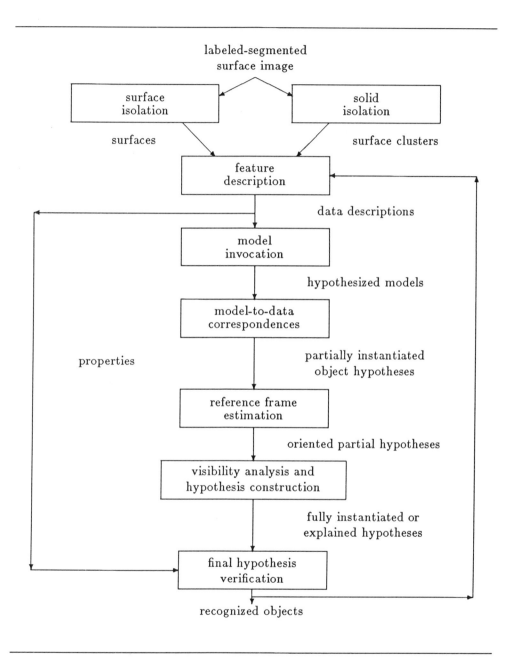

Figure 1.2: Sequence of Recognition Process Subtasks

Figure 1.3: Depth Values for the Test Scene

Data segmentation and organization are both difficult and important. Their primary justifications are that segmentation highlights the relevant features for the rest of the recognition process and organization produces, in a sense, a figure/ground separation. Properties between unrelated structure should not be computed, such as the angle between surface patches on separate objects. Otherwise, coincidences will invoke and possibly substantiate non-existent objects. Here, the raw data is segmented into regions by boundary segments labeled as shape or obscuring. Shape segmentation is based on orientation, curvature magnitude and curvature direction discontinuities. Obscuring boundaries are placed at depth discontinuities. These criteria segment the surface image into regions of nearly uniform shape, characterized by the two principal curvatures and the surface boundary. As no fully developed processes produce this data yet, the example input is from a computer augmented, hand-segmented test image. The segmentation boundaries were found by hand and the depth and orientation values were interpolated within each region from a few measured values.

The inputs used to analyze the test scene shown in Figure 1.1 are shown in Figures 1.3 to 1.6. Figure 1.3 shows the depth values associated with the scene, where the lighter values mean closer points. Figure 1.4 shows the cosine of the surface slant for each image point. Figure 1.5 shows the obscuring boundaries. Figure 1.6 shows the shape segmentation boundaries. From these pictures, one can get the general impression of the rich data available and the three dimensional character of the scene.

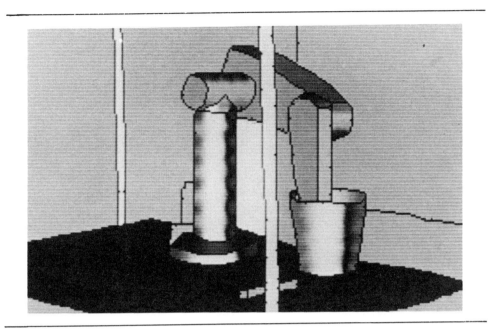

Figure 1.4: Cosine of Surface Slant for the Test Scene

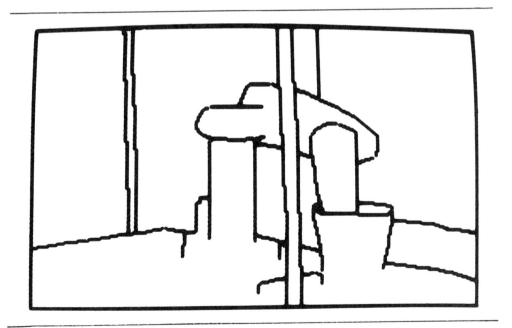

Figure 1.5: Obscuring Boundaries for the Test Scene

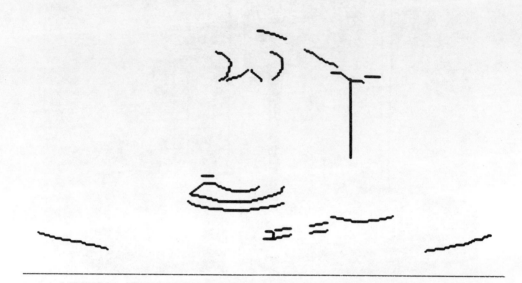

Figure 1.6: Shape Segmentation Boundaries for the Test Scene

Complete Surface Hypotheses

Image segmentation leads directly to partial or complete object surface segments. Surface completion processes (Chapter 4) reconstruct obscured portions of surfaces, when possible, by connecting extrapolated surface boundaries behind obscuring surfaces. The advantage of this is twofold: it provides data surfaces more like the original object surface for property extraction and gives better image evidence during hypothesis construction. Two processes are used for completing surface hypotheses. The first bridges gaps in single surfaces and the second links two separated surface patches. Merged surface segments must have roughly the same depth, orientation and surface characterization. Because the reconstruction is based on three dimensional surface image data, it is more reliable than previous work that used only two dimensional image boundaries. Figure 1.7 illustrates both rules in showing the original and reconstructed robot upper arm large surface from the test image.

Surface Clusters

Surface hypotheses are joined to form surface clusters, which are blob-like three dimensional object-centered representations (Chapter 5). The goal of this process is to partition the scene into a set of three dimensional solids, without yet knowing their identities. Surface clusters are useful (here) for aggregating image features into contexts for model invocation and matching. They would also be useful for tasks where identity is not necessary, such as collision avoidance.

Figure 1.7: Original and Reconstructed Robot Upper Arm Surface

A surface cluster is formed by finding closed loops of isolating boundary segments. The goal of this process is to create a blob-like solid that encompasses all and only the features associated with a single object. This strengthens the evidence accumulation used in model invocation and limits combinatorial matching during hypothesis construction. Obscuring and concave surface orientation discontinuity boundaries generally isolate solids, but an exception is for laminar objects, where the obscuring boundary across the front lip of the trash can (Figure 1.8) does not isolate the surfaces. These criteria determine the primitive surface clusters. A hierarchy of larger surface clusters are formed from equivalent depth and depth merged surface clusters, based on depth ordering relationships. They become larger contexts within which partially self-obscured structure or subcomponents can be found. Figure 1.8 shows some of the primitive surface clusters for the test scene. The clusters correspond directly to primitive model ASSEMBLYs (which represent complete object models).

Three Dimensional Feature Description

General identity-independent properties (Chapter 6) are used to drive the invocation process to suggest object identities, which trigger the model-directed matching processes. Later, these properties are used to ensure that model-to-data surface pairings are correct. The use of three dimensional information from the surface image makes it possible to compute many object properties directly (as compared to computing them from a two dimensional projection of three dimensional data).

This task uses the surfaces and surface clusters produced by the segmentation processes. Surface and boundary shapes are the key properties for surfaces. Relative feature sizes, spatial relationships and adjacency are the properties needed for solid recognition. Most of the measured properties relate to surface patches and include: local curvature, absolute area, elongation and surface intersection angles. As an example, Table 1.1 lists the estimated properties for the robot shoulder circular end panel (region 26 in Figure 3.10).

Surface-Based Object Representation

The modeled objects (Chapter 7) are compact, connected solids with definable shapes, where the complete surfaces are rigid and segmentable into regions of constant local shape. The objects may also have subcomponents joined by interconnections with degrees-of-freedom.

Identification requires known object representations with three components: a geometric model, constraints on object properties, and a set of inter-object relationships.

The SURFACE patch is the model primitive, because surfaces are the primary data units. This allows direct pairing of data with models, comparison of surface shapes and estimation of model-to-data transformation parameters. SURFACEs are described by their principal curvatures with zero, one or two curvature axes, and by their extent (i.e. boundary). The segmentation ensures that the shape (e.g. principal curvatures) remains relatively constant over the entire SURFACE.

Larger objects (called ASSEMBLYs) are recursively constructed from SURFACEs or other ASSEMBLYs using coordinate reference frame transformations. Each structure has its own local reference frame and larger structures are constructed by placing the

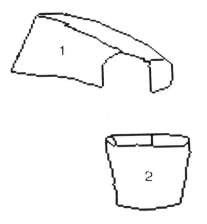

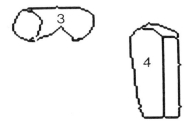

Figure 1.8: Some Surface Clusters for the Test Scene

Table 1.1: Properties of Robot Shoulder End Panel

PROPERTY	ESTIMATED	TRUE
maximum surface curvature	0.0	0.0
minimum surface curvature	0.0	0.0
absolute area	165	201
relative area	0.24	0.25
surface size eccentricity	1.4	1.0
adjacent surface angle	1.47	1.57
number of parallel boundaries	1	1
boundary curve length	22.5	25.1
boundary curve length	25.3	25.1
boundary curvature	0.145	0.125
boundary curvature	0.141	0.125
number of straight segments	0	0
number of arc segments	2	2
number of equal segments	1	1
number of right angles	0	0
boundary relative orientation	3.14	3.14
boundary relative orientation	3.14	3.14

subcomponents in the reference frame of the aggregate. Partially constrained transformations can connect subcomponents by using variables in the attachment relationship. This was used for the PUMA robot's joints. The geometric relationship between structures is useful for making model-to-data assignments and for providing the adjacency and relative placement information used by verification.

The three major object models used in this analysis are the PUMA robot, chair and trash can. (These models required the definition of 25 SURFACEs and 14 ASSEM-BLYs.) A portion of the robot model definition is shown below.

Illustrated first is the SURFACE definition for the robot upper arm large curved end panel (uendb). The first triple on each line gives the starting endpoint for a boundary segment. The last item describes the segment as a LINE or a CURVE (with its parameters in brackets). PO means the segmentation point is a boundary orientation discontinuity point and BO means the boundary occurs at an orientation discontinuity between the surfaces. The next to last line describes the surface type with its axis of curvature and radii. The final line gives the surface normal at a nominal point in the SURFACE's reference frame.

```
SURFACE uendb = PO/(0,0,0) BO/LINE
                PO/(10,0,0) BO/CURVE[0,0,-22.42]
                PO/(10,29.8,0) BO/LINE
                PO/(0,29.8,0) BO/CURVE[0,0,-22.42]
                CYLINDER [(0,14.9,16.75),(10,14.9,16.75),22.42,22.42]
                NORMAL AT (5,15,-5.67) = (0,0,-1);
```

Illustrated next is the rigid upperarm ASSEMBLY with its SURFACEs (e.g. uendb) and the reference frame relationships between them. The first triple in the relationship is the (x, y, z) translation and the second gives the (rotation, slant, tilt) rotation. Translation is applied after rotation.

```
    ASSEMBLY upperarm=
                    uside AT ((-17,-14.9,-10),(0,0,0))
                    uside AT ((-17,14.9,0),(0,π,π/2))
                    uendb AT ((-17,-14.9,0),(0,π/2,π))
                    uends AT ((44.8,-7.5,-10),(0,π/2,0))
                    uedges AT ((-17,-14.9,0),(0,π/2,3π/2))
                    uedges AT ((-17,14.9,-10),(0,π/2,π/2))
                    uedgeb AT ((2.6,-14.9,0),(0.173,π/2,3π/2))
                    uedgeb AT ((2.6,14.9,-10),(6.11,π/2,π/2));
```

The ASSEMBLY that pairs the upper and lower arm rigid structures into a non-rigidly connected structure is defined now. Here, the lower arm has an affixment parameter that defines the joint angle in the ASSEMBLY.

```
        ASSEMBLY armasm=
                    upperarm AT ((0,0,0),(0,0,0))
                    lowerarm AT ((43.5,0,0),(0,0,0))
                    FLEX ((0,0,0),(jnt3,0,0));
```

Figure 1.9 shows an image of the whole robot ASSEMBLY with the surfaces shaded according to surface orientation.

Property constraints are the basis for direct evidence in the model invocation process and for identity verification. These constraints give the tolerances on properties associated with the structures, and the importance of the property in contributing towards invocation. Some of the constraints associated with the robot shoulder end panel named "robshldend" are given below (slightly re-written from the model form for readability). The first constraint says that the relative area of the robshldend in the context of a surface cluster (i.e. the robot shoulder) should lie between 11% and 40%

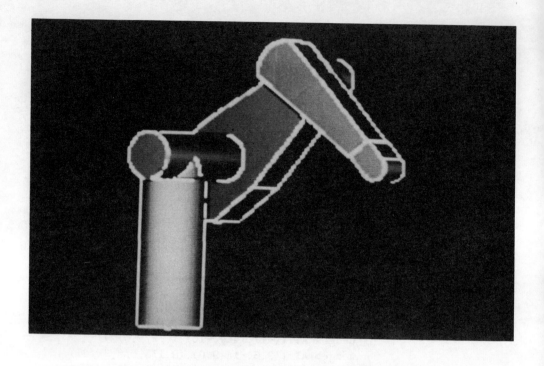

Figure 1.9: Shaded View of Robot Model

with a peak value of 25%, and the weighting of any evidence meeting this constraint is 0.5.

```
UNARYEVID 0.11 < relative_area < 0.40 PEAK 0.25 WEIGHT 0.5;
UNARYEVID 156.0 < absolute_area < 248.0 PEAK 201.0 WEIGHT 0.5;
UNARYEVID 0.9 < elongation < 1.5 PEAK 1.0 WEIGHT 0.5;
UNARYEVID 0 < parallel_boundary_segments < 2 PEAK 1 WEIGHT 0.3;
UNARYEVID 20.1 < boundary_length < 40.0 PEAK 25.1 WEIGHT 0.5;
UNARYEVID .08 < boundary_curvature < .15 PEAK .125 WEIGHT 0.5;
BINARYEVID 3.04 < boundary_relative_orientation(edge1,edge2)
                < 3.24 PEAK 3.14 WEIGHT 0.5;
```

Rather than specifying all of an object's properties, it is possible to specify some descriptive attributes, such as "flat". This means that the so-described object is an instance of type "flat" – that is, "surfaces without curvature". There is a hierarchy of such descriptions: the description "circle" given below is a specialization of "flat". For robshldend, there are two descriptions: circular, and that it meets other surfaces at right angles:

```
DESCRIPTION OF robshldend IS circle 3.0;
DESCRIPTION OF robshldend IS sapiby2b 1.0;
```

Relationships between objects define a network used to accumulate invocation evidence. Between each pair of model structures, seven types of relationship may occur: subcomponent, supercomponent, subclass, superclass, descriptive, general association and inhibition. The model base defines those that are significant to each model by listing the related models, the type of relationship and the strength of association. The other relationship for robshldend is:

```
SUPERCOMPONENT OF robshldend IS robshldbd 0.10;
```

Evidence for subcomponents comes in visibility groups (i.e. subsets of all object features), because typically only a few of an object's features are visible from any particular viewpoint. While they could be deduced computationally (at great expense), the visibility groups are given explicitly here. The upperarm ASSEMBLY has two distinguished views, differing by whether the big (uendb) or small (uends) curved end section is seen.

```
SUBCGRP OF upperarm = uside uends uedgeb uedges;
SUBCGRP OF upperarm = uside uendb uedgeb uedges;
```

Model Invocation

Model invocation (Chapter 8) links the identity-independent processing to the model-directed processing by selecting candidate models for further consideration. It is essential because of the impossibility of selecting the correct model by sequential direct comparison with all known objects. These models have to be selected through suggestion because: (a) exact individual models may not exist (object variation or generic description) and (b) object flaws, sensor noise and data loss lead to inexact model-to-data matchings.

Model invocation is the purest embodiment of recognition – the inference of identity. Its outputs depend on its inputs, but need not be verified or verifiable for the visual system to report results. Because we are interested in precise object recognition here, what follows after invocation is merely verification of the proposed hypothesis: the finding of evidence and ensuring of consistency.

Invocation is based on plausibility, rather than certainty, and this notion is expressed through accumulating various types of evidence for objects in an associative network.

When the plausibility of a structure having a given identity is high enough, a model is invoked.

Plausibility accumulates from property and relationship evidence, which allows graceful degradation from erroneous data. Property evidence is obtained when data properties satisfy the model evidence constraints. Each relevant description contributes direct evidence in proportion to a weight factor (emphasizing its importance) and the degree that the evidence fits the constraints. When the data values from Table 1.1 are associated with the evidence constraints given above, the resulting property evidence plausibility for the robshldend panel is 0.57 in the range [-1,1].

Relationship evidence arises from conceptual associations with other structures and identifications. In the test scene, the most important relationships are supercomponent and subcomponent, because of the structured nature of the objects. Generic descriptions are also used: robshldend is also a "circle". Inhibitory evidence comes from competing identities. The modeled relationships for robshldend were given above. The evidence for the robshldend model was:

- property: 0.57

- supercomponent (robshould): 0.50

- description (circle, sapiby2b):0.90

- inhibition: none

No inhibition was received because there were no competing identities with sufficiently high plausibility. All evidence types are combined (with weighting) to give an integrated evidence value, which was 0.76.

Plausibility is only associated with the model being considered and a context; otherwise, models would be invoked for unlikely structures. In other words, invocation must localize its actions to some context inside which all relevant data and structure must be found. The evidence for these structures accumulates within a context appropriate to the type of structure:

- individual model SURFACEs are invoked in a surface hypothesis context,

- SURFACEs associate to form an ASSEMBLY in a surface cluster context, and

- ASSEMBLYs associate in a surface cluster context.

The most plausible context for invoking the upper arm ASSEMBLY model was blob 1 in Figure 1.8, which is correct.

The invocation computation accumulates plausibility in a relational network of {context} × {identity} nodes linked to each other by relationship arcs and linked to the data by the property constraints. The lower level nodes in this network are general object structures, such as planes, positive cylinders or right angle surface junctions. From these, higher level object structures are linked hierarchically. In this way, plausibility accumulates upwardly from simple to more complex structures. This structuring provides both richness in discrimination through added detail, and efficiency of association (i.e. a structure need link only to the most compact levels of subdescription). Though every model must ultimately be a candidate for every image structure, the network formulation achieves efficiency through judicious selection of appropriate conceptual units and computing plausibility over the entire network in parallel.

When applied to the full test scene, invocation was generally successful. There were 21 SURFACE invocations of 475 possible, of which 10 were correct, 5 were justified because of similarity and 6 were unjustified. There were 18 ASSEMBLY invocations of 288 possible, of which 10 were correct, 3 were justified because of similarity and 5 were unjustified.

Hypothesis Construction

Hypothesis construction (Chapter 9) aims for full object recognition, by finding evidence for all model features. Invocation provides the model-to-data correspondences to form the initial hypothesis. Invocation thus eliminates most substructure search by directly pairing features. SURFACE correspondences are immediate because there is only one type of data element – the surface. Solid correspondences are also trivial because the matched substructures (SURFACEs or previously recognized ASSEMBLYs) are also typed and are generally unique within the particular model. All other data must come from within the local surface cluster context.

The estimation of the ASSEMBLY and SURFACE reference frames is one goal of hypothesis construction. The position estimate can then be used for making detailed metrical predictions during feature detection and occlusion analysis (below).

Object orientation is estimated by transforming the nominal orientations of pairs of model surface vectors to corresponding image surface vectors. Pairs are used because a single vector allows a remaining degree of rotational freedom. Surface normals and curvature axes are the two types of surface vectors used. Translation is estimated from matching oriented model SURFACEs to image displacements and depth data. The spatial relationships between structures are constrained by the geometric relationships of the model and inconsistent results imply an inappropriate invocation or feature pairing.

Because of data errors, the six degrees of spatial freedom are represented as parameter ranges. Each new model-to-data feature pairing contributes new spatial information, which helps further constrain the parameter range. Previously recognized substructures also constrain object position.

The robot's position and joint angle estimates were also found using a geometric reasoning network approach [FIS88]. Based partly on the SUP/INF methods used in ACRONYM [BRO81], algebraic inequalities that defined the relationships between model and data feature positions were used to compile a value-passing network. The network calculated upper and lower bounds on the (e.g.) position values by propagating calculated values through the network. This resulted in tighter position and joint angle estimates than achieved by the vector pairing approach.

Table 1.2 lists the measured and estimated location positions, orientations and joint angles for the robot. The test data was obtained from about 500 centimeters distance. As can be seen, the translations were estimated well, but the rotations were more inaccurate. This was because of:

Table 1.2: Measured and Estimated Spatial Parameters

PARAMETER	MEASURED	ESTIMATED
X	488 (cm)	487 (cm)
Y	89 (cm)	87 (cm)
Z	554 (cm)	550 (cm)
Rotation	0.0 (rad)	0.04 (rad)
Slant	0.793 (rad)	0.70 (rad)
Tilt	3.14 (rad)	2.97 (rad)
Joint 1	2.24 (rad)	2.21 (rad)
Joint 2	2.82 (rad)	2.88 (rad)
Joint 3	4.94 (rad)	4.57 (rad)

- insufficient surface evidence to better constrain the position of individual AS-SEMBLYs, and

- inadequacies in the geometric reasoning method, when integrating multiple AS-SEMBLYs with degrees-of-freedom.

Once position is estimated, a variety of model-driven processes contribute to completing an oriented hypothesis. They are, in order:

1. infer back-facing SURFACEs

2. infer tangential SURFACEs

3. predict visibility of remaining SURFACEs

4. search for missing visible SURFACEs

5. bind rigidly connected ASSEMBLYs

6. bind non-rigidly connected ASSEMBLYs

7. explain some incorrectly segmented SURFACEs

8. validate externally obscured structure

Hypothesis construction has a "hierarchical synthesis" character, where data surfaces are paired with model SURFACEs, surface groups are matched to ASSEMBLYs and ASSEMBLYs are matched to larger ASSEMBLYs. The three key constraints on the matching are: localization in the correct image context (i.e. surface cluster), correct feature identities and consistent geometric reference frame relationships.

Joining together two non-rigidly connected subassemblies also gives the values of the variable attachment parameters by unifying the respective reference frame descriptions. The attachment parameters must also meet any specified constraints, such as limits on joint angles in the robot model. For the robot upper and lower arm, the joint

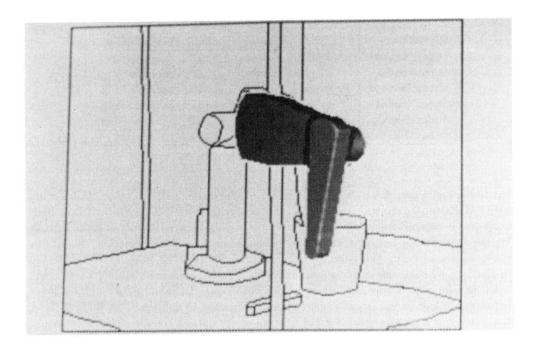

Figure 1.10: Predicted Angle Between Robot Upper and Lower Arms

angle $jnt3$ was estimated to be 4.57, compared to the measured value of 4.94. Figure 1.10 shows the predicted upper and lower arms at this angle.

Missing features, such as the back of the trash can, are found by a model-directed process. Given the oriented model, the image positions of unmatched SURFACEs can be predicted. Then, any surfaces in the predicted area that:

- belong to the surface cluster,

- have not already been previously used and

- have the correct shape and orientation

can be used as evidence for the unpaired model features.

Accounting for missing structure requires an understanding of the three cases of feature visibility, predicting or verifying their occurrence and showing that the image data is consistent with the expected visible portion of the model. The easiest case of back-facing and tangent SURFACEs can be predicted using the orientation estimates with known observer viewpoint and the surface normals deduced from the geometric model. A raycasting technique (i.e. predicting an image from an oriented model)

Table 1.3: Predicted Trash Can Visibility

SURFACE	VISIBLE PIXELS	OBSC'D PIXELS	TOTAL PIXELS	VISIBILITY
outer front	1479	8	1487	full
outer back	1	1581	1582	back-facing
outer bottom	5	225	230	back-facing
inner front	0	1487	1487	back-facing
inner back	314	1270	1584	partial-obsc
inner bottom	7	223	230	full-obsc

handles self-obscured front-facing SURFACEs by predicting the location of obscuring SURFACEs and hence which portions of more distant SURFACEs are invisible. Self-occlusion is determined by comparing the number of obscured to non-obscured pixels for the front-facing SURFACEs in the synthetic image. This prediction also allows the program to verify the partially self-obscured SURFACEs, which were indicated in the data by back-side-obscuring boundaries. The final feature visibility case occurs when unrelated structure obscures portions of the object. Assuming enough evidence is present to invoke and orient the model, occlusion can be confirmed by finding closer unrelated surfaces responsible for the missing image data. Partially obscured (but not self-obscured) SURFACEs are also verified as being externally obscured. These SUR-FACEs are noticed because they have back-side-obscuring boundaries that have not been explained by self-occlusion analysis.

The self-occlusion visibility analysis for the trash can in the scene is given in Table 1.3. Minor prediction errors occur at edges where surfaces do not meet perfectly.

Verifying missing substructure is a recursive process and is easy given the definition of the objects. Showing that the robot hand is obscured by the unrelated trash can decomposes to showing that each of the hand's SURFACEs are obscured.

Figure 1.11 shows the found robot model as predicted by the orientation parameters and superposed over the original intensity image. Though the global understanding is correct, the predicted position of the lower arm is somewhat away from its observed position because of cumulative minor rotation angle errors from the robot's base position. In analysis, all features were correctly paired, predicted invisible or verified as externally self-obscured. The numerical results in Table 1.2 also show good performance.

Identity Verification

The final step in the recognition process is verification (Chapter 10), which helps ensure that instantiated hypotheses are valid physical objects and have the correct identity. A proper, physical, object is more certain if all surfaces are connected and they enclose the object. Correct identification is more likely if all model features are accounted for, the model and corresponding image surface shapes and orientations are the same, and the model and image surfaces are connected similarly. The constraints

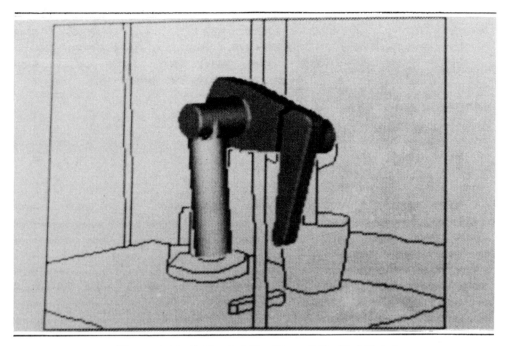

Figure 1.11: Estimated Position of Verified Robot

used to ensure correct SURFACE identities were:

- approximately correct size

- approximately correct surface shape

For solids they were:

- no duplicated use of image data

- all predicted back-facing SURFACEs have no data

- all adjacent visible model SURFACEs are adjacent in data

- all subfeatures have correct placement and identity

- all features predicted as partially self-obscured during raycasting are observed as such (i.e. have appropriate obscuring boundaries)

In the example given above, all correct object hypotheses passed these constraints. The only spurious structures to pass verification were SURFACEs similar to the invoked model or symmetric subcomponents.

To finish the summary, some implementation details follow. The **IMAGINE I** program was implemented mainly in the C programming language with some PROLOG for the geometric reasoning and invocation network compilation (about 20,000 lines of code in total). Execution required about 8 megabytes total, but this included several

256*256 arrays and generous static data structure allocations. Start-to-finish execution without graphics on a SUN 3/260 took about six minutes, with about 45% for self-occlusion analysis, 20% for geometric reasoning and 15% for model invocation. Many of the ideas described here are now being used and improved in the **IMAGINE II** program, which is under development.

The completely recognized robot is significantly more complicated than previously recognized objects (because of its multiple articulated features, curved surfaces, self-occlusion and external occlusion). This successful complete, explainable, object recognition was achieved because of the rich information embedded in the surface data and surface-based models.

Recognition Graph Summary

The recognition process creates many data structures, linked into a graph whose relationships are summarized in Figure 1.12. This figure should be referred to while reading the remainder of this book.

At the top of the diagram, the three bubbles "surface depth and orientation data", "image region labels" and "boundary and labels" are the image data input. The boundary points are linked into "boundary segments" which have the same label along their entire length. "Image region nodes" represent the individual surface image regions with their "enclosing boundary nodes", which are circularly linked boundary segments. "Adjacency nodes" link adjacent region nodes and also link to "description nodes" that record which boundary separates the regions.

The "image region nodes" form the raw input into the "surface nodes" hypothesizing process. The "surface nodes" are also linked by "adjacency nodes" and "enclosing boundary nodes". In the description phase, properties of the surfaces are calculated and these are also recorded in "description nodes". Surface shape is estimated and recorded in the "surface shape descriptors".

The surface cluster formation process aggregates the surfaces into groups recorded in the "surface cluster nodes". These nodes are organized into a "surface cluster hierarchy" linking larger enclosing or smaller enclosed surface clusters. The surface clusters also have properties recorded in "description nodes" and have an enclosing boundary.

Invocation occurs in a plausibility network of "invocation nodes" linked by the structural relations given by the "models". Nodes exist linking model identities to image structures (surface or surface cluster nodes). The invocation nodes link to each other to exchange plausibility among hypotheses.

When a model is invoked, a "hypothesis node" is created linking the model to its supporting evidence (surface and surface cluster nodes). Hypotheses representing objects are arranged in a component hierarchy analogous to that of the models. Image region nodes link to the hypotheses that best explain them.

This completes our overview of the recognition process and the following chapters explore the issues raised here in depth.

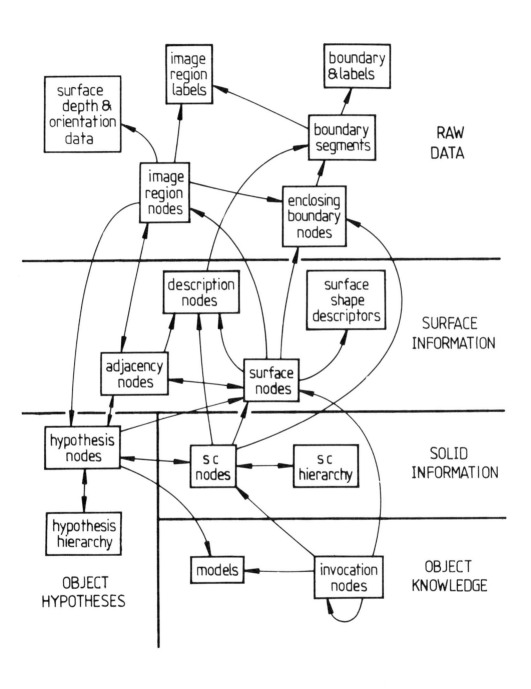

Figure 1.12: Summary of Data Structure Relationships

CHAPTER 2

Object Recognition from Surface Information

Intuitively, object recognition is the isolation and identification of structure from the midst of other detail in an image of a scene. It is also the assignment of a symbol to a group of features with the implication that those features could only belong to an object designated by that symbol. Hence, when we say we perceive (recognize) "John", we assert that there is a person named "John", who accounts for all the perceived features, and that this person is at the specified location in the given scene.

When described like this, object recognition seems little different from a general concept-matching paradigm. So, what distinguishes it as a vision problem? The answer lies in the types of data, its acquisition, the viewer-to-object geometry, the image projection relationship and the representations of structures to be recognized. This research addresses several aspects of how to perceive structure [WIT83b] visually:

- What are some of the relevant structures in the data?

- How is their appearance transformed by the visual process?

- How are they represented as a set of models?

- How are the models selected?

- How is the model-to-data correspondence established?

Visual recognition involves reasoning processes that transform between internal representations of the scene, linking the lower levels of image description to the higher levels of object description. The transformations reflect both the relationships between the representations and the constraints on the process. The most important constraints are those based on the physical properties of the visual domain and the consequent relationships between data elements.

Vision does have aspects in common with other cognitive processes – notably model invocation and generalization. Invocation selects candidate models to explain sets of data, a task that, in function, is no different from selecting "apple" as a unifying concept behind the phrase "devilish fruit". Invocation makes the inductive leap from data to explanation, but only in a suggestive sense, by computing from associations among symbolic descriptions. Generalization also plays a big role in both recognition and other processes, because one needs to extract the key features, and gloss over the irrelevant ones, to categorize a situation or object.

27

The first half of this chapter considers the problem of recognition in general, and the second half discusses previous approaches to recognition.

2.1   The Nature of Recognition

Visual recognition (and visual perception) has received considerable philosophical investigation. Three key results are mentioned, as an introduction to this section.

(1) Perception *interprets* raw sensory data. For example, we interpret a particular set of photons hitting our retina as "green". As a result, perception is an internal phenomenon caused by external events. It transforms the sensory phenomena into a reference to a symbolic description. Hence, there is a strong "linguistic" element to recognition – a vocabulary of interpretations. The perception may be directly related to the source, but it may also be a misinterpretation, as with optical illusions.

(2) Interpretations are directly dependent on the theories about what is being perceived. Hence, a theory that treats all intensity discontinuities as instances of surface reflectance discontinuities will interpret shadows as unexplained or reflectance discontinuity phenomena.

(3) Identity is based on conceptual relations, rather than purely physical ones. An office chair with all atoms replaced by equivalent atoms or one that has a bent leg is still a chair. Hence, any object with the appropriate properties could receive the corresponding identification.

So, philosophical theory implies that recognition has many weaknesses: the interpretations may be fallacious, not absolute and reductive. In practice, however, humans can effectively interpret unnatural or task-specific scenes (e.g. x-ray interpretation for tuberculosis detection) as well as natural and general ones (e.g. a tree against the sky). Moreover, almost all humans are capable of visually analyzing the world and producing largely similar descriptions of it. Hence, there must be many physical and conceptual constraints that restrict interpretation of both raw data as image features, and the relation of these features to objects. This chapter investigates the role of the second category on visual interpretation.

How is recognition understood here? Briefly, recognition is the production of symbolic descriptions. A description is an abstraction, as is stored object knowledge. The production process transforms sets of symbols to produce other symbols. The transformations are guided (in practice) by physical, computational and efficiency constraints, as well as by observer history and by perceptual goals.

Transformations are implementation dependent, and may be erroneous, as when using a simplified version of the ideal transformation. They can also make catastrophic errors when presented with unexpected inputs or when affected by distorting influences (e.g. optical, electrical or chemical). The notion of "transformation error" is not well founded, as the emphasis here is not on objective reality but on perceptual reality, and the perceptions now exist, "erroneous" or otherwise. The perceptions may be causally initiated by a physical world, but they may also be internally generated: mental imagery, dreams, illusions or "hallucinations". These are all legitimate perceptions that can be acted on by subsequent transformations; they are merely not "normal" or "well-grounded" interpretations.

Normal visual understanding is mediated by different description types over a sequence of transformations. The initial representation of a symbol may be by a set of photons; later channels may be explicit (value, place or symbol encoded), implicit (connectionist) or external. The communication of symbols between processes (or back into the same process) is also subject to distorting transformations.

In part, identity is linguistic: a chair is whatever is called a chair. It is also functional – an object has an identity only by virtue of its role in the human world. Finally, identity implies that it has properties, whether physical or mental. Given that objects have spatial extension, and are complex, some of the most important properties are linked to object substructures, their identity and their placement.

An identification is the attribution of a symbol whose associated properties are similar to those of the data, and is the output of a transformation. The properties (also symbols) compared may come from several different processes at different stages of transformation. Similarity is not a well defined notion, and seems to relate to a conceptual distance relationship in the space of all described objects. The similarity evaluation is affected by perceptual goals.

This is an abstract view of recognition. The practical matters are now discussed: what decisions must be made for an object recognition system to function in practice.

Descriptions and Transformations

This research starts at the $2\frac{1}{2}$D sketch, so this will be the first description encountered. Later transformations infer complete surfaces, surface clusters, object properties and relationships and object hypotheses, as summarized in Chapter 1.

As outlined above, each transformation is capable of error, such as incorrectly merging two surfaces behind an obscuring object, or hypothesizing a non-existent object. Moreover, the model invocation process is designed to allow "errors" to occur, as such a capability is needed for generic object recognition, wherein only "close" models exist. Fortunately, there are many constraints that help prevent the propagation of errors.

Some symbols are created directly from the raw data (e.g. surface properties), but most are created by transforming previously generated results (e.g. using two surfaces as evidence for hypothesizing an object containing both).

Object Isolation

Traditionally, recognition involves structure isolation, as well as identification, because naming requires objects to be named. This includes denoting what constitutes the object, where it is and what properties it has. Unfortunately, the isolation process depends on what is to be identified, in that what is relevant can be object-specific. However, this problem is mitigated because the number of general visual properties seems to be limited and there is hope of developing "first pass" grouping techniques that could be largely autonomous and model independent. (These may not always be model independent, as, for example, the constellation Orion can be found and declared as distinguished in an otherwise random and overlapping star field.) So, part of a sound theory of recognition depends on developing methods for isolating specific classes of objects. This research inferred surface groupings from local intersurface relationships.

The Basis for Recognition

Having the correct properties and relationships is the traditional basis for recognition, with the differences between approaches lying in the types of evidence used, the modeling of objects, the assumptions about what constitutes adequate recognition and the algorithms for performing the recognition.

Here, surface and structure properties are the key types of evidence, and they were chosen to characterize a large class of everyday objects. As three dimensional input data is used, a full three dimensional description of the object can be constructed and directly compared with the object model. All model feature properties and relationships should be held by the observed data features, with geometric consistency as the strongest constraint. The difficulty then arises in the construction of the three dimensional description. Fortunately, various constraints exist to help solve this problem.

This research investigates recognizing "human scale" rigidly and non-rigidly connected solids with uniform, large surfaces including: classroom chairs, most of a PUMA robot and a trash can. The types of scenes in which these objects appear are normal indoor somewhat cluttered work areas, with objects at various depths obscuring portions of other objects.

Given these objects and scenes, four groups of physical constraints are needed:

- limitations on the surfaces and how they can be segmented and characterized,

- properties of solid objects, including how the surfaces relate to the objects bounded by them,

- properties of scenes, including spatial occupancy and placement of objects and

- properties of image formation and how the surfaces, objects and scenes affect the perceived view.

Definition of Recognition

Recognition produces a largely instantiated, spatially located, described object hypothesis with direct correspondences to an isolated set of image data. "Largely instantiated" means that most object features predicted by the model have been accounted for, either with directly corresponding image data or with explanations for their absence.

What distinguishes recognition, in the sense used in this book, is that it labels the data, and hence is able to reconstruct the image. While the object description may be compressed (e.g. a "head"), there will be an associated prototypical geometric model (organizing the properties) that could be used to recreate the image to the level of the description. This requires that identification be based on model-to-data correspondences, rather than on summary quantities such as volume or mass distribution.

One problem with three dimensional scenes is incomplete data. In particular, objects can be partially obscured. But, because of redundant features, context and limited environments, identification is still often possible. On the other hand, there are also objects that cannot be distinguished without a more complete examination – such as an opened versus unopened soft drink can. If complete identification requires all properties to be represented in the data, any missing ones will need to be justified. Here, it is assumed that all objects have geometric models that allow appearance prediction. Then, if the prediction process is reasonable and understands physical explanations for missing data (e.g. occlusion, known defects), the model will be consistent with the observed data, and hence be an acceptable identification.

Criteria for Identification

The proposed criterion is that the object has all the right properties and none of the wrong ones, as specified in the object model. The properties will include local and global descriptions (e.g. surface curvatures and areas), subcomponent existence, global geometric consistency and visibility consistency (i.e. what is seen is what is expected).

Perceptual goals determine the properties used in identification. Unused information may allow distinct objects to acquire the same identity. If the generic chair were the only chair modeled, then all chairs would be classified as the generic chair.

The space of all objects does not seem to be sufficiently disjoint so that the detection of only a few properties will uniquely characterize them. In some model bases, efficient recognition may be possible by a parsimonious selection of properties, but redundancy adds the certainty needed to cope with missing or erroneous data, as much as the extra data bits in an error correcting code help disperse the code space.

Conversely, a set of data might implicate several objects related through a relevant common generalization, such as (e.g.) similar yellow cars. Or, there may be no physical generalization between alternative interpretations (e.g., as in the children's joke Q:"What is grey, has four legs and a trunk?" A:"A mouse going on a holiday!").

Though the basic data may admit several interpretations, further associated properties may provide finer identifications, much as ACRONYM [BRO81] used additional constraints for class specialization.

While not all properties will be needed for a particular identification, some will be essential and recognition should require these when identifying an object. One could interpret a picture of a soft drink can as if it were the original, but this is just a matter of choosing what properties are relevant. An observation that is missing some features, such as one without the label on the can, may suggest the object, but would not be acceptable as a proper instance.

There may also be properties that the object should not have, though this is a more obscure case. In part, these properties may contradict the object's function. Some care has to be applied here, because there are many properties that an object does not have and all should not have to be made explicit. No "disallowed" properties were used here.

Most direct negative properties, like "the length cannot be less than 15 cm" can be rephrased as "the length must be at least 15 cm". Properties without natural complements are less common, but exist: "adjacent to" and "subcomponent of" are two such properties. One might discriminate between two types of objects by stating that one has a particular subcomponent, and that the other does not and is otherwise identical. Failure to include the "not subcomponent of" condition would reduce the negative case to a generalization of the positive case, rather than an alternative. Examples of this are: a nail polish dot that distinguishes "his and her" toothbrushes or a back support as the discriminator between a chair and a stool.

Recognition takes place in a context – each perceptual system will have its own set of properties suitable for discriminating among its range of objects. In the toothbrushes example, the absence of the mark distinguished one toothbrush in the home, but would not have been appropriate when still at the factory (among the other identical, unmarked, toothbrushes). The number and sensitivity of the properties affects the degree to which objects are distinguished. For example, the area-to-perimeter ratio distinguishes some objects in a two dimensional vision context, even though it is an impoverished representation. This work did not explicitly consider any context-specific identification criteria.

The above discussion introduces most of the issues behind recognition, and is summarized here:

- the goals of recognition influence the distinguishable objects of the domain,

- the characterization of the domain may be rich enough to provide unique identifications even when some data is missing or erroneous,

- all appropriate properties should be necessary, with some observed and the rest deduced,

- some properties may be prohibited and

- multiple identifications may occur for the same object and additional properties may specialize them.

2.2   Some Previous Object Recognition Systems

Three dimensional object recognition is still largely limited to blocks world scenes. Only simple, largely polyhedral objects can be fully identified, while more complicated objects can only be tentatively recognized (i.e. evidence for only a few features can be found). There are several pieces of research that deserve special mention.

Roberts [ROB65] was the founder of three dimensional model-based scene understanding. Using edge detection methods, he analyzed intensity images of blocks world scenes containing rectangular solids, wedges and prisms. The two key descriptions of a scene were the locations of vertices in its edge description and the configurations of the polygonal faces about the vertices. The local polygon topology indexed into the model base, and promoted initial model-to-data point correspondences. Using these correspondences, the geometric relationship between the model, scene and image was computed. A least-squared error solution accounted for numerical errors. Object scale and distance were resolved by assuming the object rested on a ground plane or on other objects. Recognition of one part of a configuration introduced new edges to help segment and recognize the rest of the configuration.

Hanson and Riseman's VISIONS system [HAN78b] was proposed as a complete vision system. It was a schema-driven natural scene recognition system acting on edge and multi-spectral region data [HAN78a]. It used a blackboard system with levels for: vertices, segments, regions, surfaces, volumes, objects and schemata. Various knowledge sources made top-down or bottom-up additions to the blackboard. For the identification of objects (road, tree, sky, grass, etc.) a confidence value was used, based on property matching. The properties included: spectral composition, texture, size and two dimensional shape. Rough geometric scene analysis estimated the base plane and then object distances knowing rough object sizes. Use of image relations to give rough relative scene ordering was proposed. Besides the properties, schemata were the other major object knowledge source. They organized objects likely to be found together in generic scenes (e.g. a house scene) and provided conditional statistics used to direct the selection of new hypotheses from the blackboard to pursue.

As this system was described early in its development, a full evaluation can not be made here. Its control structure was general and powerful, but its object representations were weak and dependent mainly on a few discriminating properties, with little spatial understanding of three dimensional scenes.

Marr [MAR82] hypothesized that humans use a volumetric model-based object recognition scheme that:

- took edge data from a $2\frac{1}{2}$D sketch,

- isolated object regions by identifying obscuring contours,

- described subelements by their elongation axes, and objects by the local configuration of axes,

- used the configurations to index into and search in a subtype/subcomponent network representing the objects, and

- used image axis positions and model constraints for geometric analysis.

His proposal was outstanding in the potential scope of recognizable objects, in defining and extracting object independent descriptions directly matchable to three dimensional models (i.e. elongation axes), in the subtype and subcomponent model refinement, and in the potential of its invocation process. It suffered from the absence of a testable implementation, from being too serial in its view of recognition, from being limited to only cylinder-like primitives, from not accounting for surface structure and from not fully using the three dimensional data in the $2\frac{1}{2}$D sketch.

Brooks [BRO81], in ACRONYM, implemented a generalized cylinder based recognizer using similar notions. His object representation had both subtype and subcomponent relationships. From its models, ACRONYM derived visible features and relationships, which were then graph-matched to edge data represented as ribbons (parallel edge groups). ACRONYM deduced object position and model parameters by back constraints in the prediction graph, where constraints were represented by algebraic inequalities. These symbolically linked the model and position parameters to the model relationships and image geometry, and could be added to incrementally as recognition proceeded. The algebraic position-constraint and incremental evidence mechanism was powerful, but the integration of the constraints was a time-consuming and imperfect calculation.

This well developed project demonstrated the utility of explicit geometric and constraint reasoning, and introduced a computational model for generic identification based on nested sets of constraints. Its weakness were that it only used edge data as input, it had a relatively incomplete understanding of the scene, and did not really demonstrate three dimensional understanding (the main example was an airplane viewed from a great perpendicular height).

Faugeras and his group [FAU83] researched three dimensional object recognition using direct surface data acquired by a laser triangulation process. Their main example was an irregular automobile part. The depth values were segmented into planar patches using region growing and Hough transform techniques. These data patches were then combinatorially matched to model patches, constrained by needing a consistent model-to-data geometric transformation at each match. The transformation was calculated using several error minimization methods, and consistency was checked first by a fast heuristic check and then by error estimates from the transformation estimation. Their recognition models were directly derived from previous views of the object and record the parameters of the planar surface patches for the object from all views.

Key problems here were the undirected matching, the use of planar patches only, and the relatively incomplete nature of their recognition – pairing of a few patches was enough to claim recognition. However, they succeeded in the recognition of a complicated real object.

Bolles et al. [BOL83] used light stripe and laser range finder data. Surface boundaries were found by linking corresponding discontinuities in groups of stripes, and by detecting depth discontinuities in the range data. Matching to models was done by using edge and surface data to predict circular and hence cylindrical features, which were then related to the models. The key limitation of these experiments was that only large (usually planar) surfaces could be detected, and so object recognition could depend on only these features. This was adequate in the limited industrial domains. The main advantages of the surface data was that it was absolute and unambiguous, and that planar (etc.) model features could be matched directly to other planar (etc.) data features, thus saving on matching combinatorics.

The TINA vision system, built by the Sheffield University Artificial Intelligence Vision Research Unit [POR87], was a working stereo-based three dimensional object recognition and location system. Scene data was acquired in three stages: (1) subpixel "Canny" detected edges were found for a binocular stereo image pair, (2) these were combined using epipolar, contrast gradient and disparity gradient constraints and (3) the three dimensional edge points were grouped to form straight lines and circular arcs. These three dimensional features were then matched to a three dimensional wire frame model, using a local feature-focus technique [BOL80] to cue the initial matches. They eliminated the incorrect model-to-data correspondences using pairwise constraints similar to those of Grimson and Lozano-Perez [GRI84] (e.g. relative orientation). When a maximal matching was obtained, a reference frame was estimated, and then improved by exploiting object geometry constraints (e.g. that certain lines must be parallel or perpendicular).

A particularly notable achievement of this project was their successful inference of the wire frame models from multiple known views of the object. Although the stereo and wire frame-based techniques were suited mainly for polyhedral objects, this well-engineered system was successful at building models that could then be used for object recognition and robot manipulation.

More recently, Fan et al. [FAN88] described range-data based object recognition with many similarities to the work in this book. Their work initially segments the range data into surface patches at depth and orientation discontinuities. Then, they created an attributed graph with nodes representing surface patches (labeled by properties like area, orientation and curvature) and arcs representing adjacency (labeled by the type of discontinuity and estimated likelihood that the two surfaces are part of the same object). The whole scene graph is partitioned into likely complete objects (similar to our surface clusters) using the arc likelihoods. Object models were represented by multiple graphs for the object as seen in topologically distinct viewpoints. The first step of model matching was a heuristic-based preselection of likely model graphs. Then, a search tree was formed, pairing compatible model and data nodes. When a maximal set was obtained, and object position was estimated , which was used to add or reject pairings. Consistent pairings then guided re-partitioning of the scene graph, subject to topological and geometric consistency.

Rosenfeld [ROS87] proposed an approach to fast recognition of unexpected (i.e. fully data driven) generic objects, based on five assumptions:

1. objects were represented in characteristic views,

2. the key model parts are regions and boundaries,

3. features are characterized by local properties,

4. relational properties are expressed in relative form (i.e. "greater then") and

5. all properties are unidimensional and unimodal.

A consequence of these assumptions is that most of the recognition processes are local and distributed, and hence can be implemented on an (e.g.) pyramidal processor.

This concludes a brief discussion of some prominent three dimensional object recognition systems. Other relevant research is discussed where appropriate in the main body of the book. Besl and Jain [BES85] gave a thorough review of techniques for both three dimensional object representation and recognition.

2.3   Recognition Approaches

This section summarizes the four traditional approaches to object recognition, roughly in order of discriminating power. Most recognition systems use several techniques.

2.3.1   Property Based Identification

When enough model properties are satisfied by the data, recognition occurs. The properties may be scene location, orientation, size, color, shape or others. The goal is unique discrimination in the model base, so judicious choice of properties is necessary. Duda and Hart's [DUD70] analysis of an office scene typified this. Other examples include Brice and Fennema [BRI70], who classified regions by their boundary shape and defined object identity by a group of regions with the correct shapes, and Adler [ADL75], who ranked matches by success at finding components meeting structural relationships and summary properties. Property comparison is simple and efficient, but is not generally powerful enough for a large model base or subtle discriminations. The problem is always – "which properties?".

Property matchers often use pattern recognition based discrimination methods, implemented as sequential property comparison, decision trees or distance based classifiers. These are straightforward, but do not easily allow complicated recognition criteria (e.g. geometric or relational) without prior calculation of all potential properties, and treat objects at a single level of representation.

Given that properties are often continuous valued, and subject to error, a distance metric is often used to evaluate the match (e.g. [TUR74]). If the properties fit a statistical distribution, then a probabilistic classifier can be used (e.g. [DUD73]).

2.3.2   Grammatical and Graph Matching

Here, recognition is achieved when a particular grouping of data is structurally identical to a similar model pattern. This usually expresses relationships between image features, such as edges or regions, but may also refer to relationships in three dimensional data. This method requires evaluation of the match between individual features.

For objects with primitive distinguishable features that have fixed relationships (geometric or topological), two general methods have been developed. The first is the syntactic method (e.g. [MIL68], [CHA79]). Valid relationships are embodied in grammar rules and recognition is done by parsing the data symbols according to these rules. Rosenfeld [ROS72] presented a typical example of this matching method by using web grammars for analyzing two dimensional patterns. The main applications of grammatical techniques have been in fingerprint [MOA76], circuit diagram, chromosome and texture analysis. A variation on this method uses rules to recognize specific features (e.g. vegetation in an aerial image [NAG79] or urban building scenes [OHT79]).

The second general matching technique is graph matching, where the goal is to find a pairing between subsets of the data and model graphs. Two key techniques are subgraph isomorphism and maximal clique finding in association graphs [BAR74]. Barrow and Popplestone [BAR71] used a subgraph matching between their data and model graphs. Ambler et al. [AMB75] recognized by using a maximal clique method in an association graph between data and models. Combinatorial explosion can be controlled by using a hierarchy of structures [BAR72] and Turner [TUR74] exploited this method procedurally in his hierarchical synthesis matcher.

One advantage of graph matching is that it is well understood and produces understandable results through symbol matching, formal definition and computationally analyzable machinery. Unfortunately, graph methods tend to be NP-complete and are not practical unless the graph size is small. Matching would be more efficient if geometric predictions were used, allowing direct comparison instead of the complete matching that general graph matching algorithms require. Another disadvantage is that three dimensional scenes have changing viewpoints and occlusion, which distorts and fragments object descriptions (unless multiple graphs are used for alternative viewpoints).

Heuristic match criteria are still needed for comparing nodes and arcs, and for ranking subgraph matches. Barrow and Popplestone [BAR71] used a heuristic weighting to evaluate the satisfaction of a subgraph match, including a factor that favored larger matches. Ambler et al. [AMB75] used similarity of properties and relations between regions in a two dimensional parts scene. Nevatia and Binford [NEV77] evaluated matches based on components found and parameter comparisons for the primitives.

2.3.3 Geometric Matching

Here, the geometric relationships in the model, initial object location knowledge and image feature geometry combine to allow direct matching. Roberts [ROB65], Freuder [FRE77], Marr [MAR82] and others argued that partial matching of image data to object models could be used to constrain where other features were and how to classify them. Locating this data then further constrained the object's geometric location as well as increasingly confirmed its identity.

Adler [ADL75] used a top-down control regime to predict image location in two dimensional scenes, and explained data lost because of occlusion. Freuder [FRE77] described a two dimensional recognition program that used active reasoning to recognize a hammer in image region data. The program used image models to obtain <u>suggestions</u> about what features to look for next and <u>advice</u> on where to find the features.

Matching may be almost totally a matter of satisfying geometric criteria. The advantage of geometric matching is that the matching criteria are usually clear and geometric models allow directed comparisons. One might require that the accumulated error between predicted and observed features be below a threshold. For example, Faugeras and Hebert [FAU83] used the model-to-data surface pairings that passed a geometric consistency measure and had minimum transformation estimation error.

Roberts [ROB65] estimated the transformation from selected model points to image points. Transformation errors exceeding a threshold implied a bad match. Ikeuchi [IKE81] recognized and oriented objects by computationally rotating extended gaussian images until good correspondences were achieved. Hogg [HOG84] improved positional estimates using search over a bounded parameter space. The estimates were used to predict the position of edge points, and the number of verified edge points was used evaluate the estimates. Ballard and Tanaka [BAL85] used a connectionist method for deducing a polyhedral object's reference frame given network linkages specified by geometric constraints. This follows Ballard's work [BAL81a] on extracting component parameters from intrinsic images by using Hough transform techniques.

Correct geometry is a strong constraint on an object's identity. Its limitations include the need for pairing the appropriate structures, control of combinatorial matching and integration with other matchables, such as structural properties and relationships.

2.3.4 Constraint Satisfaction

Implicit in the above methods are certain constraints that the data must satisfy. These constraints may apply to individual features, or to groups of features, or to relationships between features. Some researchers have tried to generalize the constraints by making them explicit. Matching algorithms can use direct search, graph matching (where the constraints specify the node and arc match criteria) or relaxation. Relaxation algorithms can apply to discrete symbol labelings [WAL75], probabilistic labelings ([ZUC77], [ROS78], [BER83], [FAU80]) or a combination of the two [BAR76]. Barrow and Tenenbaum [BAR76] used adjacency and homogeneity constraints to deduce identity in office scenes using height, intensity and orientation data. Hinton [HIN76] formulated the substructure identity problem as a relaxation problem, with the goal of maximizing credibility subject to model constraints.

Nevatia and Binford [NEV77] matched models using connectivity relationships between generalized cylinder primitives in the model and data to constrain correspondences. In ACRONYM [BRO81], an object was identified by maximal refinement in a specialization lattice consistent with both the model constraints and image data. The refinement was by constraint satisfaction, where the constraints mainly applied to feature sizes and relationships. Constraint satisfaction was checked by inequality testing.

The constraint satisfaction approach encompasses the other methods described above. The ability of a constraint to be general is a real advantage, particularly when representing ranges of numerical values. Its weakness is it requires the choice of constraints that efficiently and adequately discriminate without rejection of minor undistinguished variants.

Most systems use a combination of the methods to recognize objects in more sophisticated scenes. For example, ACRONYM's [BRO81] matching algorithm looked for subgraph isomorphisms between the picture graph, representing located image features, and the prediction graph, which was a precompilation of the object models. This graph tried to represent the likely sizes and intercomponent relationships between primitives, as seen in typical views of the object. A node or arc match required not only local, but also global satisfaction of constraints such as requiring all features to have the same reference frame.

The goal of most algorithms (but not ACRONYM's) was to use local constraints to produce global consistency. The difficulty with these pure methods is that they excessively simplify and ignore most of the global structural relationships between nameable object features.

Matching algorithms generally follow a combinatorial tree-search approach, where each new level in the tree pairs a new data feature to a model feature. Full tree expansion is usually prevented by using constraints to remove bad expansions (e.g. those coming from predictions of positions). For example, Faugeras and Hebert [FAU83] and Grimson and Lozano-Perez [GRI84] successfully used local relative position constraints to prune the search tree dramatically.

An improvement on the above basic methods is hierarchical recognition, in which objects are structured into levels of representation, and recognition matches components at the same level. Turner [TUR74], Ambler et al. [AMB75] and Fisher [FIS83] used a bottom-up "hierarchical synthesis" process [SEL60] and Adler [ADL75] used top-down model directed analysis.

Final Comments

This completes a quick review of the philosophical and historical background to the research, and we now proceed to look at the research itself.

CHAPTER 3

Surface Data as Input for Recognition

Choosing surface data as the foundation for a theory of object recognition is not without controversy, particularly given its unsuitability for all domains and applications. None the less, it is justified in scenes where knowledge of the three dimensional scene structure is important, as discussed in this chapter.

3.1   The Labeled Segmented Surface Image

The labeled segmented surface image is the primary data input for the recognition processes described in this book. Each of these terms is discussed in greater detail below, but, by way of introduction, a surface image is a dense pointillistic two-dimensional image representation, whose geometry arises from a projective transformation of the three dimensional scene, and whose content describes properties of the visible surfaces in the scene. Segmentation partitions the surface into regions of uniform properties (namely curvature and continuity) and identifies the type of boundary between surface regions (e.g. whether obscuring or shape).

Surface Images

Surface images are an iconic representation similar in structure to traditional intensity images, except that they record surface properties, such as absolute depth and surface orientation in the camera coordinate system. The positional relationship between the scene and the image is described by projective geometry. In this way, surface images are a subset of intrinsic images [BAR78], except that here the information is solely related to the surface shape, and not to reflectance. This eliminates surface markings, shadows, highlights, image flow, shading and other illumination and observer dependent effects from the information (which are also important, but are not considered here).

A second similar representation is Marr's $2\frac{1}{2}$D sketch [MAR82]. This represents mainly surface orientation, depth and labeled boundaries with region groupings. As his work was unfinished, there is controversy over the precise details of his proposal.

There are several forms of redundancy in this information (e.g. surface orientation is derivable from distance), but here we are more concerned with how to use the information than how it was acquired or how to make it robust.

Segmentation

The surface image is segmented into significant regions, resulting in a set of connected boundary segments that partition the whole surface image. What "significant" means has not been agreed on (e.g. [WIT83b], [LOW84]), and little has been written on it in the context of surface representations. For the purposes of this research, it means **surface image regions corresponding to connected object surface regions with approximately uniform curvature and not otherwise terminated by a surface shape discontinuity.** Here, "uniform curvature" means that the principal curvatures are nearly constant over the region. The goal of this segmentation is to produce uniform regions whose shape can be directly compared to that of model SURFACEs.

The proposed criteria that cause this segmentation are:

D obscuring boundaries – points where a depth discontinuity occurs,

C1 surface orientation boundaries – points where a surface orientation discontinuity occurs,

C2m curvature magnitude boundaries – where a discontinuity in surface curvature exceeds a scale-related threshold, and

C2d curvature direction boundaries – where the direction of surface curvature has a discontinuity. This includes the change from concave to convex surfaces.

For surfaces, the curvature rules must apply in both principal directions of curvature. The idea is that a surface region should be split when the intrinsic character of the surface changes. The problem of how the boundary is found is left unsolved (here).

These four criteria are probably just minimum constraints. The first rule is obvious because, at a given scale, surface portions separated by depth should not be in the same segment. The second rule applies at folds in surfaces or where two surfaces join. Intuitively, the two sections are considered separate surfaces, so they should be segmented. The third and fourth rules are less intuitive and are illustrated in Figures 3.1 and 3.2. The first example shows a cross section of a planar surface changing into a uniformly curved one. Neither of the first two rules applies, but a segmentation near point X is clearly desired. However, it is not clear what should be done when the curvature changes continuously. Figure 3.2 shows a change in the curvature direction vector that causes segmentation as given by the fourth rule. Descriptions D, C1, C2m and C2d are sensitive to changes in scale and description D depends on the observer's position.

These criteria segment surfaces into patches of the six classes illustrated in Figure 3.3. The class labels can then be used as symbolic descriptions of the surface.

Figure 3.4 shows the segmentation of a sausage image. The segmentation produces four object surfaces (two hemispherical ends, a nearly cylindrical "back", and a saddle surface "belly") plus the background planar surface. The segmentation between the back and belly occurs because the surface changes from ellipsoidal to hyperboloidal. These segments are stable to minor changes in the sausage's shape (assuming the same scale of analysis is maintained), and are members of the six surface classes. Figure 3.10 shows the surface patches produced by the segmentation criteria for the test scene.

Figure 3.1: Segmentation at Curvature Magnitude Change in 2D

Figure 3.2: Segmentation at Curvature Direction Change in 2D

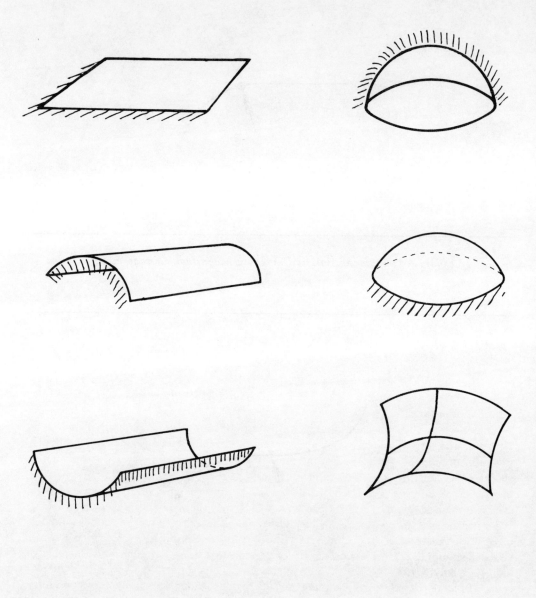

Figure 3.3: The Six Curvature Classes

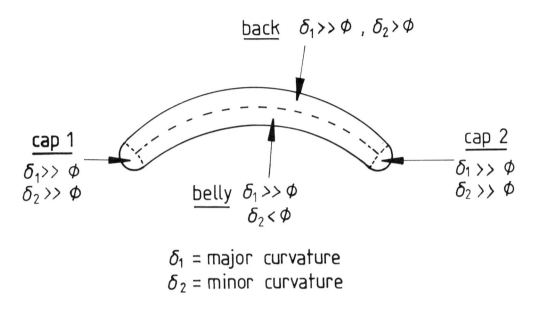

δ_1 = major curvature
δ_2 = minor curvature

Figure 3.4: Segmentation of a Sausage

The segmented sausage can be represented by the graph of Figure 3.5. Here, the nodes represent the surfaces and are labeled by the surface class, curvature values and nominal orientations. The links denote adjacency.

The theoretical grounds for these conditions and how to achieve them are not settled, but the following general principles seem reasonable. The segmentation should produce connected regions of constant character with all curvature magnitudes roughly the same and in the same direction. Further, the segmentations should be stable to viewpoint and minor variations in object shape, and should result in unique segmentations. Because the criteria are object-centered, they give unique segmentation, independent of viewpoint. As we can also apply the criteria to the models, model invocation (Chapter 8) and matching (Chapter 9) are simplified by comparing similar corresponding features. The examples used in this book were chosen to be easily and obviously segmentable to avoid controversy. Thus, image and model segmentations will have roughly corresponding surface regions, though precisely corresponding boundaries are not required.

Scale affects segmentation because some shape variations are insignificant when compared to the size of objects considered. In particular, less pronounced shape segmentations will disappear into insignificance as the scale of analysis grows. No absolute

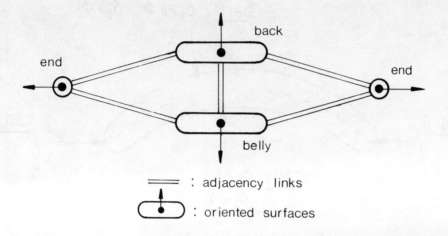

Figure 3.5: Representing the Segmented Sausage (from Figure 3.4)

segmentation boundaries exist on free-form objects, so criteria for a reasonable segmentation are difficult to formulate. (Witkin [WIT83a] has suggested a stability criterion for scale-based segmentations of one dimensional signals.)

This does not imply that the segmentation boundaries must remain constant. For some ranges of scale, the sausage's boundaries (Figure 3.4) will move slightly, but this will not introduce a new segmented surface. Invocation and matching avoid the boundary movement effects by emphasizing the spatial relationships between surfaces (e.g. adjacency and relative orientation) and not the position of intervening boundaries.

Some research into surface segmentation has occurred. Brady et al. [BRA84] investigated curvature-based local descriptions of curved surfaces, by constructing global features (i.e. regions and lines of curvature) from local properties (i.e. local principal curvatures). Besl [BES86] started with similar curvature properties to seed regions, but then used numerical techniques to fit surface models to the data (e.g. to ellipsoidal patches) and grow larger patches. This work was particularly effective. Hoffman and Jain [HOF87] clustered surface normals to produce three types of patches (planar, convex and concave). Patches were linked by four types of boundary (depth discontinuity, orientation discontinuity, tesselation and null). Null and tesselation boundaries were later removed to produce larger patches.

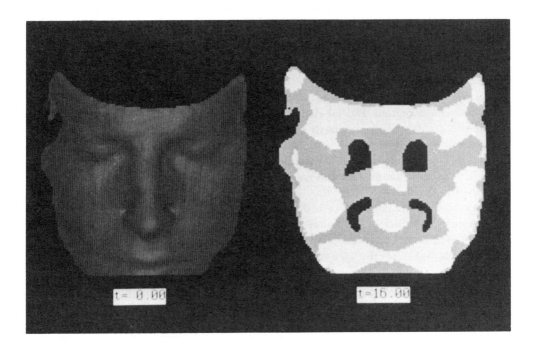

Figure 3.6: Partial Segmentation of Range Data of a Face

Following on from Besl's work, Cai [CAI89] has been investigating multiple scale segmentation of surface patches from range data. He used a modified diffusion smoothing process to blend the features and then forms surface patches from region growing based on local principal curvature estimates. Large features that remain over several scales are selected to form a stable representation. Figure 3.6 shows an intermediate stage of the segmentation of a face, where the positive ellipsoidal regions are shown in white, hyperboloidal regions are grey and negative ellipsoidal regions are black. Though there is still considerable research on segmentation to be done, features such as these are suitable for recognition with a coarse scale model.

Labeling

With the segmentation processes described above, the boundary labeling problem becomes trivial. The purpose of the labeling is to designate which boundaries result from the shape segmentations, and which result from occlusion. The type of a shape segmentation boundary is probably not important, as scale affects the labeling, so it is not used. However, the different types are recorded for completeness and the shape of the boundary helps to identify particular surfaces.

Occlusion boundaries are further distinguished into the boundary lying on a closer obscuring surface and that lying on a distant surface. All shape discontinuity boundaries are labeled as convex, concave or crack.

Inputs Used in the Research

Because the geometry of the surface image is the same as that of an intensity image, an intensity image was used to prepare the initial input. From this image, all relevant surface regions and labeled boundaries were extracted, by hand, according to the criteria described previously. The geometry of the segmenting boundaries was maintained by using a registered intensity image as the template. Then, the distances to and surface orientations of key surface points were recorded at the corresponding pixel. The labeled boundaries and measured points were the inputs into the processes described in this book.

The surface orientation was recorded for each measured point, and a single measurement point was sufficient for planar surfaces. For curved surfaces, several points (6 to 15) were used to estimate the curvature, but it turned out that not many were needed to give acceptable results. As the measurements were made by hand, the angular accuracy was about 0.1 radian and distance accuracy about 1 centimeter.

Those processes that used the surface information directly (e.g. for computing surface curvature) assumed that the distance and orientation information was dense over the whole image. Dense data values were interpolated from values of nearby measured points, using a $1/R^2$ image distance weighting. This tended to flatten the interpolated surface in the region of the data points, but had the benefit of emphasizing data points closest to the test point. A surface approximation approach (e.g. [GRI81]) would have been better. The interpolation used only those points from within the segmented surface region, which was appropriate because the regions were selected for having uniform curvature class.

We now show the input data for the test scene in greater detail. Figure 1.1 showed the original test scene and Figure 1.4 showed the depth information coded so dark means further away. Figure 3.7 shows the y component of the unit surface normal. Here, brighter means more upward facing. Figure 1.5 showed the occlusion label boundaries. Figure 3.8 shows the orientation discontinuity label boundaries and Figure 3.9 shows the curvature discontinuity boundary. Figure 3.10 shows the identifier assigned to each region and the overall segmentation boundaries.

The Region Graph

The labeled, segmented surface image was represented as a graph, because it was compact and easily exploited key structural properties of the data. These are:

1. Regions are connected sets of surface points.

2. Boundary segments are connected sets of boundary points.

3. All points in one boundary segment have the same label.

4. Every region is totally bounded by a connected chain of boundary segments.

Figure 3.7: Test Scene y Component of Surface Orientation

5. If one region is the front side of an obscuring boundary, the adjacent region is the back side.

The resulting graph structure used nodes for the surface image regions and boundaries, and the links represented adjacency. The properties of this graph are:

1. Region nodes represent complete image regions.

2. Boundary nodes represent complete boundary segments.

3. Chains of boundary nodes represent connecting boundary segments.

4. Region nodes link to chains of boundary nodes that isolate them from other regions.

5. Region nodes corresponding to adjacent regions have adjacency links.

The computation that makes this transformation is a trivial boundary tracking and graph linking process. No information is lost in the transformations between representations, because of explicit linking back to the input data structures (even

Figure 3.8: Test Scene Orientation Discontinuity Label Boundaries

if there is some loss of information in the generalization at any particular level). The only interesting point is that before tracking, the original segmented surface image may need to be preprocessed. The original image may have large gaps between identified surface regions. Before boundary tracking, these gaps have to be shrunk to single pixel boundaries, with corresponding region extensions. (These extensions have surface orientation information deleted to prevent conflicts when crossing the surface boundaries.) This action was not needed for the hand segmented test cases in this research.

3.2   Why Use Surfaces for Recognition?

It was Marr, who, in advocating the $2\frac{1}{2}$D sketch as an intermediate representation [MAR82], brought surfaces into focus. Vision is obviously a complicated process, and most computer-based systems have been incapable of coping with both the system and scene complexity. The importance of Marr's proposal lies in having a reconstructed surface representation as a significant intermediate entity in the image understanding process. This decision laid the foundation for a theory of vision that splits vision into

—

Figure 3.9: Test Scene Curvature Discontinuity Label Boundary

those processes that contribute to the creation of the $2\frac{1}{2}$D sketch and those that use its information.

A considerable proportion of vision research is currently involved in generating the $2\frac{1}{2}$D sketch (or equivalent surface representations). This work addresses the problem of what to do after the sketch is produced and some justifications for and implications of using this surface information are discussed in the sections below.

From What Sources Can We Expect to Get Surface Information?

The research presented here is based on the assumption that there will soon be practical means for producing surface images. Several promising research areas suggest that this is likely, though none of the processes described here are "perfected" yet.

Direct laser ranging (e.g. [NIT77], [JAR83], [SAM87]) computes surface depth by measuring time of flight of a laser pulse or by signal phase shift caused by path length differences. The laser is scanned over the entire scene, producing a depth image. Sonar range finding gives similar results in air, but has lower resolution and has problems because of surface specularity.

Structured illumination uses controlled stimulation of the environment to produce

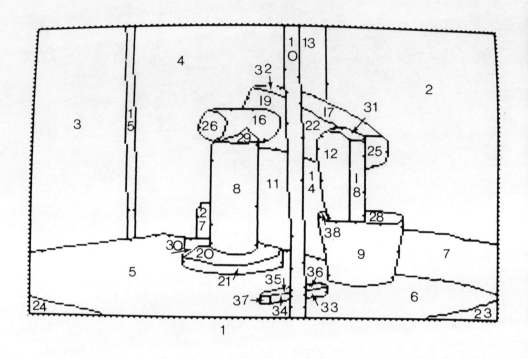

Figure 3.10: Test Scene Surface Data Patches with Region Identifiers

less ambiguous interpretations. One well known technique traces the scene with parallel light stripes ([SHI71], [AGI73], [POP75], [SHN79], [OSH81], [BOL83]). The three dimensional coordinates of individual points on the stripes can be found by triangulation along the baseline between the stripe source and sensor. Additionally, this technique highlights distinct surfaces, because all stripes lying on the same surface will have a similar character (e.g. all lines parallel), and usually the character will change radically at occlusion or orientation discontinuity boundaries. Analysis of stripe patterns may give further information about the local surface shape. Variations of this technique use a grey-code set of patterns (e.g. [INO84]) or color coding ([KAK86], [BOY87]) to reduce the number of projected patterns.

A second technique uses one or more remotely sensed light spots. By knowing the emitted and received light paths, the object surface can be triangulated, giving a depth image ([KAN81], [PIP82], [FAU83]). The advantage of using a spot is then there is no feature correspondence problem.

Besl [BES88a] gives a thorough and up-to-date survey of the techniques and equipment available for range data acquisition.

Stereo is becoming a more popular technique, because it is a significant biological process ([MAR82], [MAY80]) and its sensor system is simple and passive. The process is based on finding common features in a pair of images taken from different locations. Given the relationship between the camera coordinate frames, the feature's absolute location can be calculated by triangulation.

One major difficulty with this technique is finding the common feature in both images. Biological systems are hypothesized to use (at least) paired edges with the same sign, and from the same spatial frequency channel ([MAR82], [MAY80]). Other systems have used detected corners or points where significant intensity changes take place ([DRE81], [MOR81]). More recently, researchers have started using trinocular (etc) stereo (e.g. [OHT86]), exploiting a second epipolar constraint to reduce search for corresponding features and then produce more reliable pairings.

Another difficulty arises because stereo generally only gives sparse depth values, which necessitates surface reconstruction. This topic has only recently entered investigation, but some work has been done using a variety of assumptions (e.g. [GRI81], [TER83], [BLA84]).

The relative motion of the observer and the observed objects, causes characteristic flow patterns in an intensity image. These patterns can be interpreted to acquire relative scene distance, surface orientation, rigid scene structure and obscuring boundaries (in the viewer's coordinate system), though there is ambiguity between an object's distance and velocity. From local changing intensity patterns, it is possible to estimate the optic flow (e.g. following [HOR81], [NAG83], [HIL84]), from which one can then estimate information about the objects in the scene and their motion (e.g. [PRA79], [CLO80], [LON80], [RIE83]).

Shading, a more esoteric source of shape information well known to artists, is now being exploited by visual scientists. Horn [HOR75] elaborated the theoretical structure for solving the "shape from shading" problem, and others (e.g. [WOO79], [PEN82]) successfully implemented the theory for reasonably simple, uniform surfaces. The method generally starts from a surface function that relates reflectance to the relative orientations of the illumination, viewer and surface. From this, a system of partial differential equations is derived showing how local intensity variation is related to local shape variation. With the addition of boundary, surface continuity and singular point (e.g. highlight) constraints, solutions can be determined for the system of differential equations.

A major problem is that the solution relies on a global resolution of constraints, which seems to require a characterized reflectance function for the whole surface in question. Unfortunately, few surfaces have a reflectance function that meets this requirement, though Pentland [PEN82] has shown reasonable success with some natural objects (e.g. a rock and a face), through making some assumptions about the surface reflectance. There is also a problem with the global convex/concave ambiguity of the surface, which arises when only shading information is available, though Blake [BLA85] has shown how stereo correspondence on a nearby specular point can resolve the ambiguity. For these reasons, this technique may be best suited to only qualitative or rough numerical analyses.

Variations of this technique have used multiple light sources ([COL81], [WES82]) or polarized light [KOS79]. Explicit surface descriptions (e.g. planar, cylindrical) have been obtained by examining iso-intensity contours [TUR74] and fitting quadratic surfaces [CER83] to intensity data.

Texture gradients are another source of shape information. Assuming texture structure remains constant over the surface, then all variation in either scale ([STE79], [PEN83]) or statistics ([WIT80], [OHT81]) can be ascribed to surface slant distortion. The measure of compression gives local slant and the direction of compression gives local tilt; together they estimate local surface orientation.

The final source of orientation and depth information comes from global shape deformation. The technique relies on knowledge of how appearance varies with surface orientation, how certain patterns create impressions of three dimensional structure, and what constraints are needed to reconstruct that structure. Examples of this include reconstructing surface orientation from the assumption that skew symmetry is slant distorted true symmetry [KAN79], from maximizing the local ratio of the area to the square of the perimeter [BRA83a], from families of space curves interpreted as geodesic surface markings [STE83], from space curves as locally circular arcs [BAR83], and from characteristic distortions in known object surface boundary shapes [FIS83]. Because this information relies on higher level knowledge of the objects, these techniques probably would not help the initial stages of analysis much. However, they may provide supporting evidence at the later stages.

There are variations in the exact outputs of each of these techniques, but many provide the required data and all provide some form of useful three dimensional shape information. Further, some attributes may be derivable from measured values (e.g. orientation by locally differentiating depth).

How Can We Use Surface Information?

As the segmentation criteria are object-centered, the segments of the surface image will directly correspond to model segments, especially since boundaries are mainly used for rough surface shape alignments. Making these symbolic correspondences means that we can directly instantiate and verify object models, which then facilitates geometric inversions of the image formation process.

Surface orientation can then be used to simplify the estimation of the object's orientation. Given the model-to-data patch correspondences, pairing surface normals leaves only a single rotational degree-of-freedom about the aligned normals. Estimating the object's translation is also much simpler because the three dimensional coordinates of any image point (relative to the camera) can be deduced from its pixel position and its depth value. Hence, the translation of a corresponding model point can be directly calculated.

All together, the surface information makes explicit or easily obtainable five of the six degrees-of-freedom associated with an individual surface point (though perhaps imprecisely because of noise in the surface data and problems with making precise model-to-data feature correspondences).

Depth discontinuities make explicit the ordering relationships with more distant surfaces. These relationships help group features to form contexts for model invocation and matching, and help verify potential matches, hence simplifying and strengthening the recognition process.

Surface orientation allows calculation of the surface shape class (e.g. planar, singly-curved or doubly-curved), and correction of slant and curvature distortions of perceived surface area and elongation. The relative orientations between structures give strong constraints on the identity of their superobject and its orientation. Absolute distance measurements allow the calculation of absolute sizes.

How Can Surface Data Help Overcome Current Recognition Problems?

Recognizing real three dimensional objects is still difficult, in part because of difficulties with selecting models, matching complicated shapes, dealing with occlusion, feature description, reducing matching complexity and coping with noise. Surface information helps overcome all of these problems, as discussed below.

Selecting the correct model from the model database requires a description of the data suitable for triggering candidates from the model base. Since descriptions of the model features are given in terms of their three dimensional shapes, describing data features based on their three dimensional shapes reduces the difficulties of comparison, and hence leads to more successful model invocation.

Most current recognition programs have not progressed much beyond recognizing objects whose shapes are largely block-like. One cause of this has been a preoccupation with orientation discontinuity boundaries, which, though easier to detect in intensity images, are noticeably lacking on many real objects. Using the actual surfaces as primitives extends the range of recognizable objects. Faugeras and Hebert [FAU83] demonstrated this by using planar patch primitives to successfully detect and orient an irregularly shaped automobile part.

Viewed objects are often obscured by nearer objects and the ensuing loss of data causes recognition programs to fail. Surface images provide extra information that help overcome occlusion problems. For example, occlusion boundaries are explicit, and thus denote where relevant information stops. Moreover, the presence of a closer surface provides evidence for why the information is missing, and hence where it may re-appear (i.e. on the "other side" of the obscuring surface).

Surface patches are less sensitive to fragmentation, because pixel connectivity extends in two dimensions. Describing the surfaces is also more robust, because (usually) more pixels are involved and come from a more compact area. Globally, connectivity (i.e. adjacency) of surfaces is largely guaranteed, and slight variations will not affect description. Hence, the topology of the major patches should be reliably extracted.

Establishing model-to-data correspondences can be computationally expensive. Using surface patches helps reduce the expense in two ways: (1) there are usually fewer surface patches than, for example, the boundary segments between them and (2) patch descriptions are richer, which leads to selecting fewer locally suitable, but globally incorrect model-to-data feature pairings (such as those that occur in edge-based matching algorithms).

Noise is omnipresent. Sensor imperfections, quantization errors, random fluctuations, surface shape texture and minor object imperfections are typical sources of data variation. A surface image segment is a more robust data element, because its size leads to reduced data variation (assuming $O(n^2)$ data values as compared with $O(n)$ for linear features). This contrasts with linear feature detection and description processes, in which noise can cause erroneous parameter estimates, loss of connectivity or wandering.

Why Not Use Other Representations?

There are three alternative contenders for the primary input data representation: edges, image regions and volumes.

Edges have been used extensively in previous vision systems. The key limitations of their use are:

- ambiguous scene interpretation (i.e. whether caused by occlusion, shadows, highlights, surface orientation discontinuities or reflectance changes),

- ambiguous model interpretation (i.e. which straight edge of length 10 could it be?),

- loss of data because of noise or low contrast, and

- image areas free from edges also contain information (e.g. shading).

While these limitations have not deterred research using edge-based recognition, considerable difficulties have been encountered.

Image regions are bounded segments of an intensity image. Their meaning, however, is ambiguous and their description is not sufficiently related to three dimensional objects. For example, Hanson and Riseman [HAN80] and Ohta [OHT79] segmented green image regions for tree boughs using color, yet there is no reason to assume that trees are the only green objects in the scene nor that contiguous green regions belong to the same object. Further, the segmentations lose all the detailed structure of the shape of the bough, which may be needed to identify the type of tree. They augmented the rough classification with general context relations, which assisted in the interpretation of the data. While this type of general information is important and useful for scene analysis, it is often insufficiently precise and object-specific for identification, given current theories of image interpretation.

Volumetric primitives seem to be useful, as discussed by Marr [MAR82] and Brooks [BRO81] in their advocation of generalized cylinders. These solids are formed by sweeping a cross-section along an axis and represent elongated structures well. For volumes with shapes other than something like generalized cylinders (e.g. a head), the descriptions are largely limited to explicit space-filling primitives, which is insufficiently compact, nor does it have the power to easily support appearance deductions.

The generalized cylinder approach also leads to problems with relating volumetric features to observed visible surface data, because there is no simple transformation from the surface to the solid under most representations. Marr [MAR82] showed that generalized cylinders were a logical primitive because these are the objects with planar contour generators from all points of view (along with a few other conditions) and so are natural interpretations for pairs of extended obscuring boundaries. Unfortunately, few objects meet the conditions. Moreover, this transformation ignored most of the other information available in the $2\frac{1}{2}$D sketch, which is too useful to be simply thrown away.

Final Comments

This completes a quick review of why surface information is useful, how one might obtain the data, and how it might be segmented for use. The next chapter starts to use the data for the early stages of scene analysis.

CHAPTER 4

Making Complete Surface Hypotheses

The first step in the interpretation of surface information is the formation of surface hypotheses, which groups surface image regions to form complete surfaces of the unidentified objects. This is the first important transformation from image-based data to object-based data. Further, it reduces data complexity by representing one or more surface regions by a single symbolic entity.

If segmentation has been successful, then the surface image regions should closely correspond to the visible portions of the object's surface patches. Three problems may cause the patches to not correspond closely:

1. A data patch may correspond to several object surface patches, because of segmentation failure.

2. The object surface patch may be fragmented into several data patches, because of segmentation failure.

3. The object surface patch may be fragmented or smaller because of occlusion.

The first two problems are a concern for segmentation and are not considered closely here, though some corrective action is possible once a model has been selected (e.g. a predicted model SURFACE can be used to guide splitting or merging of patches). The third problem is the main concern of this chapter, which shows that the most common cases of occlusion can be overcome with the surfaces largely reconstructed.

Because of the pervasiveness of occlusion in natural scenes, this reconstruction is necessary. Reconstructed surfaces can only be hypothetical but, by the surface segmentation assumptions (Chapter 3), there are no extreme surface or boundary shape variations in a single segment. As many natural object boundaries exhibit surface smoothness over moderate distances (at appropriate scales), reconstruction should be possible. This is even more likely with most man-made objects.

Some research has tried to overcome occlusion directly by using visible cues. Guzman [GUZ68] used paired TEE junctions to signal the presence of occlusion and locate which two dimensional image regions should be connected. Adler [ADL75] also used TEE information to infer depth ordering between scene features. The key problem is detection of occlusion, and their work relied on the use of TEE detections, which show where one surface boundary is abruptly terminated by the obscuring boundary of a closer surface. Because a fragmented obscured surface must have a pair of

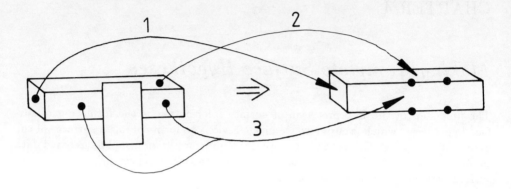

Figure 4.1: Surface Hypothesis Construction Process

TEEs at the start and end of the obscuring boundary (under normal circumstances), the detection of a matched pair of TEEs suggests a likely occlusion boundary, and hence where the invisible portion of the surface lies. In the research described here, occlusion boundaries are directly labeled, so the occlusion cueing process is no longer necessary. The TEEs are still useful for signaling where along the occlusion boundary the obscured surfaces' boundaries terminate. They would also be useful for helping cope with missing, incorrect or ambiguous data (e.g. when a correct boundary label is not available).

4.1   Reconstructing Obscured Surfaces

This process starts with the region graph described in Chapter 3. Initially, the surface hypotheses are identical to the image regions. From these, larger surface hypotheses are created based on surface extensions consistent with presumed occlusions. While it is obviously impossible to always correctly reconstruct obscured structure, often a single surface hypothesis can be created that joins consistent visible surface parts. Figure 4.1 shows a simple case of surface reconstruction.

In Figure 4.2, four cases of a singly obscured surface are shown, along with the most reasonable reconstructions possible, where the boundary arrows indicate an occlusion boundary with the object surface on the right of the arrow and the obscuring surface on the left. In the first case, the original surface boundaries meet when they are extended, and this is presumed to reconstruct a portion of the surface. If the boundaries change their curvature or direction, then reconstruction may not be possible, or it may be erroneous. (Even if erroneous, the reconstructed surface may more closely approximate the true surface than the original input.) The second case illustrates when reconstruction does not occur, because the unobscured boundaries do not intersect when extended. The third case shows an interior obscuring object removed. The fourth case shows where the surface has been split by an obscuring object and reconstructed. The label of the boundary extension always remains back-side-obscuring, because it might participate in further reconstructions.

What is interesting is that only three rules are needed for the reconstruction (see Figure 4.3). They are:

1. remove interior closer surfaces (Rule 1),

2. extend and connect boundaries on separate surface hypotheses to form a single surface hypothesis (Rule 2), and

3. extend and connect boundaries on a single surface to make a larger surface (Rule 3).

Rule 2 connects two separated surfaces if either extension of the boundaries intersect. The remaining portion of the obscuring boundary is disconnected to indicate no information about the obscured portion of the surface (until Rule 3). Rule 3 removes notches in surfaces by trying to find intersecting extensions of the two sides of the notch. Repeated application of these rules may be needed to maximally reconstruct the surface.

Reconstruction is attempted whenever surface occlusion is detected, which is indicated by the presence of back-side-obscuring labeled boundaries. Concave orientation discontinuity labelled boundaries may also mean occlusion. In Figure 4.4, the base of the obscuring cylinder rests on the plane and so has a concave shape boundary, which should be treated as part of the delineation of the obscured region of the plane. (If the two objects were separated slightly, an obscuring boundary would replace the concave boundary.) As the concave boundary does not indicate which object is in front, it is assumed that either possibility could occur.

Figure 4.5 shows a typical case where one surface sitting on another will create a TEE junction, or connect to an obscuring boundary (as in Figure 4.4).

After finding the segments indicating occlusion, the points where reconstruction can start need to be found. These are the ends of boundary segments that satisfy:

1. The endpoints must lie between obscured section boundaries (defined above), and boundaries that definitely lie on the object surface (i.e. convex or front-side-obscuring).

2. The endpoints must be at a TEE junction.

3. The true object surface boundary must be the shaft of the TEE.

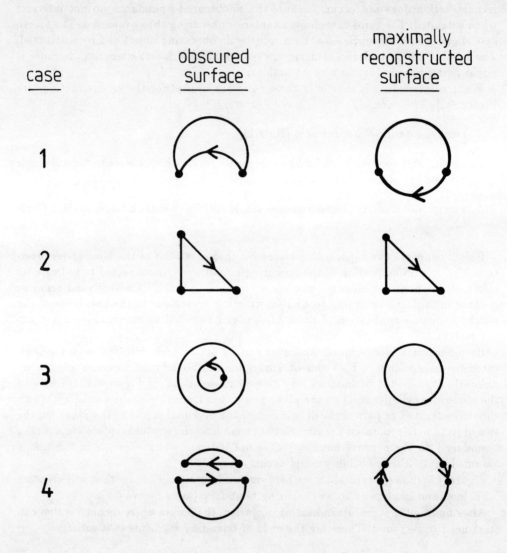

Figure 4.2: Four Occlusion Cases Reconstructed

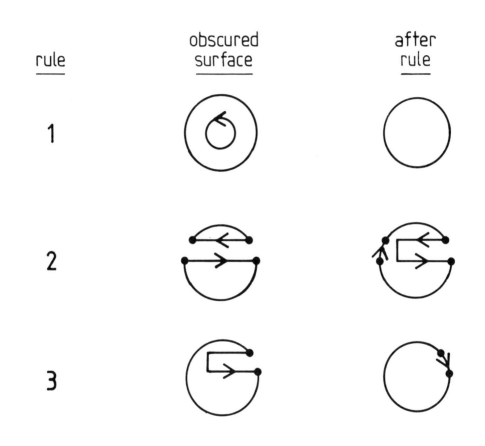

rule   obscured surface   after rule

1

2

3

Figure 4.3: Surface Construction Processes

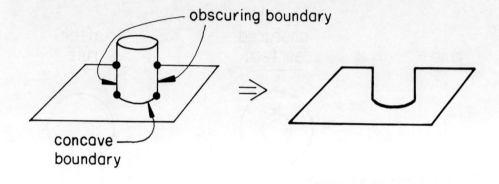

Figure 4.4: Concave Boundaries also Delineate Obscured Regions

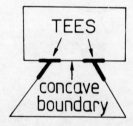

Figure 4.5: TEE Junctions Delimit Reconstruction Concave Boundaries

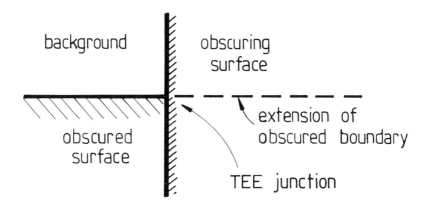

Figure 4.6: Reconstruction Starts at a TEE Junction

These points are illustrated in Figure 4.6.

For reconstruction, boundary segments must intersect when extended. As intersecting three dimensional surface curves still intersect when projected onto the image plane, extension and intersection is done only in two dimensions, thus avoiding the problems of three dimensional curve intersection. Extending the boundaries is done by estimating the curvature shortly before the terminating TEE and projecting the curve through the TEE. On the basis of the boundary segmentation assumptions (Chapter 3), segments can be assumed to have nearly constant curvature, so the extension process is justified. Segments that intersect in two dimensions can then be further tested to ensure three dimensional intersection, though this was not needed when using the additional constraints given below. Further, because of numerical inaccuracies in the range data, three dimensional intersection is hard to validate.

To prevent spurious reconstructions that arise in complex scenes with many obscuring objects, other constraints must be satisfied:

- If a portion of a surface is obscured, then that portion must be completely bounded by an appropriate type of boundary (as defined above).

- The ends of the unobscured portions of the surface boundary must be joinable.

- The joined portions of surface must lie on the same side of the boundary extension.

- The obscured portions of a surface's boundary can not intersect other boundaries of the same surface. (This rules out obscured laminar surface reconstructions, where the surface may cross underneath itself.)

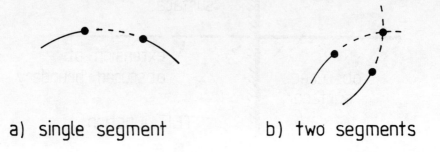

a) single segment   b) two segments

Figure 4.7: Segment Extension Process

- Reconnected surface fragments must have consistent depths, surface orientations and curvatures (because surface shape segmentation enforces the shape consistency).

- Two reconnected surfaces must not be otherwise adjacent.

There are two outputs from the reconstruction process – the boundaries and the surface itself. Because of the surface segmentation assumption, the reconstructed surface shape is an extension of the visible surface's shape. The boundary is different because, in the absence of any knowledge of the object, it is impossible to know exactly where the boundary lies. It is assumed that the obscured portion of the boundary is an extension of the unobscured portions, and continues with the same shape until intersection. The two cases are shown in Figure 4.7. In case (a), a single segment extension connects the boundary endpoints with the same curvature as the unobscured portions. In case (b), the unobscured portions are extended until intersection.

The process may incorrectly merge surface patches because of coincidental alignments, though this is unlikely to occur because of the constraints of boundary intersection and labeling and surface shape compatibility. Hence, the conservative approach to producing surface hypotheses would be to allow all possible surface reconstructions, including the original surface without any extensions. This proliferates surface hypotheses causing combinatorial problems in the later stages. So, the final surface hypotheses are made from the maximally reconstructed surfaces only. If the reconstructed surface is larger than the true surface, invocation may be degraded, but hypothesis construction would continue because the surface extension is not used. Verification avoids this problem by using the original image regions as its input.

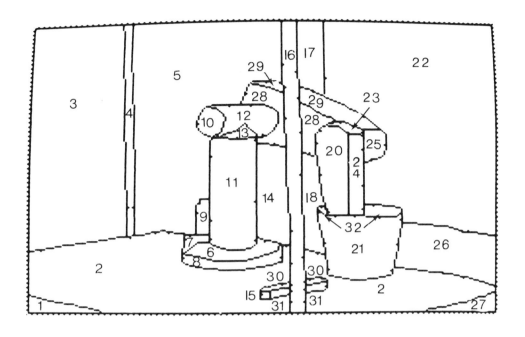

Figure 4.8: Surface Hypotheses for the Test Scene

The Surface Hypothesis Graph

The region graph (Chapter 3) forms the initial input into the explicit surface hypothesis process. The surface hypothesizing process makes the following additions to the region graph to form the surface hypothesis graph:

1. Every surface hypothesis node links to a set of region nodes.

2. A surface node is linked to a chain of boundary nodes linking to boundary segments that isolate the surface.

3. If two surface nodes have region nodes linked by adjacency nodes, then the surface nodes are linked by adjacency nodes.

4.2   Examples from the Test Scenes

Figure 3.10 showed the initial image regions and Figure 4.8 shows the final surface hypotheses formed by the processes described in this chapter (numbers in the picture are the surface index).

Figure 4.9: Observed and Reconstructed Upper Arm Surface

There are several instances of successful surface reconstructions. Figure 4.9 shows reconstruction of the robot upper arm side panel. The surface merging operation has rejoined the two sections, and the boundary extension has largely restored the missing section in the lower left corner. Because the reconstruction is only suggestive, and because the leftmost boundary was not observed as being curved, the reconstruction is a little generous and slightly exceeds the actual surface. The right end of the panel could not be reconstructed because of insufficient evidence for the true boundary, although the labeling claimed it was obscured. Other valid reconstructions included the block lying on the table and the two halves at the back of the trash can (Figure 4.10). The latter is interesting because it was a curved surface, so matching of surface shape had to account for the change in orientation. One inappropriate merging occurred: the two top panels of the robot upper arm had their real join hidden behind the vertical gantry column. As they were continuous, their orientation differed only slightly, and met all the occlusion constraints, they were merged as well. The hypothesis construction process expects this type of error, so it did not prove catastrophic.

These examples show that the obscured surface reconstructions are successful, and Figure 4.8 shows that most reasonable surfaces are made.

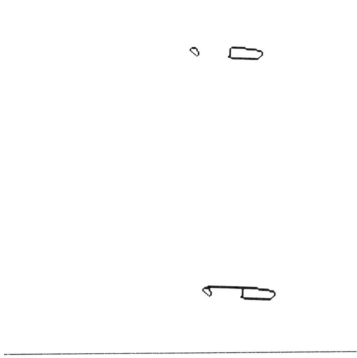

Figure 4.10: Observed and Reconstructed Trash Can Back Surface

4.3 Discussion

The major problem with the surface reconstruction constraints is unsolvable – one cannot reconstruct the invisible when the image is taken from a single viewpoint. Some examples are seen in Figure 4.11. In the first case, the extended segments never intersect, and in the second, extension creates a larger, incorrect surface. Stereo or observer movement might help reconstruct the surface, however. Feature regularity (such as symmetry) might also be exploited to aid reconstruction. As the goal was to reconstruct enough to allow the rest of recognition to proceed, a few failures should be acceptable.

Another obvious criticism is over performance when applied to rich natural images. Realistic images are likely to have missing or erroneous data, such as for line labels or surface orientation, which is likely to degrade both the quality and rate of performance. In short, the processes described in this chapter seem fine for clear laboratory images, but it is hard to predict their performance on natural scenes.

Because segmentation criteria may break up or merge surfaces at different scales, surface hypotheses need to allow for alternative representations derived as a function of a locally relevant scale. These representations are related but are not interchangeable,

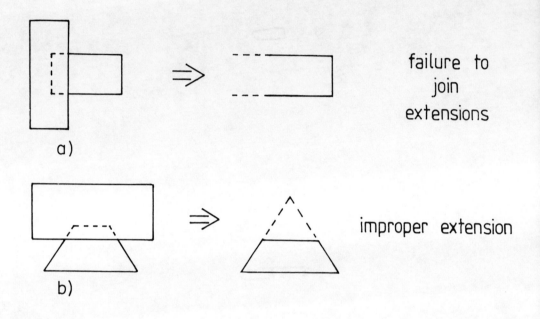

Figure 4.11: Unsuccessful Extensions

nor are they equivalent.

Scale also affects surface reconstruction, as can be seen in Figure 4.12. The first figure shows the extension based on individual teeth of the gear, whereas at the larger scale, the extension is based on the smoothed convex envelope of the gears.

To avoid the problem of redundant hypothesis formation, only the reconstructed surface is kept. An alternative solution might isolate the description of the surface, which is common to all hypotheses, from that of the boundary of the surface.

Final Comments

The test image shows that we can expect substantial occlusion in three dimensional scenes. This chapter demonstrates that much of the lost information can be inferred from the physical and modeling constraints, without generating many errors or redundant hypotheses.

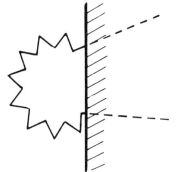

a) gear extension failure at
   higher resolution scale

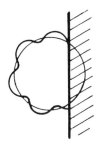

b) successful extension at
   lower resolution scale

Figure 4.12: Scale Based Extension Problems

CHAPTER 5

Surface Clusters

A competent object recognition system needs a perceptual organization mechanism, to both indicate which image features are related and delimit the object's spatial extent. To help provide this mechanism, we developed [FIS86c] a new intermediate representation, <u>surface clusters</u>, lying between the segmented surface image and the model-based three dimensional object hypotheses. This chapter describes their role in the **IMAGINE I** system.

5.1 Why Surface Clusters?

A surface cluster is a set of surface patches isolated by suitable boundaries. The goal of the surface cluster formation process is to produce a volumetric image representation for portions of the scene that might be identifiable three dimensional objects. There are three motivations for this:

1. the creation of a volumetric intermediate representation suitable for identity-independent operations,

2. the focusing of attention on an object and its associated image features and

3. the reduction of search complexity through structuring the image features.

The first motivation for a surface cluster is a competence issue – surface clusters are new representations that bridge the conceptual distance between the segmented surface image and the object. The point is to create an "unidentified, but distinct" object interpretation associated with sets of image features – a volumetric representation describing solid objects with approximate spatial relationships but without identifications. With this structure, the key image understanding representations now become (following Marr [MAR82]): image – primal sketch – $2\frac{1}{2}$D sketch – surface clusters – objects. The grouping creates a good starting point for further interpretation; it is a form of figure/ground separation for solid objects.

Such representations are needed for unidentifiable objects to allow intermediate levels of image interpretation even when full identification is not achieved, whether because of faults or lack of models in the database. Possible application areas include vehicle navigation, collision avoidance, object tracking or grasping.

The second motivation is to partition the image features into activity contexts for the later stages of recognition. This will help to focus scene understanding to make more obvious the interpretation of a group of image features and how they are matched with a model. By eliminating irrelevant and unrelated image features, it should be easier to identify and verify objects, since only features belonging to a single object will be present.

The "context" aspect of surface clusters is exploited by model invocation (Chapter 8) and hypothesis construction (Chapter 9). Model invocation requires contexts within which to accumulate evidence to hypothesize models, and surface clusters are ideal for invoking the volumetric models (the ASSEMBLY – see Chapter 7). To help fully instantiate an ASSEMBLY hypothesis, it may be necessary to search for additional evidence. Because ASSEMBLY invocation has occurred in a surface cluster context, any additional structural evidence should also come from the context. Thus, processing has been focused to a distinct region of the image.

The final motivation for creating these aggregations is one of performance – eliminating unrelated image features produces an immediate reduction in the complexity of the scene analysis. The whole interpretation has been reduced to a set of smaller independent problems, which is necessary given the quantity of data in an image.

A casual mathematical analysis supports this point. Here, we are mainly concerned with intersurface relationships (i.e. relative surface orientation and matching data surfaces to model SURFACEs). Since every surface on an object has a relationship to every other surface on the object, an object with N visible surfaces has $O(N^2)$ relationships. If there are A objects in the scene, each with B visible surfaces, there will be AB total visible surfaces. So, initially, the analysis complexity is $O((AB)^2)$. However, if the surface cluster process succeeds in partitioning the image into the A objects, then the complexity is reduced to $O(AB^2)$. For typical scenes, a nominal value for A is 20, so this can lead to a substantial improvement in performance.

5.2   Theory of Surface Clusters

The goal of the surface cluster formation process is to isolate the visible portion of each distinct three dimensional object's surface, so that later stages of the scene analysis can associate a model with the surface cluster.

The primary input into the process is the set of surface hypotheses produced as output of the processes described in Chapter 4. The surface hypotheses are linked by adjacency, and relative surface orientation at the boundaries is known.

The output of the process is a set of surface clusters hierarchically linked by inclusion, with each consisting of a set of surface patches. Though the surface cluster is not closed (i.e. it is missing the back side), it defines a solid bounded in front by the visible surfaces.

The surface cluster formation process is closely linked to the model structure known as the ASSEMBLY, which is defined in Chapter 7. The ASSEMBLY is a model of a three dimensional solid and is composed of SURFACEs or recursively defined subcomponents. Properties we would like the surface cluster formation process to have are:

- Every model ASSEMBLY is wholly contained in at least one surface cluster.

- There are surface clusters containing only a single primitive model ASSEMBLY.

- Only complete ASSEMBLYs are contained in surface clusters.

- There is a hierarchy of surface clusters corresponding to the hierarchy of model ASSEMBLYs.

However, at this stage of image analysis, models are not available to help segment the image, nor is the model base known. Hence, to achieve our goal with these properties, two assumptions must be made about the model structure independent of the actual models:

- If a set of model SURFACEs is completely surrounded by a set of concave or crack surface boundaries, then they are modeled as a distinct ASSEMBLY.

- If two model SURFACEs are adjacent across a convex surface boundary, then they are in the same model ASSEMBLY.

For example, a nose on a face, or a handle on a coffee cup would thus be in separate ASSEMBLYs.

The process of creating the surface clusters has three steps:

1. Classify adjacent surface regions as connected or unconnected.

2. Form primitive surface clusters from connected groups of surfaces. (Primitive surface clusters are those that cannot be split further.)

3. Merge primitive surface clusters to form larger surface clusters.

These steps are described in detail below.

The algorithm is conservative, in that it tries to avoid splitting the smallest model ASSEMBLYs between surface clusters at the price of creating clusters containing several ASSEMBLYs. Splitting an object between several different surface clusters would be catastrophic because it asserts that the segregated components are unrelated. Creating clusters larger than single objects is mainly an annoyance, because the rest of the recognition process then has more work to identify the objects.

Determining Surface Connectivity

The segmented surface image can be thought of as a graph, where the nodes of the graph represent the surface patches and the arcs of the graph represent surface adjacency. These arcs will be labeled as connecting or segmenting, according to criteria based on boundary type and configuration. The connection criteria are simple and logical, except for a laminar surface case (described shortly) and are based on obvious three dimensional properties of surface connectivity and object depth ordering. Splitting the graph at segmenting boundaries partitions the scene into sets of connected surfaces – forming the primitive surface clusters.

We assume that the modeled objects are segmented into subcomponents at chains of connected concave boundaries. As concave model boundaries are observed as concave

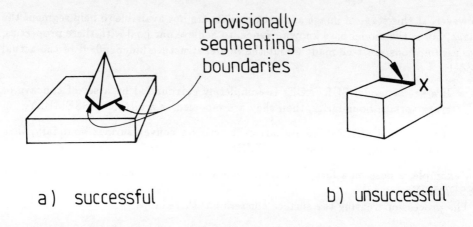

Figure 5.1: Concave Boundaries Provisionally Segment

image boundaries, the latter are potentially segmenting. In Figure 5.1 part (a), the concave boundary is truly segmenting.

Further, distinct objects are often on opposite sides of concave surface orientation boundaries. For example, a block sitting on a table has concave boundaries isolating it from the table. Nameable subcomponents of natural objects often fit flushly with concave boundaries, as in the nose-to-face junction. Because the boundary is concave, it is indeterminate whether the two surfaces are joined or merely in contact. Moreover, it is usually impossible to tell which surface passes underneath the other past the point of the observed concave boundary. So, the conservative approach suggests that this boundary causes a segmenting arc. Assuming concave boundaries necessarily imply segmentation leads to contradictions as seen in Figure 5.1 part (b), where there is no reasonable shape boundary at point X to continue segmentation. If there are other connections between the two surfaces that do not involve a segmenting boundary, then the final surface cluster will include both surfaces.

A more complicated case occurs with crack-type boundaries. Here, two surfaces may be coincidentally aligned, or part of a flush contact boundary (as often occurs with revolute joints). Because of the ambiguity, it is assumed that connectivity does not hold across crack-type joints.

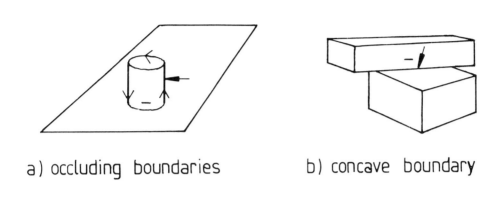

a) occluding boundaries   b) concave boundary

Figure 5.2: Object Ordering Causes Concave and Obscuring Boundaries

Whenever one object sits in front of or on top of another, the intervening boundary is always either concave or obscuring, as illustrated in Figure 5.2. To complete the isolation of the cylinder in part (a) from the background plane, a rule is needed to handle obscuring boundaries. As these usually give no clues to the relation between opposing surfaces (other than being depth separated), surfaces will usually be segmented across these, and so segmenting arcs join the nodes representing these surfaces.

Connectivity holds across some obscuring boundaries. Disregarding coincidental alignments, the one exception found occurs when laminar objects fold back on themselves, as illustrated in Figure 5.3. This figure shows a leaf folded over and the two surfaces of a trash can. The arrows on the boundary mean that it is an obscuring type boundary with (here) the front surface lying to the left when looking along the boundary in the direction of the arrow. In both cases, the two surfaces are connected, even though an obscuring boundary intervenes, and so here a connecting arc is used. Fortunately, this case has a distinctive signature: the arrow vertices shown at the right side of the figure are paradigmatic of the junction formed by a folding laminar surface. Viewpoint analysis (by octant) shows that these are the only special trihedral vertex label cases needed for two connected laminar surfaces. Curved laminar surfaces are (here) treated locally as two connecting planar laminar surfaces.

Two surfaces lying on opposite sides of convex boundaries ordinarily belong to the same object, though coincidental alignment may also produce this effect. Hence, surfaces on opposite sides of convex boundaries cause connecting arcs. A surface orientation boundary that is both concave and convex in places is broken up by the curve segmentation assumptions.

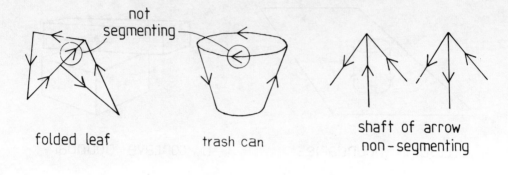

Figure 5.3: Connectivity Holds Across Some Obscuring Boundaries

To summarize, the constraints that specify the connectivity of surface patches are:

- Connectivity holds across convex shape boundaries.

- Connectivity does not hold across concave and crack shape boundaries.

- Connectivity does not hold across obscuring boundaries, except when the boundaries are configured as in Figure 5.3.

Forming Primitive Surface Clusters

Primitive surface clusters are formed by collecting all surface patch nodes that are directly or transitively connected in the graph, once all arcs are labeled as "segmenting" or "connecting". Thus, image features that can only belong to the same object lie in the same surface cluster, and features that possibly belong to other objects do not lie in the cluster.

Depth Merged Surface Clusters

The goal of the surface cluster process is to associate all components of an object in some surface cluster. All components of a model may not occur in the same primitive surface cluster for several reasons:

- The object may consist of several subcomponents, each of which appears in smaller surface clusters.

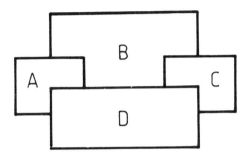

Figure 5.4: Depth Merging Example

- The object may fold back on itself, and thus be observed as two different components separated by an obscuring boundary.

In the test image, the upper and lower robot arms lie in separate primitive surface clusters, but the model ASSEMBLY joining them does not yet have a surface cluster. Depth merged surface clusters are intended to provide the context for complete objects.

This merging process is constrained by the following observation, referring to Figure 5.4. If there are four surface clusters (A, B, C, and D), an object might be wholly contained in only one of these, but it might also obscure itself and be in more than one. Hence, reasonable groupings of surface clusters containing whole objects are AB, AD, BC, BD, CD, ABC, ABD, ACD, BCD and ABCD. AC is an unlikely grouping because there is no obvious relation between them.

Merging all surfaces behind a given surface does not solve the problem. If only surfaces ABC were present in the above scene, then merging behind does not produce a containing surface cluster if the true object was ABC. Similarly, the technique of merging all surfaces in front fails if both the object and grouping were ACD. Neither of these processes individually produce the correct clusters. To avoid this problem, a more combinatorial solution was adopted.

Before the computational constraints for depth merging are given, one refinement is necessary. Rather than considering depth merging for all surface clusters, certain sets of surface clusters can be initially grouped into equivalent depth surface clusters. These occur when either surface clusters mutually obscure each other, or when there is no obvious depth relationship (e.g. they lie across a concave surface boundary). An example of where two surface clusters mutually obscure is with the robot lower arm and trash can surface clusters in the test image. When these cases occur, all such primitive surface clusters can be merged into a single equivalent depth surface cluster. Thereafter, the combinatorial depth merging process only considers the equivalent depth surface clusters.

The properties defining the equivalent depth clusters are:
Let:

$\{P_1, ...P_n\}$ be the primitive surface clusters

$\text{front}(P_i, P_j)$ means P_i is in front of P_j, which holds if there is a
surface in P_i with an obscuring relation to a surface in P_j

$\text{beside}(P_i, P_j)$ means P_i is beside P_j, which holds if there is a surface
in P_i that shares a concave or crack boundary with a
surface in P_j

$\{E_1, ...E_m\}$ be the equivalent depth clusters

$E_i = \{P_{i1}, ...P_{is}\}$

Then, the relationship between the P_i and the E_i is defined by:

(1) If $\mid E_i \mid \neq 1$, for any $P_{ia} \in E_i$, there is a $P_{ib} \in E_i$ such that:

$$\text{front}(P_{ia}, P_{ib}) \text{ and front}(P_{ib}, P_{ia})$$

or

$$\text{beside}(P_{ia}, P_{ib})$$

(2) If $\mid E_i \mid = 1$ and $E_i = \{ P_i \}$, then for all $P_j \neq P_i$

$$\text{not front}(P_i, P_j) \text{ or not front}(P_j, P_i)$$

and

$$\text{not beside}(P_i, P_j)$$

(3) The E_i are maximal (i.e. no E_i contains another E_j).

Equivalent depth surface clusters that only contain a single primitive surface cluster are replaced by that primitive surface cluster (for compactness).

Then, using the same definitions, the depth merged surface clusters are sets of equivalent depth surface clusters:

Let:

efront(E_i, E_j) mean equivalent depth surface cluster E_i is in front of equivalent depth surface cluster E_j, which occurs if there are primitive surface clusters $P_{ia} \in E_i$ and $P_{jb} \in E_j$ such that front(P_{ia}, P_{jb})

linked(E_i, E_j) holds if efront(E_i, E_j) or efront(E_j, E_i)

$\{D_1, ... D_n\}$ be the depth merged clusters

$D_i = \{E_{i1}, ... E_{it}\}$

Then:

the D_i are all subsets of $\{E_1, ... E_m\}$ such that for any $E_{ia} \in D_i$ there is a $E_{ib} \in D_i$ satisfying linked(E_{ia}, E_{ib})

The implementation of these definitions is straightforward and leads first to the construction of primitive surface clusters, then to formation of equivalent depth clusters and finally to the linking of these into larger depth merged surface clusters. The background and picture frame surfaces are omitted.

The surface clusters are linked into the image description graph started in Chapter 3 by the following additions:

1. Every surface cluster node is linked to a set of surface hypotheses.

2. Surface clusters are linked into a hierarchy by containment.

3. Surface clusters are linked to chains of boundary elements that surround them.

5.3 Examples of Surface Cluster Formation

To show that the implemented computation produced suitable results, an example is given here, using the surface hypotheses of the test image (see Figure 4.8). Some of the surface clusters for this scene are shown in Figures 5.5, 5.6 and 5.7.

As can be seen in these examples, the surface clusters form object level "chunks" of the image, and correspond to the primitive ASSEMBLYs of the models given in Chapter 7. In Table 5.1, there is a listing of the surface cluster to model ASSEMBLY correspondences for the test image. Clearly, the surface cluster formation process isolates the key features into what corresponds to structurally based intuitive "objects".

Figure 5.8 shows the surface clusters of Table 5.1 organized to make explicit their hierarchical relationships. Clusters designated by squares closely correspond to models.

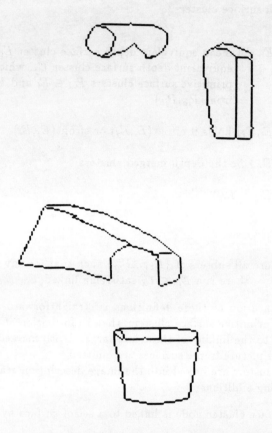

Figure 5.5: Several Primitive Clusters

For the example above, the primitive and equivalent depth surface clusters are appropriate. What seems to be a problem is the number of depth merged surface clusters, which depend on combinatorial groupings of equivalent depth surface clusters. For the test scene, there are 9 primitive, 3 equivalent depth and 6 depth merged surface clusters. Here, the number of depth merged surface clusters is not such a problem as the object also has a strong depth order, so 2 of the 6 correspond to ASSEMBLYs. In other test images, shallower depth ordering causes more serious combinatorial grouping. Hence, an alternative process should be considered.

Though several surface clusters contained multiple ASSEMBLYs, this caused no recognition failures.

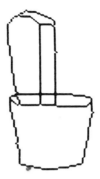

Figure 5.6: An Equivalent Depth Cluster

5.4   Relation to Other Work

In early two dimensional scene understanding work, Shirai [SHI75] and Waltz [WAL75] achieved a rough separation of objects from the background by assuming external boundaries of regions were the separator. Heuristics for adding isolated background regions, based on TEE matching, were suggested. These techniques required that the background be shadow free, and that the objects did not contact the image boundary.

Both of these approaches concentrated on finding relevant objects by eliminating the irrelevant (i.e. the background). This was later seen to be unprofitable because relevance is usually determined at a higher level. The methods were also incapable of decomposing the object grouping into smaller object groups.

Guzman [GUZ68] started a sequence of work on surface segmentation using image topology. Starting from line drawings of scenes, he used heuristics based on boundary configurations at junctions to link together image regions to form complete bodies. Huffman [HUF71] and Clowes [CLO71] put Guzman's heuristics into a more scientific form by isolating distinct bodies at connected concave and obscuring boundaries in two dimensional images.

Sugihara [SUG79] proposed two heuristics for separating objects in an edge labeled

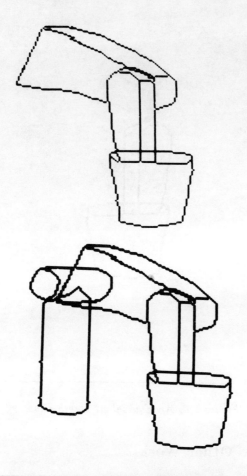

Figure 5.7: Several Depth Merged Clusters

three dimensional light-stripe based range data image. The first separated objects
where two obscuring and two obscured segments meet, depending on a depth gap being
detectable from either illumination or viewer effects. The second heuristic separated
bodies along concave boundaries terminating at special types of junctions (mainly
involving two obscuring junctions). Other complexities arose because of the disparate
illumination and sensor positions.

Kak et al. [KAK86] described segmentation from a labeled edge diagram that connects "cut"-type vertices with obscuring and concave edges, producing a segmentation
similar to the primitive surface clusters.

The work described here extends the previous work for application to objects with
curved surfaces, some laminar surface groupings and hierarchical object structure. In
particular, obscuring boundaries can become connecting (in certain circumstances)

Table 5.1: Surface Cluster To Model Correspondences

SURFACE CLUSTER	CLUSTER TYPE	IMAGE REGIONS	MODEL
1	PRIMITIVE	20,21,30	
2	PRIMITIVE	27	
3	PRIMITIVE	16,26	robshldbd
4	PRIMITIVE	8	robbody
5	PRIMITIVE	29	robshldsobj
6	PRIMITIVE	33,34,35,36,37	
7	PRIMITIVE	12,18,31	lowerarm
8	PRIMITIVE	9,28,38	trashcan
9	PRIMITIVE	17,19,22,25,32	upperarm
10	EQUIVALENT	20,21,27,30	
11	EQUIVALENT	8,16,26,29	robshould + robbody
12	EQUIVALENT	9,12,18,28,31,38	lowerarm + trashcan
13	DEPTH	9,12,17,18,19,22, 25,28,31,32,38	armasm + trashcan
14	DEPTH	8,16,17,19,22, 25,26,29,32	
15	DEPTH	8,9,12,16,17, 18,19,22,25,26, 28,29,31,32,38	link + robot + trashcan
16	DEPTH	8,16,20,21,26, 27,29,30	
17	DEPTH	8,16,17,19,20, 21,22,25,26,27, 29,30,32	
18	DEPTH	8,9,12,16,17, 18,19,20,21,22, 25,26,27,28,29, 30,31,32,38	

which allows the two laminar surfaces in the folded leaf problem to become joined into a single surface cluster (Figure 5.3). Further, concave boundaries defining ambiguous depth relationships can be exploited to limit combinatorial explosion in the creation of larger surface clusters, which is necessary to provide the image context for structured object recognition.

Given the current input data, it is possible to directly infer from surface depth and orientation the type of surface discontinuity boundaries (i.e. obscuring, convex, concave). If the orientation data were missing, then topological analysis like that from the two dimensional blocks world analysis (e.g. [HUF71], [CLO71], [WAL75], [MAC73], [TUR74], [KAN79], [WAL75]) can sometimes uniquely deduce the three dimensional

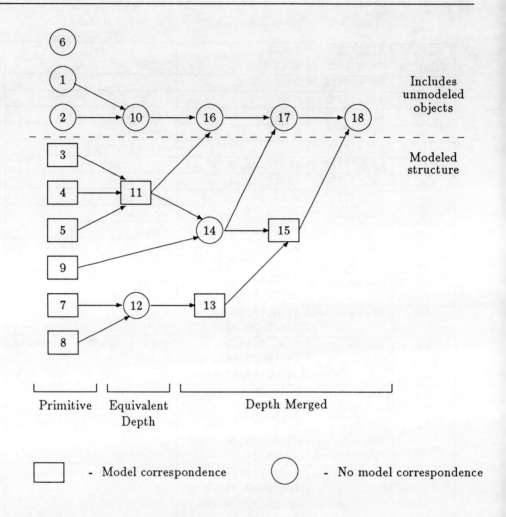

Figure 5.8: Surface Cluster Hierarchy

boundary type. Labeling rules could also correct some data errors (e.g. [FAL72]).

These projects also introduced the boundary labels of types obscuring (front surface, back surface) and shape discontinuity (convex, concave) that are used for the reasoning described here. Also useful is the understanding of how boundary junctions relate to observer position and vertex structures (e.g. Thorpe and Shafer [THO83]).

5.5   Discussion

Surface clusters need not be perfect, as the goal of the process is to produce a partitioning without a loss of information. They may be incomplete, as when an object is split up by a closer obscuring object, though the surface hypothesizing may bridge the occlusion. They may also be over-aggregated – from images where there is insufficient evidence to segregate two objects. These failures may reduce recognition performance (i.e. speed), but not its competence (i.e. success): incompletely merged surface clusters will be merged in a larger context and insufficiently split surface clusters will just cause more searching during hypothesis construction.

The process of forming primitive surface clusters is particularly interesting because it is a local process (i.e. connectivity is determined by classifications made in the neighborhoods of vertices and single boundary segments) that produces a global organization of the image. This also holds for the formation of the equivalent depth surface clusters, but not the depth merged clusters. Locality is important because (1) it is often required for efficient parallelization and (2) it is often the hallmark of a robust process.

A criticism concerns the combinatorial formation of the depth merged surface clusters. The general goal is to create hypotheses that correspond to the complete visible surface of an object and nothing more, necessitating merging surface clusters. Unfortunately, in the absence of context or object knowledge, there is no information yet to determine whether a surface cluster is related to the surfaces behind. As an object may be associated with any two consecutive surfaces, it is likely that the merging process needs to be based on either merging all surface clusters linked to the current one, or all possible combinations of consecutive depths. As each surface may be in front of more than one other surface, the latter alternative most likely leads to a combinatorial explosion, whereas the former leads to enlarged surface clusters. The combinatorial process, however, probably has better future potential, provided some further merging constraints can be elucidated and implemented. The use of equivalent depth clusters helped control the problem, and as seen in Table 5.1, most of the surface clusters correspond to object features, an object was never split between surface clusters, and usually only one new model was appropriate for each new level of surface cluster.

A general criticism about the surface cluster is that, as formulated here, it is too literal. A more suggestive process is needed for dealing with natural scenes, where segmentation, adjacency and depth ordering are more ambiguous. The process should be supported by surface evidence, but should be capable of inductive generalization – as is needed to see a complete surface as covering the bough of a tree. The complexity of natural scenes is also likely to lead to combinatorial problems, because of the many objects overlapping each other in dense scenes.

Final Comments

Surface clusters provide a good intermediate visual representation between the segmented surface patches and the object hypotheses. In the chapters that follow, we will see how they are used to accumulate evidence to select models and reduce the complexity of model matching.

CHAPTER 6

Description of Three Dimensional Structures

The recognition of complex objects cannot be based on raw image data because of its quantity and inappropriate level of representation. What reduces the data to a manageable level is the process of **feature description**, that produces symbolic assertions such as "elongation(S,1.2)" or "shape(S,flat)".

Besides providing the data compression that makes recognition computationally tractable, description allows recognition processes to be more independent of the specific type of raw data, thus promoting generality. It may also simplify relationships; for example, an apple is approximately described as a "reddish spheroid".

One might ask: "What is the distinction between recognition and description?", because recognition also reduces sets of data to descriptions. We would be more inclined to say an image curve is "described as straight" than is "recognized as a straight line", whereas the reverse would apply to a person's face. Thus, one criterion is simplicity – descriptions represent simple, consistent, generic phenomena. They are also more exact – "convex" allows approximate local reconstruction of a surface fragment, whereas "face" can hardly be more than representative.

If a description is dependent on a conjunction of properties, then it is probably not suitable for use here (e.g. a "square" is a "curve" with equal length "side"s, each at "right angle"s). Hence, another criterion is general applicability, because "straight" is a useful description to consider for any boundary, whereas "square" is not.

The descriptions presented here are simple unary and binary three dimensional properties of curves, surfaces and volumes such as curvature, area or relative orientation. They are not reducible to subdescriptions (i.e. they are not structured). Because we have three dimensional range data available, it is possible to directly compute these properties, as contrasted to the difficulties encountered when using two dimensional intensity data (though two dimensional data is also useful). The use of three dimensional data also allows richer and more accurate descriptions.

Pattern recognition techniques often estimate properties from two dimensional projections of the structures, but cannot always do so correctly, because of the information lost in the projection process. To overcome this, some researchers have exploited constraints available from the real properties of objects, such as the relationship between area and contour [BRA83a], from assuming that curves are locally planar [STE83] or by assuming that a surface region is a particular model patch [FIS83].

Some of the properties considered below are viewpoint invariant. These properties are important because they further the goal of viewpoint independent recognition.

Moreover, the key invariant properties are local (e.g. curvature) as compared to global (e.g. area), because objects in three dimensional scenes are often partially obscured, which affects global properties.

Some Three Dimensional Structural Descriptions

Here, three classes of structures acquire descriptions: boundaries, surfaces and surface clusters. The structures are interrelated and at times their descriptions depend on their relationships with other entities. We have identified a variety of descriptions, some of which are listed below. Those numbered have been implemented and their computations are described in the given section. Those that are viewpoint invariant are signaled by a "(V)" annotation.

- Boundary descriptions

    - three dimensional boundary curvature (Section 6.1) (V)

    - three dimensional boundary length (Section 6.2)

    - three dimensional symmetry axis orientation

    - parallel boundary orientation (Section 6.3) (V)

    - relative boundary segment orientation (Section 6.4)

    - relative boundary segment size

- Surface descriptions

    - surface principal curvatures (Section 6.5) (V)

    - surface curvature axis orientation (Section 6.5) (V)

    - absolute surface area (Section 6.6)

    - surface elongation (Section 6.7)

    - relative surface orientation (Section 6.8) (V)

    - relative surface size (Section 6.9)

    - relative surface position

- Surface cluster descriptions

    - surface cluster volume

    - surface cluster elongation

    - surface cluster elongation axis orientation

    - surface cluster symmetry

    - surface cluster relative volume

    - surface cluster relative axis orientation

These three dimensional descriptions are reminiscent of the types of features used in traditional two dimensional pattern recognition approaches to computer vision (e.g. [BAL82], pages 254-261). With these, one attempts to measure enough object properties to partition the feature space into distinct regions associated with single object classes. These techniques have been successful for small model bases containing simple, distinct unobscured two dimensional objects, because the objects can then be partially and uniquely characterized using object-independent descriptions. Unfortunately, three dimensional scenes are more complicated because the feature values may change as the object's orientation changes, and because of occlusion.

The description processes discussed below extract simple global properties of curves and surfaces. The processes assume constant shape, but the actual features are not always uniform, resulting in descriptions that are not always exact (e.g. the chair back is not a perfect cylinder, though it is described as such). However, the segmentation assumptions produce features with the correct shape class (e.g. locally ellipsoidal), and so a first-order global characterization is possible. This property is exploited to approximately characterize the features.

To estimate the global properties, global methods are used, as shown below. In retrospect, I feel that some of the methods are less theoretically ideal or practically stable than desired, and perhaps other approaches (e.g. least-squared error) might be better. That being said, the algorithms are generally simple and fast, using a few measurements from the data feature to estimate the desired property. There is a modest error, associated with most of the properties, but this is small enough to allow model invocation and hypothesis construction to proceed without problems.

6.1 Boundary Curvature

The calculation of three dimensional boundary curvature is trivial – the difficulty lies in grouping the boundary segments into sections that might belong to the same feature. Fortunately, the input boundary is labeled with both the type of the segmentation boundary (between surfaces) and the type of discontinuities along the boundary (Chapter 3). This allows sections to be grouped for description with the goal of finding segments that directly correspond to model boundary segments.

Boundaries are not arbitrary space curves, but are associated with surfaces. Hence, the surface determines which boundary sections will be described. Boundaries labeled as:

- convex shape discontinuity boundaries are true object features, and are thus described.

- concave boundaries may be true surface boundaries or may occur where one object rests on another; in either case they are described.

- <back-side-obscuring> are definitely not true object boundaries (relative to the current surface) and are not described.

- <front-side-obscuring> boundaries may be either orientation discontinuities or extremal boundaries; in either case they are described.

The ring of boundary segments surrounding a surface is partitioned into describable sections by the following criteria:

1. If a segment has the label <back-side-obscuring>, then it is deleted.

2. If the point where two segments join is labeled as a boundary segmentation point, then split the ring at this point.

3. If two adjacent boundary segments have different labels, then split the ring at their junction point.

Each set of connected boundary segments that remain after the splitting process is described.

For example, assume that the object in Figure 6.1 is sitting on a surface, that it is a box with an opening at surface 1, that boundary segment l belongs to the background and that the labelings are:

SEGMENT	SURFACE	LABEL
a	1	<front-side-obscuring>
b	1	<back-side-obscuring>
b	2	<front-side-obscuring>
c	1	<back-side-obscuring>
c	3	<front-side-obscuring>
d	2,3	<convex>
e	2	<front-side-obscuring>
f	3	<front-side-obscuring>
g	2	<concave>
h	3	<concave>
i	1	<front-side-obscuring>
l	?	any

VERTEX	SEGMENTING JUNCTION?
v_1	yes (orientation discontinuity)
v_2	yes (orientation discontinuity)
v_3	yes (orientation discontinuity)
rest	irrelevant

Then, the only describable boundary section for surface 1 is {a,i}. As b and c are <back-side-obscuring>, they are not used. Segments a and i are not separated by any criterion, so are treated as a single section. For surface 2, each segment is isolated. Between b and d the label changes, as between e and g. Between b and e there is a

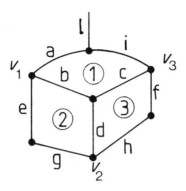

Figure 6.1: Boundary Segment Grouping Example

boundary segmentation point (placed because of an orientation discontinuity in the boundary), as between d and g. Surface 3 is similar to surface 2.

One goal of the boundary segmentation described in Chapter 3 was to produce boundary sections with approximately uniform curvature character. Hence, assuming a boundary section is approximately circular, its curvature can be estimated as follows (referring to Figure 6.2):

Let:

$\vec{e_1}$ and $\vec{e_2}$ be the endpoints of the section
$\vec{b}$ be the bisecting point of the section
$\vec{m}$ be the midpoint of the bounding chord $= (\vec{e_1} + \vec{e_2})/2$

If:

$\vec{m} = \vec{b}$, then the segment is straight,

Otherwise:

$s = |\vec{m} - \vec{b}|$
$t = |\vec{m} - \vec{e_1}|$

And:

$curvature = 2s/(s^2 + t^2)$

A heuristic declares nearly straight segments as straight. The curvature estimates

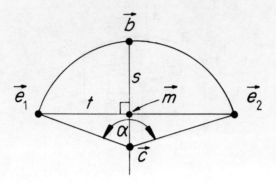

Figure 6.2: Radius Estimation Geometry

Table 6.1: Boundary Curvature Estimates

REGION	SEGMENTS	ESTIMATED CURVATURE	TRUE CURVATURE
26	1	0.131	0.125
26	2	0.120	0.125
8	3,4,5	0.011	0.0
8	6	0.038	0.111
8	7,8,9,10	0.010	0.0
9	11,12	0.0	0.0
9	13	0.083	0.090
9	14,15,16	0.012	0.0
9	17,18,19,20	0.054	0.069

for some of the complete boundaries in the test image (using segment labels shown in Figure 6.3) are given in Table 6.1.

The estimation of curvature is accurate to about 10%. Some straight lines have been classified as slightly curved (e.g. segments 3-4-5) but they received large radius estimates (e.g. 90 cm). Some curvature errors arise from point position errors introduced during surface reconstruction. This factor particularly affects boundaries lying on curved surfaces.

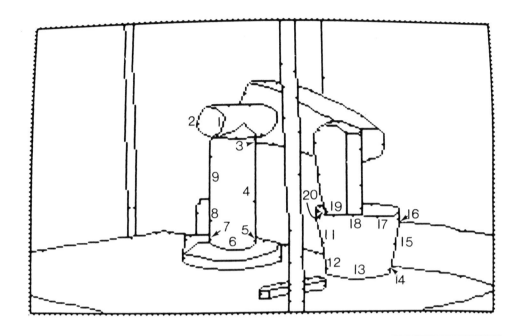

Figure 6.3: Test Image Boundary Numbers

6.2 Boundary Length

Given the three dimensional data, the length of boundary segments can be estimated directly. If the segment is straight, then its length is just the distance between its endpoints. Otherwise, given the groupings described in the previous section, the calculated curvature and the geometric definitions, the length of a curved segment is given as follows (referring to Figure 6.2):

Let:

$\vec{u}$ be the unit vector in the direction $\vec{m} - \vec{b}$

$\vec{c} = \vec{b} + \vec{u}/curvature$ be the center of the arc

$\vec{r_i}$ be the unit vector from $\vec{c}$ to $\vec{e_i}$

Then:

$\alpha = arccos(\vec{r_1} \circ \vec{r_2})$ is the angle subtended by the arc, and

$length = \alpha/curvature$

Table 6.2: Boundary Length Estimates

REGION	SEGMENTS	ESTIMATED LENGTH	TRUE LENGTH	% ERROR
26	1	31.9	25.2	26
26	2	37.0	25.2	47
8	3,4,5	51.1	50.0	2
8	6	27.3	28.2	3
8	7,8,9,10	46.1	50.0	8
9	11,12	28.0	27.2	3
9	13	30.1	34.5	12
9	14,15,16	25.3	27.2	7
9	17,18,19,20	32.7	45.5	28

The boundary length estimates for some of the complete boundaries in the test image (segment labels from Figure 6.3) are shown in Table 6.2.

The average error for boundary length is about 20%, but there are larger errors. On the whole, the estimates are generally acceptable, though not accurate. The poor estimates for segments 1 and 2 result from data errors.

6.3 Parallel Boundaries

A distinctive surface feature is the presence of parallel boundary sections. Hence, one potential description for surfaces is the number of groups of parallel boundaries. In this context, parallel means in three dimensions, and requires:

- vectors between endpoints to be parallel, and

- direction of arc curvature to be parallel.

The endpoint vector calculation is trivial given the three dimensional data. The direction vectors are the $\bar{u}$ defined in the previous section, so the second test is also easy. The results for the test image are given in Table 6.3. No errors occurred.

6.4 Relative Boundary Orientation

The angular relationships between sections of a segmented boundary are also a distinctive characteristic of the surface. The angle between the tangents before and after the segmentation point is a potential measurement, but this would not discriminate between a short and a long arc smoothly joined to a straight segment (recalling that the boundary is segmented by orientation and curvature discontinuities). Further, estimation of the tangent angle is less reliable. Hence, the measurement chosen was the angle between the vectors through the segment endpoints, as illustrated in Figure 6.4. Partial occlusion of the boundary will affect this measurement for curved segments.

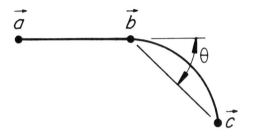

Figure 6.4: Angle Between Boundary Sections

Table 6.3: Parallel Boundary Group Counts

REGION	BOUNDARIES PARALLEL IN DATA	BOUNDARIES PARALLEL IN MODEL
8	2	2
9	2	2
16	2	2
26	1	1
29	0	0

However, if enough of the boundary is visible, the estimate will be close (assuming small curvatures).

Some of the join angles for complete object surfaces are reported in Table 6.4. The average angular estimation error is about 0.1 radian, so this estimation process is acceptable.

6.5 Surface Curvature

By the surface shape segmentation assumptions (Chapter 3), each surface region can be assumed to have constant curvature signs and approximately constant curvature magnitude. Using the orientation information, the average orientation change per im-

Table 6.4: Boundary Join Angles

REGION	SEGMENTS	DATA ANGLE	MODEL ANGLE	ERROR
26	1 - 2	3.14	3.14	0.0
26	2 - 1	3.14	3.14	0.0
8	3,4,5 - 6	1.40	1.57	0.17
8	6 - 7,8,9,10	1.79	1.57	0.22
9	11,12 - 13	1.73	1.70	0.03
9	13 - 14,15,16	1.64	1.70	0.06
9	14,15,16 - 17,18,19,20	1.45	1.44	0.01
9	17,18,19,20 - 11,12	1.45	1.44	0.01

Table 6.5: Surface Shape Classes

	$\kappa_1 < 0$	$\kappa_1 = 0$	$\kappa_1 > 0$
$\kappa_2 < 0$	CONCAVE ELLIPSOID	CONCAVE CYLINDER	HYPERBOLOID SURFACE
$\kappa_2 = 0$	CONCAVE CYLINDER	PLANE	CONVEX CYLINDER
$\kappa_2 > 0$	HYPERBOLOID SURFACE	CONVEX CYLINDER	CONVEX ELLIPSOID

age distance is estimated and this is then used to estimate absolute curvature. This description separates surface regions into curvature classes, which provides a first level of characterization. The absolute magnitude of the curvature then provides a second description.

Following Stevens [STE81] and others, the two principal curvatures, κ_1 and κ_2, are used to characterize the local shape of the surface (along with the directions of the curvatures). These are the maximum and minimum local curvatures of the planar curves formed by intersecting a normal plane with the surface. (The rotation angles at which these curvatures occur are orthogonal – a property that will be used later.) The signs of the two curvatures categorize the surfaces into six possible surface shape classes (Table 6.5). The curvature sign is arbitrary, and here convex surfaces are defined to have positive curvature.

Turner [TUR74] classified surfaces into five different classes (planar, spherical, conical, cylindrical and catenoidal) and made further distinctions on the signs of the curvature, but here the cylindrical and conical categories have been merged because they are locally similar. Cernuschi-Frias, Bolle and Cooper [CER83] classified surface regions as planar, cylindrical or spherical, based on fitting a surface shading model for quadric surfaces to the observed image intensities. Both of these techniques use intensity data, whereas directly using the surface orientation data allows local computation of shape. Moreover, using only intensity patterns, the methods give a qualitative evaluation of shape class, instead of absolute curvature estimates. More recently, Besl [BES86] used the mean and gaussian curvature signs (calculated from range data) to produce a similar taxonomy, only with greater differentiation of the hyperboloidal surfaces.

Brady et al. [BRA84] investigated a more detailed surface understanding including locating lines of curvature of surfaces and shape discontinuities using three dimensional surface data. This work gives a more accurate metrical surface description, but is not as concerned with the symbolic description of surface segments. Agin and Binford [AGI73] and Nevatia and Binford [NEV77] segmented generalized cylinders from light-stripe based range data, deriving cylinder axes from stripe midpoints or depth discontinuities.

To estimate the curvature magnitude, we use the difference in the orientation of two surface normals spatially separated on the object surface. The ideal case of a cross-section perpendicular to the axis of a cylinder is shown in Figure 6.5. Two unit normals $\vec{n_1}$ and $\vec{n_2}$ are separated by a distance L on the object surface. The angular difference θ between the two vectors is given by the dot product:

$$\theta = arccos(\vec{n_1} \circ \vec{n_2})$$

Then, the curvature estimate at this cross-section orientation is:

$$\kappa = 2 * sin(\theta/2)/L$$

To find the two principal curvatures, the curvature at all orientations must be estimated. The planar case is trivial, and all curvature estimates are $\kappa = 0$.

If the curvature is estimated at all orientations using the method above, then the minimum and maximum of these estimates are the principal curvatures. Part (a) of Figure 6.6 shows the path of the intersecting plane across a cylinder. For simplicity, assume that the orientation (β) of the plane intersecting the surface starts perpendicular to the axis of the cylinder. Further, assume that the cylinder surface is completely observed, so that the points at which the surface normals $\vec{n_1}$ and $\vec{n_2}$ are measured are at the extrema of the surface. Then, the normals are directly opposed, so that θ equals π in the above expression. The curvature is then estimated for each orientation β. While the intersection curve is not always a circle, it is treated as if it is one.

Let R be the cylinder radius. The chord length L observed at orientation β is:

$$L = 2 * R/ \mid cos(\beta) \mid$$

Hence, the curvature estimate (from above) is:

$$\kappa = 2 * sin(\theta/2)/L = \mid cos(\beta) \mid /R$$

For the ellipsoid case (part (b) of Figure 6.6), the calculation is similar. Letting R_1 and R_2 be the two principal radii of the ellipsoid (and assuming that the third is large relative to these two) the length measured is approximately:

$$L = 2 * R_1 * R_2/\sqrt{T}$$

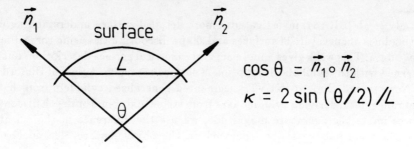

$$\cos \theta = \vec{n}_1 \circ \vec{n}_2$$
$$\kappa = 2 \sin (\theta/2)/L$$

Figure 6.5: Surface to Chord Length Relationship

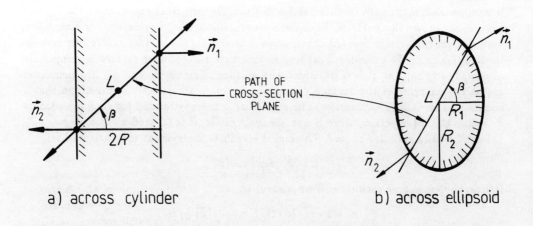

a) across cylinder   b) across ellipsoid

Figure 6.6: Cross-Section Length Relationships

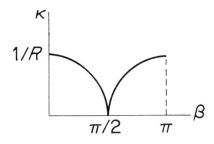

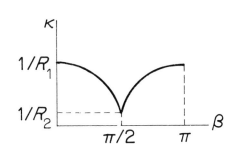

a) cylindrical surface   b) ellipsoid surface

Figure 6.7: Ideal Estimated Curvature Versus Orientation

where:
$$T = (R_1 * sin(\beta))^2 + (R_2 * cos(\beta))^2$$

Hence, the curvature estimate (from above) is:

$$\kappa = 2 * sin(\theta/2)/L = \sqrt{T}/(R_1 * R_2)$$

The special case of the cylinder can be derived from this by looking at the limit as R_2 approaches infinity.

This analysis gives the estimated curvature versus cross-section orientation β. If β is not aligned with a principal curvature axis, then the cross-section has a shifted phase. In any case, the minimum and maximum values of these estimates are the principal curvatures. The maximum curvature occurs perpendicular to the major curvature axis (by definition) and the minimum curvature occurs at $\pi/2$ from the maximum. Figure 6.7 shows a graphical presentation of the estimated curvature versus β.

For simplicity, this analysis used the curvature estimated by picking opposed surface normals at the extremes of the intersecting plane's path. Real intersection trajectories will usually not reach the extrema of the surface and instead we estimate the curvature with a shorter segment using the method outlined at the beginning of this section. This produces different curvature estimates for orientations not lying on a curvature axis. However, the major and minor axis curvature estimates are still correct, and are still the maximum and minimum curvatures estimated. Then, Euler's relation for the local curvature estimated at orientations θ (not necessarily aligned with the principal curvatures) is exploited to find an estimate of the curvatures:

$$\kappa(\beta) = \kappa_1 * cos^2(\beta) + \kappa_2 * sin^2(\beta) = \kappa_2 + (\kappa_1 - \kappa_2) * cos^2(\beta)$$

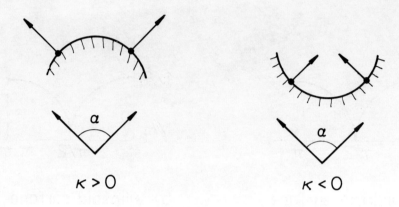

Figure 6.8: Convex and Concave Surface Similarities

One might ask why the global separated normal vector approach to curvature estimation was used, rather than using derivatives of local orientation estimates, or the fundamental forms? The basis for this decision is that we wanted to experiment with using the larger separation to reduce the error in the orientation difference θ when dealing with noisy data. This benefit has to be contrasted with the problem of the curvature changing over distance. But, as the changes should be small by the segmentation assumption, the estimation should still be reasonably accurate. Other possibilities that were not tried were least-squared error fitting of a surface patch and fitting a curve to the set of normals obtained along the cross-section at each orientation β.

We now determine the sign of the curvature. As Figure 6.8 shows, the angle between corresponding surface normals on similar convex and concave surfaces is the same. The two cases can be distinguished because for convex surfaces the surface normals point away from the center of curvature, whereas for the concave case the surface normals point towards it.

Given the above geometric analysis, the implemented surface curvature computation is:

1. Let $\vec{P}$ be a nominal point in the surface image region.

2. Generate the curvature estimate versus β function as outlined above, for cross-sections through $\vec{P}$:

    (a) find cross-section length L

    (b) find surface orientation angle difference θ

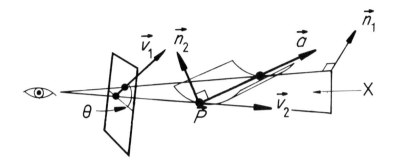

viewer intersection
plane determination

Figure 6.9: Curvature Axis Orientation Estimation (Find Axis Plane)

   (c) estimate curvature magnitude $| \kappa |$

3. Fit $cos^2(\alpha)$ to the curvature versus β function to smooth estimates and determine the phase angle.

4. Extract maximum and minimum curvature magnitudes.

5. At maximum and minimum curvature orientations, check direction of surface normal relative to surface.

   (a) if towards the center, then $\kappa < 0$

   (b) if away from the center, then $\kappa > 0$

The estimation of the major axis orientation for the surface region is now easy. (The major axis is that about which the greatest curvature occurs.) The plane case can be ignored, as it has no curvature. Figures 6.9 and 6.10 illustrate the geometry for the axis orientation estimation process.

We calculate the axis direction by calculating the direction of a parallel line $\vec{a}$ through the nominal point $\vec{P}$. We start by finding a plane X that this line lies in (see Figure 6.9). Plane X contains the viewer and the nominal point $\vec{P}$. Hence, the vector $\vec{v_2}$ from the viewer to the nominal point lies in the plane. Further, we assume that line $\vec{a}$ projects onto the image plane at the image orientation θ at which the minimum

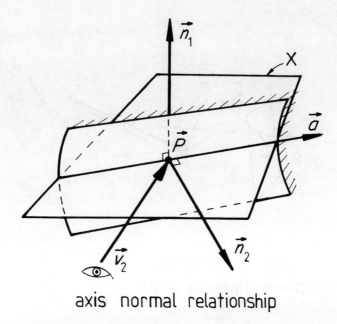

axis normal relationship

Figure 6.10: Curvature Axis Orientation Estimation (Find Vector)

curvature is estimated. Hence, the vector $\vec{v_1} = (cos(\theta), sin(\theta), 0)$ also lies in plane X. As the two vectors are distinct ($\vec{v_1}$ is seen as a line, whereas $\vec{v_2}$ is seen as a point), the normal $\vec{n_1}$ to plane X is:

$$\vec{n_1} = \vec{v_1} \times \vec{v_2}$$

Line $\vec{a}$ lies in this plane (see Figure 6.10) so it must be perpendicular to the plane's normal $\vec{n_1}$. It is also perpendicular to the surface normal $\vec{n_2}$. Hence, the direction of line $\vec{a}$ is:

$$\vec{a} = \vec{n_1} \times \vec{n_2}$$

This vector is used as an estimate of the major curvature axis direction. The minor curvature axis direction is given by $\vec{a} \times \vec{n_2}$.

The curvature and axis orientation estimation process was applied to the test scene. The curvatures of all planar surfaces were estimated correctly as being zero. The major curved surfaces are listed in Tables 6.6 and 6.7, with the results of their curvature and axis estimates. (If the major curvature is zero in Table 6.6, then the minor curvature is not shown.) In Table 6.7, the error angle is the angle between the measured and estimated axis vectors.

The estimation of the surface curvature and axis directions is both simple and mainly accurate, as evidenced by the above discussion and the results. The major error is on the small, nearly tangential surface (region 31), where the curvature estimates are acceptable, but the algorithm had difficulty estimating the orientation, as might be

Table 6.6: Summary of Surface Curvature Estimates

IMAGE REGION	MAJOR(MJ) MINOR(MN)	ESTIMATED CURVATURE	TRUE CURVATURE
8	MJ	.11	.11
	MN	0	0
9	MJ	.09	.08
	MN	0	0
12	MJ	0	0
16	MJ	.15	.13
	MN	0	0
18	MJ	0	0
25	MJ	.19	.13
	MN	0	0
26	MJ	0	0
29	MJ	.12	.13
	MN	0	0
31	MJ	.07	.09
	MN	0	0

Table 6.7: Summary of Curved Surface Curvature Axis Estimates

IMAGE REGION	ESTIMATED AXIS	TRUE AXIS	ERROR ANGLE
8	(0.0,0.99,-0.1)	(0.0,1.0,0.0)	0.10
16	(-0.99,0.0,0.0)	(-0.99,0.0,0.1)	0.09
25	(-0.99,0.07,0.11)	(-0.99,0.0,0.1)	0.13
31	(-0.86,-.21,-0.46)	(-0.99,0.0,0.1)	0.53
9	(-0.09,0.99,-0.07)	(0.0,1.0,0.0)	0.12
29	(-.14,0.99,0.0)	(0.0,1.0,0.0)	0.14

expected. Again, as the depth and orientation estimates were acquired by hand, this is one source of error in the results. Another source is the inaccuracies caused by interpolating depth and orientation estimates between measured values.

The major weak point in this analysis is that the curvature can vary over a curved surface segment, whereas only a single estimate is made (though the segmentation assumption limits its variation). Choosing the nominal point to lie roughly in the middle of the surface helps average the curvatures, and it also helps reduce noise errors by giving larger cross-sections over which to calculate the curvature estimates.

6.6   Absolute Surface Area

The surfaces of man-made objects typically have fixed surface areas, and many natural objects also have surfaces whose areas fall within constrained ranges. Thus surface area is a good constraint on the identity of a surface. Consequently, we would like to estimate the absolute surface area of a segmented surface region, which is possible given the information in the surface image. Estimation applies to the reconstructed surface hypotheses (Chapter 4).

The constraints on the estimation process are:

- The surface region image area is the number of pixels inside the surface region boundaries.

- The image area is related to the surface area of a fronto-parallel planar surface at a given depth by the camera parameters.

- The area of a fronto-parallel planar surface is related to the area of an oriented planar surface by its surface orientation.

- The area of a curved surface is related to the area of the equivalent projected planar surface by the magnitude of its curvature.

The effects of surface curvature are approximately overcome using two correction factors for the principal curvatures, which are calculated in the following manner. In Figure 6.11 part (a), the case of a single dimension is considered. A curved segment of curvature C subtends an angle θ . Hence, it has length θ/C. This appears in the image as a straight segment of length L. So, the curvature correction factor relating the length of a curved segment to the equivalent chord is:

$$F = \theta/(L * C)$$

where the angle θ is given by:

$$\theta = 2 * arcsin(L * C/2)$$

Hence, the complete curvature correction factor is (if $C > 0$):

$$F = 2 * arcsin(L * C/2)/(L * C)$$

else

$$F = 1$$

Now, referring to Figure 6.11 part (b), the absolute surface area is estimated as follows:

Let:

I be the image area in square pixels

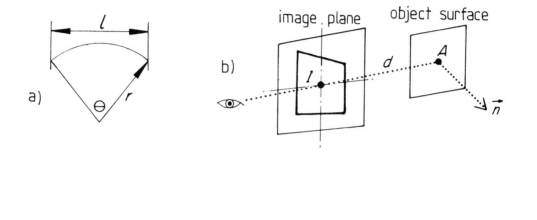

(a)   curvature   correction   (b)   projection   correction

Figure 6.11: Image Projection Geometries

D be the depth to a nominal point in the surface region

$\vec{n}$ be the unit surface normal at the nominal point

G be the conversion factor for the number of pixels per centimeter of object length when seen at one centimeter distance

F, f be the major and minor principal curvature correction factors

$\vec{v}$ be the unit vector from the nominal point to the viewer

Then, the slant correction relating projected planar area to true planar area is given by:

$$\vec{v} \circ \vec{n}$$

and the absolute surface area is estimated by:

$$A = I * (D/G)^2 * (F * f)/(\vec{v} \circ \vec{n})$$

Table 6.8: Summary of Absolute Surface Area Estimation

IMAGE REGION	PLANAR OR CURVED	ESTIMATED AREA	TRUE AREA	% ERROR
8	C	1239	1413	12
9	C	1085	1081	0
16	C	392	628	38
26	P	165	201	17
29	C	76	100	24

The (D/G) term converts one image dimension from pixels to centimeters, the $\vec{v} \circ \vec{n}$ term accounts for the surface being slanted away from the viewer, and the $F * f$ term accounts for the surface being curved instead of flat.

In the test image, several unobscured regions from known object surfaces are seen. The absolute surface area for these regions is estimated using the computation described above, and the results are summarized in Table 6.8.

Note that the estimation error percentage is generally small, given the range of surface sizes. The process is also often accurate, with better results for the larger surface regions and largest errors on small or nearly tangential surfaces. The key sources of error are pixel spatial quantization, which particularly affects small regions, and inaccurate shape data estimation.

From the above discussion, the estimation process is obviously trivial, given the surface image as input. Since the goal of the process is only to acquire a rough estimate, the implemented approach is adequate.

6.7 Surface Elongation

The elongation of a surface region is also a distinguishing characteristic. This has been a traditional pattern recognition measurement applied to two dimensional regions, but a three dimensional version can also be obtained.

For a planar surface, elongation is the ratio of the longest to the shortest dimension of a planar rectangular box circumscribing the surface, which is similar to the two dimensional definition. The definition can be adapted to curved surfaces by using the maximum and minimum arc lengths of the intersection of the surface and a plane normal to the surface. The arc length should be calculated for all intersections of the surface, but this is time-consuming. Instead, only the cross-section widths about a central point are used.

The four factors involved in the estimation of the surface's dimensions are: the image region's dimensions, the surface slant relative to the viewer, the curvature of the surface, and the distance from the viewer. It is possible to approximate the elongation after separating the effects of these factors.

Figure 6.12 part (a) shows a sketch of the viewing relationship at one cross-section through the surface. By the discussion in the previous section, the cross-section length

a) projection geometry   b) slant correction

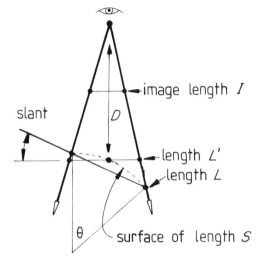

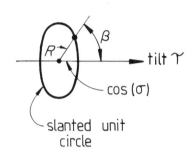

Figure 6.12: Cross-Section Length Distortions

S is approximately related to the chord length L as:

$$S = L * \theta/(2 * sin(\theta/2))$$

Then, if the cross-section is slanted away from the viewer by an angle α, the observed slanted length L' is approximately related to the chord length L (assuming the viewing distance is large) by:

$$L' = L * cos(\alpha)$$

Finally, the observed image length I for the surface at depth D with conversion factor G (as in Section 6.6) is:

$$I = L' * (G/D)$$

This analysis is then modified for observed slant compression at angles other than the tilt angle. Figure 6.12 part (b) shows the geometry used for the following analysis. This figure shows a unit circle compressed by a slant angle σ in the direction τ and orthographically projected onto the image plane. Elementary trigonometry and algebra show that the observed length R at the angle β is:

$$R = 1/\sqrt{1 + (tan(\sigma) * cos(\beta))^2}$$

The computation of the elongation value is then:

Let:

$\vec{N}$ be a nominal point in the center of the surface image region

$w(\alpha)$ be the image cross-section width at image angle α about $\vec{N}$

$\theta(\alpha)$ be the change in surface orientation across the cross-section at image angle α

$(P, Q, -T)$ be the unit surface normal at $\vec{N}$

D be the distance from the viewer to $\vec{N}$

G be the conversion factor for the number of pixels per centimeter of object length when seen at one centimeter distance

$\vec{v}$ be the unit vector pointing to the viewer from the point $\vec{N}$

Then, the tilt angle is:

$$\tau = arctan(Q/P)$$

the relative slant direction β is:

$$\beta = \alpha - \tau$$

the slant angle σ is:

$$\sigma = arccos(\vec{v} \circ (P, Q, -T))$$

the slant correction factor is:

$$M = \sqrt{1 + (tan(\sigma) * cos(\beta))^2}$$

the projected chord length L' is:

$$L'(\alpha) = w(\alpha) * (D/G)$$

the unprojected chord length L is:

$$L(\alpha) = L'(\alpha) * M$$

and the estimated three dimensional cross-section is:

$$cross(\alpha) = L(\alpha) * \theta(\alpha)/(2 * sin(\theta(\alpha)/2))$$

Table 6.9: Summary of Estimated Elongations

IMAGE REGION	PLANAR OR CURVED	ESTIMATED ELONGATION	TRUE ELONGATION
8	C	3.3	2.0
9	C	1.8	1.7
16	C	2.9	1.5
26	P	1.4	1.0
29	C	3.6	3.1

Finally, the elongation is:

$$E = max_\alpha(cross(\alpha))/min_\alpha(cross(\alpha))$$

The elongations for all unobscured image regions that directly correspond to model SURFACEs are listed in Table 6.9.

These results show that the estimation process gives approximate results when applied to unobscured regions. In part, small regions should be more affected because single pixel errors are significant, but this is not always the case.

A weakness of the process is that it only estimates the dimensions based on reconstructions about a single point, which produces lower bounds for the maximum and upper bounds for the minimum cross-sections. This should result in an estimate that is lower than the true elongation. However, the key source of error is the small size of the regions coupled with image quantization. Other sources of error are the hand measured surface data, surface interpolation and the curvature correction process assuming uniform curvature along the cross-section path. However, the approximations were felt to be justifiable on practical grounds and the above results show that the approach is acceptable.

6.8 Relative Surface Orientation

Given surface orientation and some elementary geometry, it is possible to estimate the angle at which two surfaces meet (defined as the angle that the solid portion of the junction subsumes). This description is useful for two reasons: (1) extra information is always useful for recognition and (2) the measurement is dependent on the surface's relationship with its neighbors, whereas many other descriptions relate only to the structure in isolation. Hence, context can enhance the likelihood of identification.

This description is only applied to surfaces that are adjacent across a shape boundary and so emphasizes group identification. (Surfaces across an obscuring boundary may not be related.)

The factors involved in the description's calculation are the orientation of the surfaces, the shared boundary between the surfaces and the direction to the viewer. As the boundary is visible, the viewer must be in the unoccupied space sector between the two surfaces.

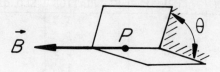

Figure 6.13: Two Adjacent Surfaces

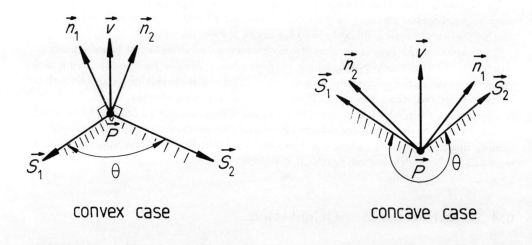

convex case   concave case

Figure 6.14: Surface Normals and the Two Surface Cases

Because surfaces can be curved, the angle between them may not be constant along the boundary; however, it is assumed that this angle will not vary significantly without the introduction of other shape segmentations. Consequently, the calculation obtained at a nominal point is taken to be representative.

Figure 6.13 shows two surfaces meeting at a boundary. Somewhere along this boundary a nominal point $\vec{P}$ is chosen and also shown is the vector of the boundary direction at that point $(\vec{B})$. Through this point a cross-section plane is placed, such that the normals $(\vec{n})$ for the two surfaces lie in the plane. Figure 6.14 shows the two cases for this cross-section.

The essential information that determines the surface angle is the angle at which the two normals meet. However, it must also be determined whether the surface junction is convex or concave, which is the difficult portion of the computation. The details of the solution are seen in Figure 6.14. Let vectors $\vec{S}_1$ and $\vec{S}_2$ be tangential to the respective surfaces in the cross-section plane. By definition, the vector $\vec{B}$ is normal to the plane in which the $\vec{n}_i$ and $\vec{S}_i$ vectors lie. Hence, each individual $\vec{S}_i$ vector is normal to both the corresponding $\vec{n}_i$ vector and the $\vec{B}$ vector, and can be calculated by a cross product.

These $\vec{S}_i$ vectors may face the wrong direction (e.g. away from the surface). To obtain the correct direction, a track is made from the point $\vec{P}$ in the direction of both $\vec{S}_i$ and $-\vec{S}_i$. One of these should immediately enter the surface region, and this is assumed to be the correct $\vec{S}_i$ vector.

Because the boundary must be visible, the angle between the vector $\vec{v}$ from the nominal point to the viewer and a surface vector $\vec{S}_i$ must be less than π. Hence, the angle between these vectors is guaranteed to represent open space. Then, the angle between the two surfaces is 2π minus these two open spaces. This computation is summarized below:

Let:

$\vec{P}$ be a nominal point on the boundary between the two surfaces

$\vec{n}_1$, $\vec{n}_2$ be the two surface normal vectors at $\vec{P}$

$\vec{v}$ be the vector from the nominal point to the viewer

Then, the boundary vector $\vec{B}$ is:

$$\vec{B} = \vec{n}_1 \times \vec{n}_2$$

and the surface vectors $\vec{S}_i$ are:

$$\vec{S}_i = \vec{B} \times \vec{n}_i$$

which are then adjusted for direction, as described above.

Given this, the surface angle is:

$$\theta = 2\pi - |arccos(\vec{v} \circ \vec{S}_1)| - |arccos(\vec{v} \circ \vec{S}_2)|$$

The true and estimated surface angles for the modeled objects are summarized in Table 6.10. Further, only rigid angles between surfaces in the same primitive surface clusters are reported (these being the only evidence used).

The estimation procedure is accurate for orientation discontinuities. The major source of errors for this process is the measurement of the surface orientation vectors by hand, and interpolating their value to the nominal point. This contributed

Table 6.10: Summary of Relative Surface Orientation

IMAGE REGIONS	ESTIMATED ANGLE	TRUE ANGLE	ERROR	NOTE
16,26	1.47	1.57	0.10	
16,29	2.96	3.14	0.18	
12,18	1.53	1.57	0.04	
12,31	1.60	1.57	0.03	
18,31	2.03	2.14	0.11	
17,25	2.09	3.14	1.05	*
17,22	1.56	1.57	0.01	

* – large error across a curvature discontinuity

Table 6.11: Summary of Relative Surface Area Estimation

IMAGE REGION	PLANAR OR CURVED	IMAGE CONTEXT	ESTIMATED PROPORTION	VALID RANGE
8	C	8	1.00	1.00
9	C	9,28,38	0.92	0.6 - 1.0
16	C	16,26	0.70	0.76
26	P	16,26	0.29	0.24
29	C	29	1.0	1.0

substantially to the error at the curvature discontinuity, where interpolation flattened out the surface.

6.9   Relative Surface Area

Because a surface generally appears with a known set of other surfaces, its proportion of the total visible surface area is another constraint on its identity in the complete object context. This proportion can vary because of self-occlusion, but is otherwise a constant. The precise relative area is, in theory, determinable for all viewing positions, but in practice only the range defined by representative positions is considered.

The relative surface area calculation is trivial once the individual component's absolute areas have been calculated. The surface cluster (Chapter 5) is the context for the relative area calculation.

Table 6.11 summarizes the results of the relative surface area calculation for the same image regions as in Table 6.8. Again, the same good performance is noted. A point to note about the relative area is that valid evidence can still be computed even if only the relative distances (as compared to the absolute distances) to the object's surfaces are available. This point also holds for objects with fixed geometry, but variable size: the relative proportion of the total size remains the same.

Final Comments

This chapter showed that surface data allowed a variety of general identity-independent three dimensional properties. These were directly computable for curves, surfaces and surface clusters, using simple computations that estimated the properties acceptably. More work is needed to extend the number of properties, improve the algorithms and determine their stability over a wider range of objects.

CHAPTER 7

Object Representation

To recognize objects, one must have an internal representation of an object suitable for matching its features to image descriptions. There are several approaches to modeling, and this research uses a surface-based object representation distinguished by its use of shape segmentable surfaces organized in a subcomponent hierarchy. This approach provides the information needed to efficiently recognize and locate complicated articulated structures (like a robot) when using the input data described in Chapter 3.

This chapter also briefly describes the SMS modeling approach [FIS87a], whose development was based on experience with the **IMAGINE I** system.

7.1 The Geometric Model

The model is what the system knows about an object. Paraphrasing Binford [BIN82]: a capable vision system should know about object shape, and how shape affects appearance, rather than what types of images an object is likely to produce. Geometric models explicitly represent the shape and structure of an object, and from these, one can (1) deduce what features will be seen from any particular viewpoint and where they are expected to be and (2) determine under what circumstances a particular image relationship is consistent with the model. Both of these conditions promote efficient feature selection, matching and verification. Hence, this approach is intrinsically more powerful than the property method, but possibly at the expense of complexity and substantial computational machinery. However, a practical vision system may also incorporate redundant viewer-centered descriptions, to improve efficiency.

The geometric body model used here introduces a uniform level of description suitable for a large class of objects (especially man-made). It specifies the key primitive elements of an object representation, and how they are positioned relative to the whole object.

Some Requirements on the Model

The models should emphasize the relevant aspects of objects. As this research is concerned with model shape and structure, rather than reflectance, these are: surface shape, intersurface relationships (e.g. adjacency and relative orientation), surface-object relationships and subcomponent-object relationships. To recognize the objects in the test scene, the geometric models will have to:

- make surface information explicit – to easily match image surface data,

- have three dimensional, transformable object-centered representations – because objects can take arbitrary, unexpected spatial locations and orientations,

- have geometric subcomponent relationships – because of the structuring of the surface clusters and the physical constraints on their placement,

- represent solid and laminar objects – to handle the variety in the scene and

- have attachments with degrees-of-freedom – for recognizing articulated objects (e.g. the robot).

These are general requirements; more specific requirements for geometric information are discussed below.

As model invocation (Chapter 8) is based on both image property evidence and component associations, it additionally needs:

- size, shape and curvature parameters of individual surfaces and boundary segments,

- non-structural object relations, such as subtype or subclass,

- adjacency of surfaces and their relative orientation and

- typical configurations of visible components.

Hypothesis construction and verification (Chapters 9 and 10) instantiate and validate invoked models by pairing image data or previously recognized objects with model components. To build the hypotheses, the matcher will have to search the image and its results database for evidence. Verification ascertains the soundness of the instantiated models by ensuring that the substructures have the correct geometric relationship with each other and the model as a whole, and that the assembled object forms a valid and compact solid. Together, the two processes require:

- the type of substructures needed and

- the geometric relationships between the substructures and the object.

Model Primitives

Model surfaces and boundaries are usually segmented according to the same criteria discussed in Chapter 3 for image data (essentially shape discontinuities). Hence, the same primitives are also used for the models to reduce the conceptual distance to the data primitives, and thus simplify matching. The primitive element of the model is the SURFACE, a one-sided bounded two dimensional (but not necessarily flat) structure defined in a three dimensional local reference frame. A SURFACE has two primary characteristics – surface shape, and extent.

Surface shape is defined by its surface class, the curvature axes and the curvature values. The surface classes are planar, cylindrical and ellipsoidal/hyperboloidal. The curvature values can be positive or negative, representing convex or concave principal curvatures about the curvature axes. The minor curvature axis (if any) is orthogonal to both the surface normal and the major curvature axis. (This is always locally true and it also holds globally for the surface primitives used here.) These model patches are exactly the same as the data patches shown in Figure 3.10, except for where the data patches are not fully seen because of occlusion or inappropriate viewpoint. While many other surface shape representations are used, this one was chosen because:

- surface shape is characterized by two parameters only (the principal curvatures), and it is felt that these can be successfully estimated from image data (e.g. [BRA84]). Further, it is felt that it will be difficult to reliably estimate more detailed information.

- Even if the precise curvature values are not extractable, shape class should be, using a variety of shape cues (e.g. specularity, shadows, shading, etc.).

The definition of surface shapes is straightforward for the planar and cylindrical (and conical) patches. Each SURFACE is defined relative to a local coordinate system. The plane is implicitly defined to pass through $(0, 0, 0)$ with a normal of $(0, 0, -1)$ and has infinite extent. A cylinder is convex or concave according to the sign of its curvature, has a defined curvature magnitude and axis of curvature, and has infinite extent.

Surfaces that curve in two directions are not well represented here. The problem is that on these surfaces, curvature varies everywhere (except for on a perfect sphere), whereas we would like to characterize the surface simply and globally. Given the segmentation criteria, one feature that does remain constant is the sign of the principal curvatures. To make the characterization more useful, we also include the magnitudes and three dimensional directions of the curvatures at a nominal central point. While this is just an approximation, it is useful for model matching.

When it is necessary to draw or predict instances of these SURFACEs, the model used is $(r_1 = radius_1, r_2 = radius_2)$:

$$sign(r_1) * \frac{(x')^2}{r_1^2} + sign(r_2)\frac{(y')^2}{r_2^2} + \frac{(z)^2}{r_z^2} = 1$$

where $r_z = 50$ (an arbitrary choice) and (x', y') are in a coordinate system that places x' along the major curvature axis.

Surfaces with twist are neither modeled nor analyzed.

All SURFACEs are presumed to bound solids; laminar surfaces are formed by joining two model SURFACEs back to back. Hence, the normal direction also specifies the outside surface direction.

The extent of a SURFACE is defined by a three dimensional polycurve boundary. The surface patch lies inside the boundary, when it is projected onto the infinite surface. These patches are intended to be only approximate as: (1) it is hard to characterize when one surface stops and another starts on curved surfaces, and (2) surface extraction and description processes do not reliably extract patch boundaries except near strong orientation discontinuities. This implies that surface patches may not smoothly join. However, this is not a problem as the models are defined for recognition (which does not require exact boundaries), rather than image generation.

The polycurve boundary is specified by a few three dimensional points and connecting segments: "point – curve – point – curve – ...". The connecting curve descriptions are either straight lines or portions of circular arcs.

The surface feature that causes the curve or surface segmentation is recorded as part of the model. The surface segmentation boundary labels are (refer to Chapter 3 for their definition):

BN – non-segmenting extremal boundary
BO – surface-orientation
BC – surface-curvature-magnitude
BD – surface-curvature-direction

The curve segmentation point labels are:

PO – boundary-orientation
PC – boundary-curvature-magnitude
PD – boundary-curvature-direction

These labels were not used by the recognition process, but can provide stronger constraints on the identity of surface groupings.

An example of a full SURFACE description of the small curved end surface of the robot upper arm (called "uends") is:

```
SURFACE uends =
     PO/(0,0,0) BC/LINE
     PO/(10,0,0) BO/CURVE[0,0,-7.65]
     PO/(10,15,0) BC/LINE
     PO/(0,15,0) BO/CURVE[0,0,-7.65]
     CYLINDER[(0,7.5,1.51),(10,7.5,1.51),7.65,7.65]
     NORMAL AT (5,7.5,-6.14) = (0,0,-1);
```

This describes a convex cylinder with a patch cut out of it. The next to last line defines the cylinder axis endpoints and the radii at those points. Here, we see that the axis is parallel to the x-axis. The four lines above that define the polycurve boundary, using four points linked by two line and two circular arc sections. All boundary sections are connected at orientation discontinuities (PO), while the surface meets its neighbors across orientation (BO) and curvature magnitude (BC) discontinuities at the given boundary section. The final line records the direction of the surface normal at a nominal central point. Figure 7.1 shows the surface and boundary specifications combined to model the end patch.

ASSEMBLY Definition

Whole objects (called ASSEMBLYs) are described using a subcomponent hierarchy, with objects being composed of either SURFACEs or recursively defined subcomponents. Each ASSEMBLY has a nominal coordinate reference frame relative to which all subcomponents are located. The geometric relationship of a subcomponent to the

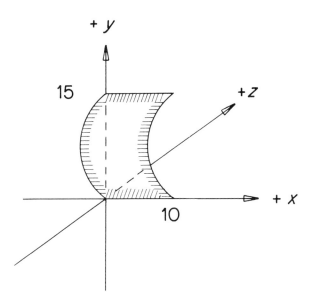

Figure 7.1: Upperarm Small Curved End Patch

object is specified by an AT coordinate system transformation from the subcomponent's reference frame to the object's. This is equivalent to the ACRONYM [BRO81]
affixment link. The transformation is specified using an xyz translation and a rotation-
slant-tilt reorientation of the subcomponent's coordinate system relative to the AS-
SEMBLY's. The transformation is executed in the order: (1) slant the subcomponent's
coordinate system in the tilt direction (relative to the object's xy plane), (2) rotate the
subcomponent about the object's z-axis and (3) translate the subcomponent to the
location given in the object's coordinates. The affixment notation used in the model
definition (Appendix A) is of the form:

$$((trans_x, trans_y, trans_z), (rotation, slant, tilt))$$

Figure 7.2 shows an example of the transformation:

$$((10, 20, 30), (0, \pi/2, \pi/2))$$

Figure 7.3 shows the robot hand ASSEMBLY defined from three SURFACEs: hand-
sidel (the long lozenge shaped flat side), handsides (the short rectangular flat side)

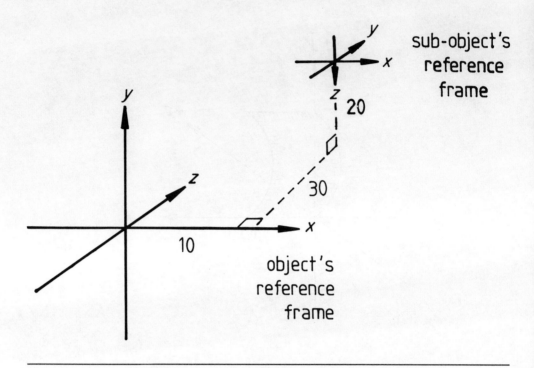

Figure 7.2: Coordinate Reference Frame Transformation

and handend (the cylindrical cap at the end). Assuming that all three SURFACEs are initially defined as facing the viewer, the ASSEMBLY specification is:

```
ASSEMBLY hand =
         handsidel AT ((0,-4.3,-4.3),(0,0,0))
         handsidel AT ((0,4.3,4.3),(0,π,π/2))
         handsides AT ((0,-4.3,4.3),(0,π/2,3π/2))
         handsides AT ((0,4.3,-4.3),(0,π/2,π/2))
         handend AT ((7.7,-4.3,-4.3),(0,π/2,0));
```

The SURFACEs do not completely enclose the ASSEMBLY because the sixth side is never seen. This causes no problem; a complete definition is also acceptable as the hypothesis construction process (Chapter 9) would deduce that the SURFACE is not visible when attempting to fully instantiate a hypothesis.

Affixments with degrees-of-freedom are specified by using a FLEX (or SYM) option, which allows unspecified translations and rotations of the subcomponent, *in its local reference frame*, about the affixment point. The partially constrained attachment

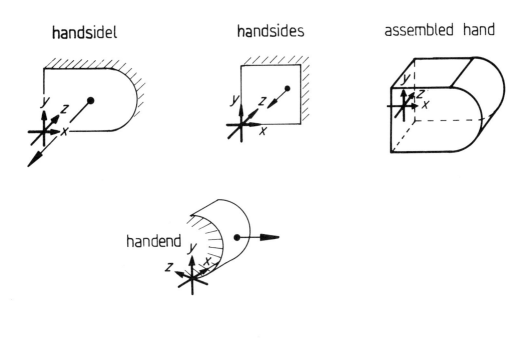

Figure 7.3: Robot Hand ASSEMBLY

definitions use one or more symbolic parameters. The distinction between the FLEX and SYM option is as follows:

- *FLEX* is used for orientable objects with a partially constrained affixment between them. The variables in the definition are bound to values when the components are linked during recognition.

- *SYM* is used for unorientable, rotationally symmetric objects. Any value can be matched to the variable during recognition, and the variables always have values during enquiry (nominally 0.0). Examples of this from the models used in this research include the chair legs.

The AT and FLEX (or SYM) transformations are largely equivalent, and so could be algebraically combined, but this complicates the definition task. A subcomponent's partially constrained position is usually specified relative to the subcomponent, not the ASSEMBLY. The affixment to the ASSEMBLY, however, is usually about a point

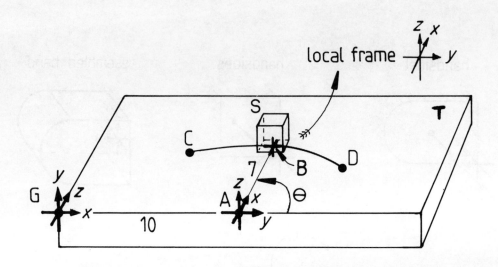

Figure 7.4: Partially Constrained ASSEMBLY Example

that is defined in the ASSEMBLY's reference frame, so that the two transformations are separated.

An ASSEMBLY S with a rotational degree-of-freedom is shown in Figure 7.4. It is attached to the table T and rotates rigidly (to angle Θ) along the path CD. S and T are part of ASSEMBLY Q. Both T and Q have their coordinate frames located at G and S has its at B. The ASSEMBLY is defined:

ASSEMBLY Q =
  T AT $((0,0,0),(0,0,0))$ % T is at G
  S AT $((10,0,0),(3\pi/2,\pi/2,0))$ % from G to A
    FLEX $((-7,0,0),(\Theta,0,0))$;   % from A to B

The recursive subcomponent hierarchy with local reference frames supports a simple method for coordinate calculations. Assume that the hierarchy of components is:

ASSEMBLY P_0 =
    P_1 AT A_1
    FLEX F_1
ASSEMBLY P_1 =
    P_2 AT A_2
    FLEX F_2

ASSEMBLY $P_2 =$

P_3 AT A_3
FLEX F_3

(etc.)

Let A_i and F_i be simplified homogeneous coordinate matrices representing the reference frame transformations given above. Then, each of these 4*4 matrices has the form:

$$\begin{pmatrix} R_i & \vec{T_i} \\ \vec{0}^t & 1 \end{pmatrix}$$

where R_i is the 3×3 rotation matrix and $\vec{T_i}$ is the translation vector. Each matrix represents the transformation $\vec{T_i} + R_i * \vec{v}$ of a vector $\vec{v}$ in the subcomponent to the object coordinate system. If:

G is the matrix transforming the ASSEMBLY's top level coordinate system
into global coordinates, and
C transforms from global coordinates into those of the camera,

then a point $\vec{p}$ in the local coordinate system of ASSEMBLY P_n can be expressed in camera coordinates by the calculation:

$$CG(A_1 F_1^{-1})(A_2 F_2^{-1})...(A_n F_n^{-1})\vec{p}$$

There are many ways to decompose a body into substructures, and this leads to the question of what constitutes a good segmentation. In theory, no hierarchy is needed for rigidly connected objects, because all surfaces could be directly expressed in the top level object's coordinate system. This is neither efficient (e.g. there may be repeated structure) nor captures our notions of substructure. Further, a chain of multiple subcomponents with partially constrained affixments represented in a single reference frame would have a complicated linkage definition.

Some guidelines for the decomposition process are:

1. Object surfaces are segmented according to the shape discontinuity criteria of Chapter 3.

2. Non-rigidly connected substructures are distinct ASSEMBLYs.

3. Repeated structures become distinct ASSEMBLYs (e.g. a common surface shape, like a chair leg).

4. Surface groups surrounded by concave surface shape discontinuities become ASSEMBLYs (e.g. where the nose joins to the face). This is because one cannot distinguish a connecting-to from a sitting-on relationship, and so data segmentation must take the conservative choice. Hence, the models should follow this as well. Figure 7.5 illustrates this problem for a structure that might be a rivet or a cylinder on a plane.

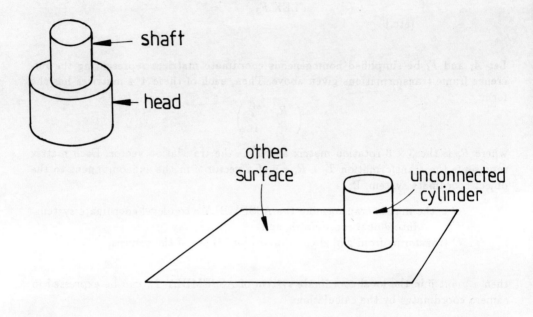

Figure 7.5: Segmenting a Rivet Versus a Cylinder on a Plane

Examples of the Models

A range of solid and laminar structures were modeled. The robot model (Figure 1.9) has four rigid subcomponents: the cylindrical base, the shoulder, the upper arm and the lower arm/gripper. Each of these is an ASSEMBLY, as are several of their subcomponents. These four components are joined hierarchically using the FLEX option to represent the partially constrained joint angles. The shoulder body and robot body are defined using non-segmenting boundaries to correspond to the observed extremal boundaries (as discussed below).

The chair (Figure 7.6) and trash can (Figure 7.7) illustrate laminar surfaces and symmetric subcomponents (SYM). The chair legs are defined as thin cylinders, which are attached by a SYM relation to the chair, as is the seat. The seat and back are both laminar surfaces defined using two back-to-back SURFACEs (with their associated surface normals outward-facing). A similar construction holds for the trash can. Its model has six SURFACEs, because both the outer and inner cylindrical surfaces were split into two, with non-segmenting boundaries joining.

The complete model for the robot is given in Appendix A.

Figure 7.6: Chair Model

Discussion on the Geometric Model

There are several major inadequacies with the geometric modeling system. Object dimensions have to be fixed, but this was largely because no constraint maintenance mechanism was available (unlike in ACRONYM [BRO81]). Uniform surface and boundary segment curvatures were also simplifications. However, because major curvature changes cause segmentations, deviations between the models and observed objects should be minor. The point was to segment the models in a similar manner to the data, to promote direct feature matching through having a similar representation for both.

Of course, some surfaces do not segment into conceptual units strictly on shape discontinuities, such as when a chair leg continues upward to form part of the chair back (Figure 7.8). Here, the segmentation requires a boundary that is not in the data. This is part of the more general segmentation problem, which is ignored here.

The surface matching process described in Chapter 9 recognizes image surfaces by pairing them with model SURFACEs. Because non-planar surfaces can curve away from the viewer's line-of-sight, the observed surface patch may not correspond to the full modeled patch. Moreover, extremal boundaries will be seen, and these will not

Figure 7.7: Trash Can Model

correspond with the patch boundaries.

As the matching process can not properly account for this phenomenon, it was necessary to ensure that the models were defined to help avoid the problem. This required splitting large curved surfaces into patches corresponding to typically obscured surfaces. For example, full cylindrical surfaces were split into two halves, because only one half could be seen from any viewpoint. The new cylindrical patch boundaries approximately correspond to the extremal boundaries (i.e. subset of the front-side-obscuring boundaries) of the observed surface.

For surfaces with an extent that distinguishes orientation, this approach needs extension. A key instance where this splitting was adequate but not general was with the cylindrical robot shoulder, because the shoulder had an irregular notch where it connected to the base. As with the cylindrical surface, the patch was split at its apex to give a boundary that could be matched with the observed extremal boundary, and a roughly corresponding surface patch. If the robot had been viewed from an orientation substantially above or below that actually seen in Figure 1.1, the shoulder patch may not have been recognized.

Surfaces have been represented with a single boundary, and so must not have any holes. The important issues of scale, natural variation, surface texture and object

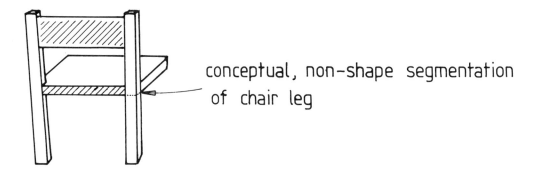
conceptual, non-shape segmentation of chair leg

Figure 7.8: Chair Leg Becomes Part of Chair Back

elasticity/flexibility are also ignored, but this is true of almost all modeling systems.

This surface-based representation method seems best for objects that are primarily man-made solids. Many other objects, especially natural ones, would not be well represented. The individual variation in a tree would not be characterizable, except through a surface smoothing process that represented the entire bough as a distinct solid with a smooth surface, over the class of all trees of the same type. This is an appropriate generalization at a higher level of conceptual scale. Perhaps a combination of this smoothing with Pentland's fractal-based representation of natural texture [PEN83] could solve this problem.

According to the goals of the recognition system, an object probably should not be completely modeled, instead only the key features need description. In particular, only the visually prominent surfaces and features need representation and these should be enough for initial identification and orientation.

Finally, any realistic object recognition system must use a variety of representations, and so the surface representation here should be augmented. Several researchers (e.g. [NEV77],[BRO81],[MAR82]) have shown that axes of elongated regions or volumes are useful features, and volumetric models are useful for recognition. Reflectance, gloss and texture are good surface properties. Viewer-centered and sketch models provide alternative representations.

7.2   Other Model Information

Object models include more than just shape and structure, and this section discusses
the remaining information and its representation. Model invocation (Chapter 8) needs
three types of object-linked information. (The work described below is by both myself
([FIS86a], [FIS87c]) and Paechter [PAE87].) The details and the use of this information
is described in depth in Chapter 8.

The first type is interobject relationships, which provides indirect evidence. Seven
types of relationships are allowed: subcomponent, supercomponent, supertype (fam-
ily), subclass (specialization), superclass (simplification), arbitrary association and
inhibiting. The model also includes a weight to express the importance of the relationship. The information is represented as:

> relation OF objecttype1 IS objecttype2 weight

For example:

> SUPERTYPE OF trash_can_outer_surface IS positive_cylinder 1.0

The second requirement is for constraints on feature properties (Chapter 6) specified
by the acceptable value ranges and a contribution weight. Examples of this information
are the expected areas of surfaces or angles at which surfaces meet. The value ranges
are based on normal distributions about peak values, and may include or exclude the
values near the peak. Additionally, some properties may just be required to be above
(or below) the peak value. Altogether, six forms for property requirements are used.

The final invocation requirement is for subcomponent groups, which are lists of the
immediate subcomponents seen from each distinct viewpoint.

Some of the extra information could have been derived from the geometric models
(e.g. subcomponent relationships). For others, such as the importance of an attribute
to the invocation of a model, the relationships or the methods for automatically extracting the information (i.e. for deciding on the key visible feature groups) are not
well understood. Hence, the extra information is represented explicitly.

7.3   The SMS Object Representation Approach

Based on the experience of this and more recent research, the SMS object representation system [FIS87a] was designed. Extensions over the geometric model approach
described above include: multiple, alternative representations (curve, surface or first
and second-order volumetric primitives), surfaces that extend around the objects, and
can have holes, key feature models, parameterized feature sizes and properties (e.g.
surface curvatures), unconstrained degrees-of-freedom in reference frame transformations, multiple levels of scale-based representation and viewpoint dependent visibility
information.

The goal of SMS is to represent the visual aspects of an object that characterize
its identity, rather than describe its shape. Hence, the modeling approach aims to
provide representations that closely correspond to reliably extractable image features.
This implies that:

1. all object features may not be represented, but instead only the most salient,

2. model representations may not be exact enough for precise reconstruction of the object (e.g. shapes may be simplified to correspond to expected data features or surface patches may not join up neatly) and

3. there may be a variety of alternative (structural or scale-based) representations, depending on the expected data.

The SMS structural models are linked by a subcomponent hierarchy similar to that described for **IMAGINE I**, where subcomponents can be joined to form larger models by reference frame transformations. SMS allows partially constrained relationships, either through the use of variable parameters in the transformation, or by use of an unconstrained degree-of-freedom relationship that, for example, aligns a subcomponent axis vector with a given vector direction in the main model.

The primitive ASSEMBLY structure (i.e. one without subcomponent ASSEMBLYs) can have three non-exclusive representations based on curve, surface or volumetric primitives. The main motivation for the structural alternatives is that different sensors produce different data features (e.g. stereo produces good edge features, ranging produces good surface features and bodyscanners produce good volumetric features). SMS allows one to use the same model to interpret data from all of these scenes; whether this is useful is not known yet.

The curve representations are piecewise circular, elliptic and straight arcs, segmented by the curvature discontinuity criteria proposed in Chapter 3. Surface patches are similar to those described above, except that SURFACEs can now be connected on all sides (e.g. a complete cylinder instead of two arbitrarily segmented patches) and may have holes. Patches are carved out of infinite planes, cylinders and cones, or (finite) tori. Volumetric primitives are based on those proposed by Shapiro et al. [SHA80]. They used a rough three dimensional object model based on sticks (one primary dimension of extension), plates (two dimensions) and blobs (three dimensions) and structural interrelationships. This approach allowed development of more stable relational models, while still symbolically characterizing object structure. The SMS modeling system also has some second-order volumetric representations [FIS87d] for small positive features (bump, ridge, fin and spike) and negative features (dent, groove, slot and hole). The volumetric primitives provide model primitives that can be matched to rough spatial characterizations of the scene - such as when stereo provides only a sparse depth image.

In Figure 7.9 we can see first a surface characterization of a "widget" and then a volume and curve based model. Each representation approach captures the "feel" of the object differently.

There is a simplification hierarchy in SMS, which links together models through scale relationships. This development is more speculative, and tries to fuse the ideas of Marr and Nishihara [MAR78] and Brooks [BRO81] on scale-based refinement of model representations and generalization hierarchies. At each new level in the simplification hierarchy, models have their features simplified or removed, resulting in broader classes of objects recognizable with the model. Figure 7.10 shows a coarse and fine scale model of an ashtray (which is also considerably more free-form than the "widget"). The main

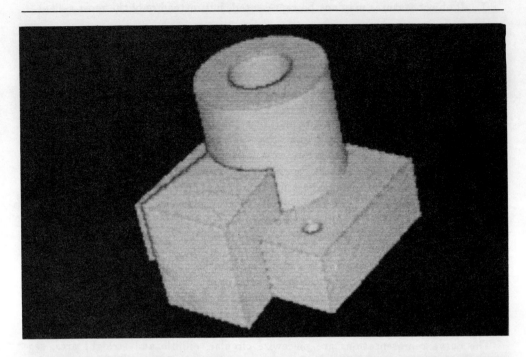

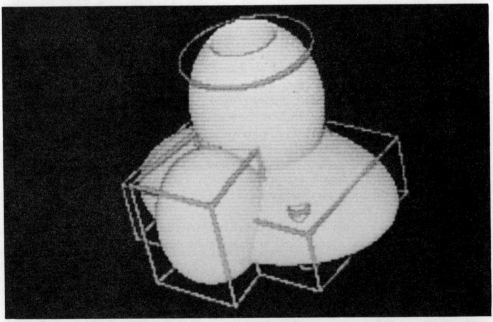

Figure 7.9: Surface and Volume/Curve Model of "Widget"

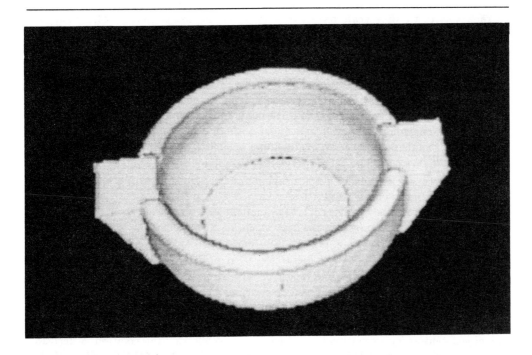

Figure 7.10: Coarse and Fine Scale Model of Ashtray

difference between the two representations is the simplification of the cigarette rest corrugations in the fine scale model to a plane in the coarse model. The plane is a suitable representation for when the object is too distant from the observer to resolve the fine detail.

Following ACRONYM [BRO81], all numerical values can be symbolic variables or expressions, as well as constants. This has been used for generic model representation, by allowing size variation amongst the recognizable objects. Variables are defined as either local or global to a model and are bound by a dynamic scoping mechanism. For example, one could define a robot finger with an external scale parameter and an internal joint angle parameter. When defining a robot hand using several instances of the fingers, than each finger would have its own joint position, but all fingers would have the same scale parameter. Figure 7.11 shows the ashtray with parameter changes causing a wider and deeper shape.

Besides the structural model, each SMS model has a set of constraints and descriptions. Some constraints are expressed in algebraic form, following ACRONYM, and affect the model variables (e.g. feature sizes and joint angles). These constraints can be exploited in the simplification hierarchy, as in ACRONYM. Evidence constraints bound properties such as area, curvature or relative position. These are used primarily for model invocation, as discussed in Section 7.2. Finally, relations between the volumetric primitives can be given [SHA80], such as "a STICK touches a PLATE".

Each SMS model has some visibility information directly represented along with the object-centered information described above. While this information is derivable from the geometric model, in principle, experience with **IMAGINE I** showed that these derivations were time-consuming, because a full raycast image was synthesized and then analyzed. (Chapter 9 elaborates on this).

The visibility information is organized into visibility groups, where each group corresponds to a different topological viewpoint of the immediate subcomponents. While this is still an open research problem, our work suggests that the complexity of the viewsphere [KOE82] of a complicated object, can be reduced by (1) only considering occlusion relationships between immediate subcomponents of a model, thus creating a hierarchy of viewspheres, and (2) only considering large scale relationships, like surface ordering. Each visibility group records which subcomponents are visible or tangential (i.e. possibly visible) and for the visible ones, which are partially obscured. New viewpoint dependent features are also recorded, such as surface relative depth ordering, TEE junctions and extremal boundaries on curved surfaces. Each viewpoint has a set of algebraic constraints that specify the range of object positions over which the given viewpoint is visible.

As can be seen, the SMS models are considerably richer than those used for **IMAGINE I**, and form the basis for the **IMAGINE II** system currently being developed (see Chapter 11). The rest of this book describes the results obtained using the **IMAGINE I** models.

7.4   Other Object Representation Approaches

Marr [MAR82] proposed five criteria for evaluating object representations:

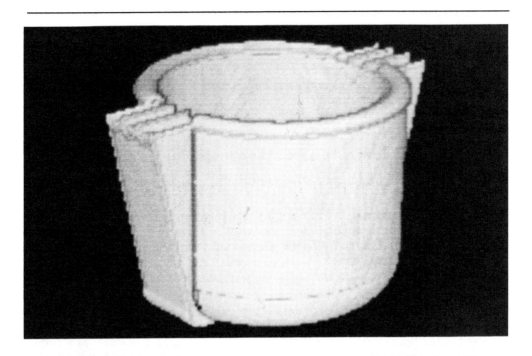

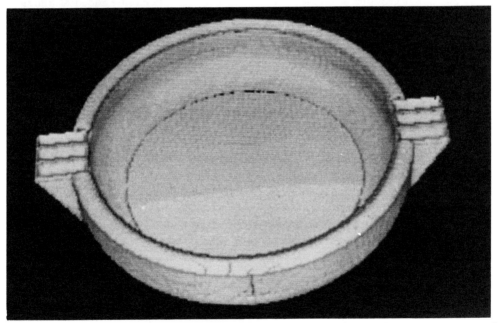

Figure 7.11: Parameter Changes Give Deep and Wide Ashtray

1. accessibility – needed information should be directly available from the model rather than derivable through heavy computation,

2. scope – a wide range of objects should be representable,

3. uniqueness – an object should have a unique representation,

4. stability – small variations in an object should not cause large variations in the model and

5. sensitivity – detailed features should be represented as needed.

We will use these criteria to help understand the relationships between different model schemes.

The model representation scheme defined above generally satisfies these criteria, except that the uniqueness criterion is weakened to become: an object should have only a few representations and these should be easily derivable from each other. The problem with the uniqueness criterion appears when one considers the subcomponent hierarchy. At present, there is no strong understanding of when to describe a set of features at one level in a model hierarchy versus creating a separate subcomponent for them. Further, given that the image data is typically seen from only one viewpoint, it is conceivable that the properties that were used in organizing the model may not be observed in the image data. An example where this might occur is with: (a) a teapot body and spout grouped at one level of description with the handle added at a higher level versus (b) grouping all three features at the same level.

The problems of model hierarchies suggest that another criterion of a good representation is **conceptual economy**, and I have identified two justifications for it. First, economy dictates that there should be only a single representation of any particular shape, and multiple instances of that shape should refer to the single representation. Second, features that are distinctly characterized as a whole, irrespective of their substructures, should be represented simply by reference to that whole, with the details of that feature represented elsewhere.

Brady [BRA83b] proposed three additional criteria for analyzing representation schemes: rich local support, smooth extension and subsumption of representations and reference frame propagation. Since surface patch types are defined by the principal curvatures, the first additional criterion is partially satisfied. The second one does not seem to apply (Brady investigated merging local descriptions to form larger descriptions). The reference frame propagation criterion also seems to be satisfied because, here, all model features have well defined local reference frames and data descriptions also have local reference frames (though there may be degrees-of-freedom, as with a cylindrical patch).

Modeling schemes in computer vision mainly belong to two families:

- Property representations – that define objects by properties or constraints (without recourse to an explicit geometric model) the satisfaction of which should lead to unique identification.

- Geometric representations – that represent object shape and structure.

The representations may be expressed implicitly in a computer program or explicitly as an identifiable defined model. The implicit model is not different in competence from the explicit model, but is ignored here because of its lack of generality. We discuss the two families in greater detail in the following subsections. (These representations are closely related to the matching algorithms discussed in Chapter 2.)

Property Representations

A typical property representation associates lists of expected properties with each object. Some examples of this are:

- color, size and height for image regions in office scenes [DUD70],

- rough object sizes, colors and edge shapes for desk top objects [SHI78] and

- face shape, edge lengths and two dimensional edge angles for identifying polyhedra [FAL72].

One can also include relationships that have to be held with other structures (e.g. [BAR76]), such as in Adler's program [ADL75] that interpreted two dimensional Peanuts cartoon figure scenes.

Property and relationship representations often take the form of a graph. Here, object features become nodes in the graph, relationships between the features become the arcs and properties of the features are labels on the nodes. For example, Barrow and Popplestone [BAR71] represented visible object regions and their interrelationships, (like adjacency and relative size).

Graph representations have the advantage of adding some structure to the object properties, and providing a common representation method for many problems. One problem is all object details tend to be represented at the same level, so the graphs can become large without benefit. Adding more detail increases the computational difficulties of matching rather than easing them. Barrow et al. [BAR72] investigated hierarchical graph representations in matching to try to overcome the computational complexity.

Various researchers ([HAN78b], [NAG79], [OHT79]) have augmented property representations with weak geometric shape (e.g. parallel, square) and relationships (e.g. above, near).

Property representations mainly satisfy Marr's scope and accessibility criteria. Further, graph and property representations are usually two dimensional, whereas we are interested in three dimensional objects and scenes, where changes in viewpoint make drastic changes in the representation. Property representations offer simplicity at the expense of having weak descriptive powers and providing no support for active deduction. However, it is still difficult to represent natural objects geometrically so their recognition must depend heavily on these property representations.

Geometric Representations

Early geometric models were based on three dimensional point or line descriptions. Point models (e.g. [ROB65]) specify the location of significant points relative to the whole object. This method is simple but problematic, because of difficulties in correctly establishing model-to-data correspondences. Edge models (e.g. [FAL72]) specify the location, orientation and shape of edges (typically orientation discontinuities). These characterize the wire-frame shape of an object better than the point models and have stronger correspondence power, but lead to difficulties because of the ambiguity of scene edges and the difficulty of reliably extracting the edges. Further, it is difficult to define and extract intrinsic linear features on curved surfaces. Point and edge models have trouble meeting Marr's scope and sensitivity criteria.

Surface models describe the shape of observable surface regions and their relationship to the whole object (and sometimes to each other). Key questions include how to describe the shape of the surfaces and what constitutes an identifiable surface primitive.

Surface regions can be represented by their bounding space curves in wire frame models ([BOL83], [BAL82], page 291). Planar surfaces are most easily represented, but curved surfaces can also be represented by judicious placement of lines. While useful for computer-aided design and graphics, the surface information needed for recognition tends to be hard to access.

Surface patch models can give arbitrarily accurate representations of object surfaces. One approach to surface representation is by bicubic spline patches ([YOR81], [BAL82], page 269), where cubic polynomials approximate the surface between fixed control points, giving both positional and derivative continuity. Lack of uniqueness and stability are weak aspects of these models. Also, these modeling approaches ignore the problem of shape discontinuities (i.e. surface orientation).

A second popular approach uses polygonal patches (e.g. [BOI81]), with subdivision of the patches to achieve the required accuracy. These represent surfaces well, but give no conceptual structure to the surface and also suffer over the stability criterion. Faugeras and Hebert [FAU83] used planar patches derived from depth data to partially bound a three dimensional rigid object. Here, the model did not characterize well the full object, rather, it concentrated on nearly planar regions. Other researchers have created planar and cylindrical surface models from light-stripe range data (e.g. [POP75], [DAN82]).

On the whole, surfaces represent the actual visibility of an object well and allow direct comparison of appearance, but do not easily characterize the mass distribution of an object. Further, techniques for describing surfaces that are curved or have natural variation for recognition have not yet been well formulated.

Volumetric models represent the solid components of an object in relation to each other or the whole object. Examples include space filling models (e.g. [BAL82], page 280) that represent objects by denoting the portions of space in which the object is located, and constructive solid geometry (CSG) models, that start from geometric primitives like cubes, cylinders or half-spaces (e.g. [REQ77], [CAM84]) and then form more complex objects by merging, difference and intersection operations. With these, three dimensional character is directly accessible, but appearance is hard to deduce without the addition of surface shape and reflectance information. Matching with solids requires finding properties of images and solids that are directly comparable, such as obscuring boundaries and axes of elongation. These volumetric representations tend to meet only Marr's scope and sensitivity criteria.

Recently, Pentland [PEN88] introduced a superquadric-based volumetric model representation. The advantage of the superquadrics was that a great variety of primitive volumes can be described using only a few parameters. Natural appearance was improved by adding fractal-based surface texture afterwards. Larger objects and scenes were formed by scaling and positioning instances of the primitives. Pentland demonstrated several techniques for locally estimating a global superquadric decomposition (from local shape analysis and global subsumption) that was particularly effective on elongated features. He also demonstrated estimation of fractal parameters from local shape spatial frequency spectra and showed how these could be used to segment texture regions. However, as with the CSG primitives, superquadric models seem to be more useful for graphics, and appear to have difficulties with uniqueness and access of the correct feature for model matching. This remains an open research area.

Another promising volumetric model for computer vision is the generalized cylinder (or cone) ([BIN71], [MAR78], [AGI79], [HOG84]), which have had their most significant usage in the ACRONYM system [BRO81].

The primitive unit of representation is a solid specified by a cross-sectional shape, an axis along which to sweep the cross-section and a sweeping rule describing how the shape and orientation of the cross-section vary along the axis.

The axis was the key feature because of its relation to axes directly derivable from image data. Many "growth" based natural structures (e.g. tree branches, human limbs) have an axis of elongation, so generalized cylinders make good models. It also represents many simple man-made objects well, because the manufacturing operations of extrusion, shaping and turning create reasonably regular, nearly symmetric elongated solids.

In Marr's proposal [MAR82], objects were described by the dominant model axis and the names and placement of subcomponents about the axis. Subcomponents could be refined hierarchically to provide greater detail. The specification used dimensionless units, which allowed scale invariance, and the relative values were represented by quantized value ranges that provided both the symbolic and approximate representation needed for stability to variation and error.

Brooks [BRO81] used generalized cylinders in the ACRONYM system, where they could be directly matched to image boundary pairs (i.e. ribbons). Subcomponents were attached by specifying the rotation and translation relating the object and subcomponent reference frames. All primitive or affixment relationship specifications could contain variables, but the subcomponents used in ACRONYM's airplane example were all rigidly connected to the main model. Hogg [HOG84] used variable attachments to represent joint variation in a human model, with a posture function constraining relative joint position over time.

For matching, ACRONYM's geometric models were compiled into a prediction graph, where key generalized cylinders became the nodes and placement relationships between the cylinders defined the relations. Because the image data being matched was two dimensional, the prediction graphs represented typical two dimensional views of the objects, derived from the full three dimensional geometric model. The advantage of this was that the full constraints of the geometric model could be employed in the uniform graph matching method. Substantial reasoning was needed to derive the prediction graph from the three dimensional models.

The most important contribution of ACRONYM's modeling was the use of algebraic constraints that limit the range of model variables in relation to either fixed values or other variables. An example would be: "the length of a desk top is greater than the width, but less than twice the width", where both length and width are variable parameters.

Variables and constraints together support generic class models, at least in structural terms (as opposed to functional). The structural aspects of the model define the essential components and their attachments, symbolic parameters denote the type of variation and the constraints specify the range of variation. The effect of the algebraic constraints is to structure the space of all possible models with the same logical part relationships into a generalization hierarchy, where more restrictive constraints define generic specializations of the model. Subclasses are defined by more tightly constrained (or constant) parameters, or additional constraints.

A criticism of the generalized cylinder/cone representation concerns its choice of primitive element. Many natural and man-made objects do not have vaguely cylindrical components: a leaf, a rock, the moon, a crumpled newspaper, a tennis shoe. Though some aspects of these objects could be reasonably represented, the representation would omit some relevant aspects (e.g. the essential two dimensionality of the leaf), or introduce other irrelevant ones (e.g. the axis of a sphere). Hence, other primitives should at least be included to increase its scope.

Secondly, what is perceived is the surface of objects. Hence, it seems reasonable that the preferential representation for object recognition should make surface-based information explicit. The near-parallel, tangential obscuring boundaries of a generalized cylinder ("ribbon") are reasonable features for detection, and the orientation of the figure's spine constrains its three dimensional location, but this is about all the information that is easily derivable from the cylinder representation. Surface shape comparisons are non-trivial, because it is difficult to determine the visible surfaces of the cylinder and what it will look like from a given viewpoint. It is often hard to decide with what model feature an image feature should correspond.

These models are structured, so that they meet the sensitivity criterion and give unique representations. When modeling objects formed from hierarchical collections of elongated primitive shapes, the generalized cylinder method also meets the scope and stability criteria. The key problem of these models is accessibility – it can be hard to deduce much about the appearance of an object from its volumetric description and much about which model to use from the observed appearance.

These considerations, however, are most relevant when recognizing objects whose three dimensional surface shape and structure is apparent at the scale of analysis. The ACRONYM examples, aerial photographs of airport scenes, were largely two dimensional as almost all objects were reduced to laminar surfaces viewed perpendicularly. Hence, treating nearly parallel intensity boundaries as potentially observable extremal boundaries of generalized cylinders was appropriate.

The reduction of generics to numerical ranges of parameter values is simplistic, although an important first step. Sometimes it is inappropriate: a model adequate for recognizing a particular type of office chair probably would not specialize to any other chair. Any chair model that includes most office chairs would probably require a functional definition: seating surface meets appropriate back support surface.

Brooks attempted to introduce structural variation through parameter variation, but his solution seems inappropriate. For example, an integer variable ranging from 3 to 6 was used to state that an electric motor had 3, 4, 5 or 6 flanges, and a second variable stated that a motor did or did not have a base by constraining its value to 0 to 1. More complicated algebraic inequalities stated that motors with bases have no flanges. Uniform representation is a laudable goal, but these examples suggest that a more powerful representation should be considered. Hence, the physical variation within a class (i.e. size and affixment variations), that constraints represent well, should be separated from the conceptual relationships involved in generalization, where logical/relational constraints would be better.

There has been little work on object representations for non-rigid objects, other than ACRONYM, as just described. Grimson [GRI87] defined and recognized piecewise linear two dimensional models that could scale, stretch along one axis or have subcomponents joined by a revolute joint. Terzopolous et al. [TER87] described symmetry-seeking models based on deformable parametric tube and spine primitives. The shapes of the models were controlled by energy constraints on the deformation of the spine, the symmetry of the tube and the relative position of the two. These models allowed the successful reconstruction of three dimensional natural shapes (e.g. a crook-neck squash) from only the two dimensional image contours. It is unclear, however, if this approach is suitable for object recognition, because of the many parameters required.

Most geometric representations are object-centered, though Minsky [MIN75] proposed a frame representation for recording features visible from typical distinct viewpoints, thus adding viewer-centered information. Chakravarty [CHA82] applied this notion in classifying the topologically distinct views of polyhedral scenes, for use in object recognition. Koenderink and van Doorn [KOE82] considered the application of such ideas to generic smooth objects, by analyzing the discontinuities of occlusion and visibility relationships.

Final Comments

This completes our discussion on object representation. Other discussions of three dimensional object representation techniques can be found in [BAL82], [BES85] and [FIS87b]. A particularly thorough review was given by Besl [BES88b] and covers geometric techniques for space-curves, surfaces, volumes and four dimensional (i.e. moving) objects. His review also summarized well the basic geometric matching techniques that are typically used with each class of object.

With the models defined in this chapter, we can now start to recognize the objects in the scene. The recognition process will make heavy use of the surface-based geometric models, and of the subcomponent hierarchy. The first step of recognition is to select potential models for the image features, which is the topic of the next chapter.

CHAPTER 8

Model Invocation

One important and difficult task for a general model-based vision system is selecting the correct model. Model-based vision is computationally intractable without reducing the large set of objects that potentially explain a set of data to a few serious candidates that require more detailed analysis. Since there may be 1,000 – 100,000 distinct objects in a competent general vision system's range, and even a modest industrial vision system may have 100 distinct objects in its repertoire, the problem is too large to undertake model-directed comparisons of every known object in every viewpoint. The problem remains even if the potentially massive parallelism of the brain or VLSI are considered.

Visual understanding must also include a non-attentive element, because all models need be accessible for interpreting all image data. So, the solution must consider both efficiency and completeness of access.

There is also a more crucial competence aspect to the problem. A vision system needs to be capable of (loosely) identifying previously unseen objects, based on their similarity to known objects. This is required for non-rigid objects seen in new configurations, incompletely visible objects (e.g. from occlusion) or object variants (e.g. flaws, generics, new exemplars). Hence, "similar" models must be invoked to help start identification, where "similar" means sharing some features or having an identically arranged substructure.

In view of all these requirements, model invocation is clearly a complex problem. This chapter presents a solution that embodies ideas on association networks, object description and representation, and parallel implementations. In the first section, the relevant aspects of the problem are discussed. The second presents a theoretical formulation of the proposed solution, the third shows examples of the process, the fourth discusses related work, and the last evaluates the theory.

The work described here builds on the original work by Fisher [FIS86a] and many significant improvements by Paechter [PAE87].

8.1 Some Characteristics of the Invocation Process

Invocation is Suggestion

Invocation is the result of the directed convergence of clues that suggest identities for explaining data. On the street, one occasionally sees a person with a familiar figure,

Figure 8.1: Picasso-like Figure Invokes Human Model

face and style, but who on closer inspection turns out not to be the acquaintance. The clues suggest the friend, but direct examination contradicts the suggestion.

Invocation also supports the "seeing" of nonexistent objects, as in, e.g., Magritte's surrealist paintings, where configurations of features give the impression of one object while actually being another. Figure/ground reversals and ambiguous interpretations such as the vase and faces illusion could occur when multiple invocations are possible, but only a single interpretation is held at any instant, because of mutual inhibition, as suggested by Arbib [ARB79] and others.

Invocation is Mediated by Relationships

Invocation is computed through associations or relationships with other objects. The effect is one of suggestion, rather than confirmation. For example, a red spheroid might suggest an apple, even though it is a cherry. Another example is seen in the Picasso-like picture drawn in Figure 8.1. Though many structural relationships are violated, there are enough suggestions of shapes, correct subcomponents and rough relationships for invoking a human face.

While there are many types of relationship between visual concepts, two key ones are mediated by class and component relationships as discussed below. Other relationship types include context (robots are more often found in factories than in trees) or temporal (a red traffic light is often seen after a yellow traffic light). Altogether, the

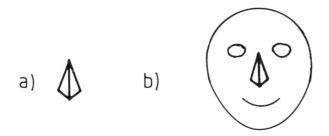

Figure 8.2: Pyramid in Face Context Invokes Nose Model

work here integrates eight different evidence types: subcomponent, supercomponent, subclass, superclass, description (i.e. generic shape), property, general association and inhibiting (i.e. competing).

Associations Have Varying Importances

The importance of a particular feature in invoking a model is a function of the feature, model, context and viewing system.

Some objects share common features, such as planar faces in blocks world scenes. Other objects have distinct features, such as the shape of the Eiffel Tower, an ear or the characteristic blue light used by emergency vehicles. Hence, some features may dramatically reduce the set of potential models.

Context is also important, because the *a priori* likelihood of discovering an object influences the importance of a feature. Wheels (generic) when seen in a garage are more likely cues for automobiles than when seen in a bicycle shop. Part (a) of Figure 8.2 shows is a standard pyramid that is unlikely to invoke any models other than its literal interpretation. Yet, in Figure 8.2 part (b), the same pyramid invokes the "nose" model acceptably. Obviously, the context influences the likely models invoked for a structure. The viewing system is also a factor, because its perceptual goals influence the priorities of detecting an object. For example, industrial inspection systems often concentrate on a few distinctive features rather than on the objects as a whole.

Statistical analysis could determine the likelihood of a feature in a given context, but is unhelpful in determining the importance of the feature. Further, because contexts may change, it is difficult to estimate the object and feature *a priori* distributions needed for statistical classification. Finally, feature importance may change over time as factors become more or less significant (e.g. contexts can change). Hence, importance assessment seems more properly a learning than an analysis problem.

Evidence Starts with Observed Properties

Property evidence is based on properties extracted from the input data. Here, the evidence will be common unary or binary properties. An example is surface shape evidence, which may have zero, one or two magnitudes and axes of curvature.

The properties are absolute measurements constrained by bounds (like ACRONYM [BRO81]). Some properties must lie in a range, such as expected surface area. Others are merely required to be above or below a limit, as when requiring positive maximum principal curvature. Other property values may be excluded, such as zero principal curvature.

Evidence is acquired in "representative position" [COW83]. Features that remain invariant during data acquisition over all observer positions are few (e.g. reflectance, principal curvatures). As this research is concerned with surface shape properties, the potential evidence is more limited and includes angles between structures, axis orientations, relative feature sizes and relative feature orientations. Invocation features should be usually visible. When they are not, invocation may fail, though there may be alternative invocation features for the privileged viewing positions.

Evidence Comes from Component Relationships

The presence of an object's subcomponents suggests the presence of the object. If we see the legs, seat and back of a chair, the whole chair is likely although not guaranteed to be there, as we could be seeing an unassembled set of chair parts. Hence, verified or highly plausible subcomponents influence the plausibility of the object's presence. The reverse should also occur. If we are reasonably sure of the chair's presence (e.g. because we have found several subcomponents of the chair), then this should enhance the plausibility that nearby leg-like structures are chair legs. This information is useful when such structures are partially obscured, and their direct evidence is not as strong.

Figure 8.3 shows an abstract head. While the overall face is unrepresentative, the head model is invoked because of the grouping of correct subcomponents.

Evidence Comes from Configurations of Components

Configurations of subcomponents affect invocation in two ways: (1) only a subset of subcomponents is visible from any particular viewpoint, and (2) the spatial distribution of subcomponents can suggest models as well. The first case implicates using visibility groups when integrating evidence. For a chair, one often sees the top of the seat and the front of the back support, or the bottom of the seat and back of the back support, or the top of the seat and the back of the back support, but seldom any of the other twelve groupings of the four subcomponents. These groupings are directly related to the major visibility regions in the visual potential scheme suggested by Koenderink and van Doorn [KOE77]. They showed how the sphere of all potential viewing positions of an object could be partitioned according to what components

Figure 8.3: Identified Subcomponents Invoke Models

were visible in each partition and when various features became self-obscured. Minsky [MIN75] suggested that distinguishable viewer-centered feature groupings should be organized into separate frames for recognition.

It is well known that the many small features of a normal object lead to a great many regions on the view potential sphere. To avoid this problem, two ideas were adopted here. First, rather than creating a new visibility region whenever an occlusion event occurs (i.e. when an edge is crossed), the regions are formed only according to changes in the visibility of large-scale features (i.e. SURFACEs and ASSEMBLYs). That is, a new group is formed whenever new subcomponents are seen, or when feature ordering relationships are different. Second, the visibility and feature ordering analysis only applies to the immediate subcomponents of the object, and disregards any visibility relationships between their own subcomponents. Thus, visibility complexity is reduced by reducing the number of features and the details of occlusion relationships considered, by exploiting the subcomponent hierarchy, and by ignoring less likely visibility groupings.

Figure 8.4 shows the sphere of viewpoints partitioned into the topologically distinct regions for a trash can. At a particular scale, there are three major regions: outside bottom plus adjacent outside surface, outside surface plus inside surface and outside, inside and inner bottom surfaces. There are other less significant regions, but these are ignored because of their minor size.

During invocation, these visibility groupings are used to collect subcomponent evidence, and the invocation of a group implies a rough object orientation. Here, invocation is the important result, which will lead to initial structure assignments for hypothesis construction (Chapter 9), from which orientation is estimated directly.

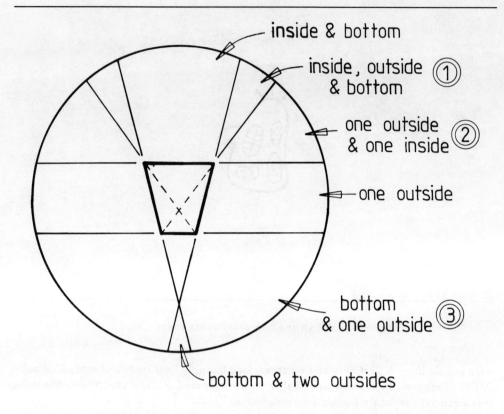

inside & bottom

inside, outside ①
& bottom

one outside ②
& one inside

one outside

bottom ③
& one outside

bottom & two outsides

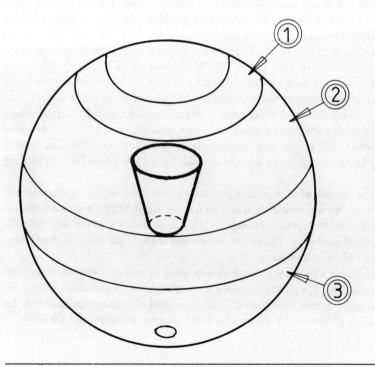

Figure 8.4: Distinct Viewing Regions for Trash Can

Figure 8.5: Spatial Configurations Invoke Models

The second aspect of spatial configurations is how the placement of components, rather than their identity, suggests the model. Figure 8.5 shows the converse of Figure 8.3, where all subcomponents have the wrong identity but, by virtue of their position, suggest the face model.

Spatial configuration evidence is represented by binary evidence types that constrain relationships like relative position, orientation or size. The evidence for these relationships should probably be stronger if the features involved in the relationship also have the correct types. That is, the two eye-like features in Figure 8.5 help suggest a face, but they would do so more strongly if they were individually more like eyes.

Evidence Comes from Class Relationships

An object typically has several generalizations and specializations, and evidence for its invocation may come from any of these other hypotheses. For example, a generic chair could generalize to "furniture", or "seating structure", or specialize to "dentist chair" or "office typing chair". Because of the unpredictabilities of evidence, it is conceivable that any of the more generalized or specialized concepts may be invoked before the generic chair. For the more general, this may occur when occlusion leaves only the seating surface and back support prominent. Conversely, observation of a particular distinguishing feature may lead to invocation of the more specific model first. In either case, evidence for the categorically related structures gives support for the structure.

Class prototypes are useful when a set of objects share a common identity, such as "chair". General properties of an object class are more important for invocation (as compared to verification, which needs the details of shape).

There are some superficial relationships with the generic identification scheme in ACRONYM [BRO81], where identification proceeds by descent through a specialization hierarchy with increasingly stringent constraints. Here, the hierarchy and notion of refining constraints are similar, but: (1) the goal is suggestion, not verification, so the property constraints are not strict, and (2) the flow of control is not general to specific: identification could locally proceed in either direction in the hierarchy.

There is a Low-Level Descriptive Vocabulary

There is a vocabulary of low level, object independent and special intermediate shapes and configurations. The purpose of the descriptions is to introduce generic, sharable structures into the invocation process. Examples of the symbols include: "positive-cylindrical-surface" and "square-planar-polygon". However, this vocabulary does not usually refer to identifiable real objects, but instead to ideal generalizations of some particular aspects of the object. For the "positive-cylindrical-surface", it does not say anything about the identity of the patch, nor the extent or curvature, but concisely characterizes one aspect of the object.

The symbols structure the description of an object, thus simplifying any direct model-to-data comparisons and increase efficiency through shared features. A description hierarchy arises from using subdescriptions to define more complex ones. An example of this is in the chain of descriptions: "polygon" - "quadrilateral" - "trapezoid" - "parallelogram" - "rectangle" - "square", where each member of the chain introduces a new property constraint on the previous. The hierarchy helps reduce the model, network and matching complexity. Rather than specify all properties of every modeled object, the use of common descriptions can quickly express most properties and only object-specific property constraints need be added later.

This is important to invocation efficiency, because of the filtering effect on recognitions, whereby image data invoke low level visual concepts, which then invoke higher level concepts.

If object descriptions are sufficiently discriminating, a vision system may be able to accomplish most of its interpretation through only invocation with little or no model-directed investigation.

Invocation is Incremental

Evidence can come from a variety of sources and as more supporting evidence accumulates the desirability of invoking a model increases. The invocation process must continue even though some evidence is missing because of occlusion or erroneous descriptions. Complementary evidence should contribute to plausibility and conflicting evidence should detract from it. The process should degrade gracefully: less evidence should lower the desirability of invocation rather than prevent it totally.

These factors suggest that invocation is mediated by a continuous plausibility.

Invocation Occurs in Image Contexts

There must be contexts for grouping property evidence and for associating subcomponents, so that related evidence is integrated and unrelated evidence is excluded.

Individual Evidence Values Need to be Integrated

Evidence needs to be integrated several times: when individual properties are merged to provide a total property evidence value, when individual subcomponent evidence values are combined and when all eight evidence types are combined. This integration is complicated by the different implications of the evidence types and their relative importances. Moreover, the quantity of evidence associated with different evidence types implies evidence weighting is required.

8.2 Theory: Evidence and Association

We now describe the invocation process in detail, based on the intuitions of the previous section.

The first consideration of invocation is from its externally viewed characteristics – its function and its input and output behavior. Formally, the inputs to invocation are:

- A set $\{C_i\}$ of image contexts.

- A set $\{(d_j, v_{ij}, C_i)\}$ of image descriptions of type (d) with value (v) for the data in these contexts.

- A database $\{(t_i, M_j, M_k, w_{ijk})\}$ of model-to-model (M) relationships of different types (t) with weights (w).

- A database $\{(M_i, \{(d_{ij}, l_{ij}, h_{ij}, u_{ij}, x_{ij}, w_{ij})\})\}$ of desired description constraints for each model, where d is the description type, l is the lower acceptable value for the description, h is the expected peak value, u is the upper acceptable value, x specifies whether the desired value is included or excluded in the range and w is a weight.

The basic structural unit of invocation is a <u>model instance</u> for a model M_j in an image context C_i. The output of invocation is a set $\{(M_j, C_i, p_{ij})\}$ of the plausibility measures for each model instance. This implies that each object type is considered for each context. Fortunately, the context formulation has already achieved a reduction of information.

Invocation always takes place in an image context. This is because objects are always connected and their features are always spatially close. The context defines where image data can come from and what structures can provide supporting evidence. For this research, the two types of contexts are the surface hypothesis (Chapter 4) and the surface cluster (Chapter 5), which localize evidence for model SURFACEs and ASSEMBLYs respectively. The surface cluster also groups surfaces and contained surface clusters, so is a suitable context for accumulating subcomponent plausibilities.

Model invocation calculates a plausibility representing the degree to which an object model explains an image structure. Plausibility is a function of the model, the data context, the data properties, the desired properties, the model-to-model relationships, current object hypotheses, and the plausibilities of all related model-to-data pairings.

A plausibility measure is used instead of direct indexing because:

1. many objects have similar features and a plausibility measure expresses the similarity between models,

2. generic models may not exactly match a real specific object,

3. it allows weak evidence support from associated model-to-data pairings,

4. it supports accumulating unrelated evidence types, and

5. it provides graceful degradation as image descriptions fail because of noise, occlusion or algorithmic limits.

Given the plausibility ranking, when should a model be invoked? Even if a model instance has the highest plausibility, it should not invoke the model if the absolute plausibility is low, as when analyzing an image with no identifiable objects in it. The measure used lies in the range $[-1, 1]$, and when it is positive, the model can be invoked. Because the invocation network described below favors positive plausibilities as supporting and negative plausibilities as contradicting, a threshold of zero was used.

Plausibility is a function of property evidence arising from observed features and relationship evidence arising from hypotheses that have some relationship with the current one. For example, a toroidal shape gives property evidence for a bicycle wheel, whereas a bicycle frame gives relationship evidence.

The foundation of plausibility is property evidence and is acquired by matching descriptions of image-based structures to model-based evidence constraints. The constraints implement the notion that certain features are important in distinguishing the structure.

Relationship evidence comes from associated model instances. Although there are many types of relationships, this work only considered the following ones (treating object A as the model of current interest):

1. Supercomponent: B is an structure of which A is a subcomponent.

2. Subcomponent: B is a subcomponent of structure A.

3. Superclass: B is a more generic class of object than A.

4. Subclass: B is a more specific class of object than A.

5. Description: Every property of B is a property of A.

6. Inhibition: Identity B competes with identity A.

7. Association: The presence of object B makes the presence of A more likely.

These seven relationships have been made explicit because each embodies different forms of visual knowledge and because their individual evidence computations are different. Component relationships give strong circumstantial evidence for the presence of objects. An object necessarily requires most of its subcomponents for it to be considered that object, whereas the reverse does not hold. The presence of a car makes the presence of wheels highly plausible, but cannot say much about whether a particular image feature is a wheel. The presence of automobile wheels also makes the presence of a car plausible (though the latter implication is weaker), but does not mean that any containing image context is likely to contain the car.

The final issue is evidence integration. Evidence is cumulative: each new piece of valid evidence modifies the plausibility of a structure. Evidence is also suggestive: each item of support is evaluated independently of the others and so does not confirm the identity of any structure. Because there are eight different evidence types, the problem of how to compute a single plausibility value arises. We wish to use all the evidence, as data errors, missing values, and object variations are alternative causes for weak evidence, as well as having the wrong identity. The solution given below treats the different evidence values on the same scale, but integrates the values according to the evidence type.

The different model hypotheses in the different contexts are represented as nodes in a network linked by property and relationship evidence arcs. Many of the arcs also connect to arithmetic function nodes that compute the specific evidence values, as discussed in detail below. Property evidence provides the raw plausibility values for a few of the nodes, and the other nodes acquire plausibility by value propagation through the relationship arcs.

An abbreviated example is shown in Figure 8.6, where a simplified network is shown with the given relationship links ("G" denotes a class relationship, "D" denotes a description relationship, "I" denotes an inhibiting relationship and "C" denotes a component relationship). The precise formulation of the calculations is given in later sections, and the point here is to introduce the character of the computation (while glossing over the details). Supposing there was property evidence for there being a $< torus >$ and a $< vehicle >$ in the current context, the question then is what the plausibility of the $< wheel >$ is. This value comes from integrating description evidence from the $< torus >$ and component evidence from the $< car >$ and $< bike >$, and competing generic evidence from the $< polo\ mint >$.

When a model has been invoked, it is subject to a model-directed hypothesis construction and verification process. If the process is successful, then the plausibility value for that object is set to 1.0. Alternatively, failure sets the plausibility to -1.0. These values are permanently recorded for the hypotheses and affect future invocations by propagating through the network.

In the discussion of each of the relationship types below, three major aspects are considered: the type of relationship, the calculation of the relationship's invocation contribution and the context from which the relationship evidence is taken.

8.2.1   Property Evidence

Property evidence is calculated by evaluating the fit of structural properties (Chapter 6) to model requirements (Chapter 7). An example of a set of requirements would be a particular surface must be planar and must meet all adjacent connected surfaces at right angles.

There is some controversy over what constitutes evidence, but here, evidence is based only on primitive image properties, such as relative curve orientation, rather than

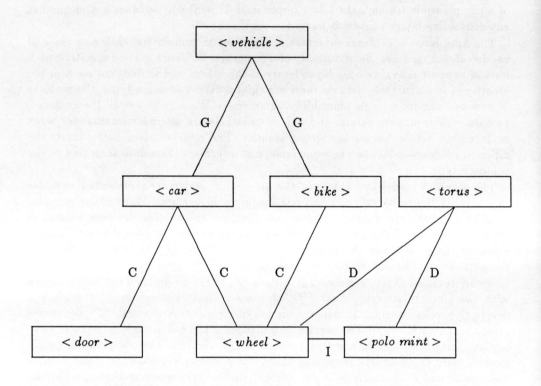

Figure 8.6: A Simplified Invocation Network

higher level descriptions, such as "rectangular". This decision is partly made because "rectangular" is a distinct conceptual category and, as such, would be included as a distinct generic element in the invocation network. It would then have a description relationship to the desired model.

The context within which data is taken depends on the structure for which property evidence is being calculated. If it is a model SURFACE, then properties come from the corresponding surface hypothesis. If it is an ASSEMBLY, then the properties come from the corresponding surface cluster.

Unary evidence requirements are defined in the model database in one of six forms, depending on whether the values are required or excluded, and whether there are upper, lower or both limits on their range. The complete forms are:

central include:
UNARYEVID *low* < evidence_type < *high* PEAK *peak* WEIGHT *wgt*

above include:
UNARYEVID *low* < evidence_type PEAK *peak* WEIGHT *wgt*

below include:
UNARYEVID evidence_type < *high* PEAK *peak* WEIGHT *wgt*

central exclude:
UNARYEVID *low* < evidence_type < *high* PEAK *peak* ABSENT
WEIGHT *wgt*

above exclude:
UNARYEVID *low* < evidence_type PEAK *peak* ABSENT WEIGHT *wgt*

below exclude:
UNARYEVID evidence_type < *high* PEAK *peak* ABSENT WEIGHT *wgt*

If the peak value is the mean of the upper and lower limit, it need not be specified. Each requirement has a weight that scales the contribution of this evidence in the total property evidence evaluation.

Binary evidence requirements are defined similarly, with the key difference that the model also specifies the types of the substructures between which the properties are to hold. The model specification for the binary "central include" form is:

BINARYEVID *low* < evidence_type(type1,type2) < *high* PEAK *peak*
WEIGHT *wgt*

In **IMAGINE I**, all evidence types were considered to be unary. If a binary property between two features was expressed, then evidence evaluation would take the best instance of the binary relationship. **IMAGINE II** made the relationship explicit. The properties used in **IMAGINE I** were:

NUMLINB – number of straight lines in boundary
NUMARCB – number of curves in boundary
DBPARO – number of groups of parallel lines in boundary
NUM90B – number of perpendicular boundary junctions
NUMEQLB – number of groups of equal length boundary segments
DCURV – boundary segment curvature
DCRVL – boundary segment length
DBRORT – boundary segment relative orientation
MINSCURV – minimum surface curvature
MAXSCURV – maximum surface curvature
SURSDA – relative surface orientation

ABSSIZE – surface area
RELSIZE – percent of surface area in surface cluster
SURECC – eccentricity of surface

It is possible to generate automatically most of the evidence types from the geometric models, if heuristics for setting the ranges and weight values are given, but all these values were manually chosen here. Appendix A shows some of the evidence constraints for the modeled objects.

Models inherit evidence from their descriptions (discussed in Section 8.2.4), so only additional evidence (i.e. refinements) need be specified here.

Finally, we consider how the total evidence value is calculated from the individual pieces of evidence. The constraints on this computation are:

- Each piece of evidence should contribute to the total value.

- The contribution of a piece of evidence should be a function of its importance in uniquely determining the object.

- The contribution of a piece of evidence should be a function of the degree to which it meets its constraints.

- Negative evidence should inhibit more strongly than positive evidence support.

- Each piece of evidence should only be evaluated by the best fitting constraint (allowing disjunctive evidence constraints).

- All constraints need evidence.

- Every property must meet a constraint, if any constraints of the appropriate type exist.

- Not all properties are constrained (i.e. some are irrelevant).

- Binary property evaluations are also a function of the plausibility that the two substructures have the desired identities.

Based on the "degree of fit" requirement, a function was designed to evaluate the evidence from a single description. The function is based on a scaled gaussian evaluation model, with the evaluation peaking at the desired value, having positive value within the required range (which need not be symmetric), and tailing off to -1.0. Because there are six types of evidence requirements, six different evidence evaluation functions are needed. However, the excluded types are the negatives of the included types, and the below types are the mirror image of the above types. So, only the "central include" and "above include" are described here. Based on the model definitions above, the "central include" function for the ith evidence constraint is:

Let:
$$d_j = j^{th} \text{ data value}$$

If: $d_j > peak_i$

then: $f_{ij} = \left(\frac{(d_j - peak_i)}{(high_i - peak_i)} * 1.1774\right)^2$

else: $f_{ij} = \left(\frac{(peak_i - d_j)}{(peak_i - low_i)} * 1.1774\right)^2$

And the evaluation e_j is:

$$g_{ij} = 2 * exp\left(-\frac{f_{ij}}{2}\right) - 1$$

The constant 1.1774 ensures the evaluation equals 0 when the data value equals *high* or *low*. The "above include" function for the ith evidence constraint is:

Let:
$$d_j = j^{th} \text{ data value}$$

If: $d_j > peak_i$

then: $f_{ij} = 0.0$

else: $f_{ij} = \left(\frac{(peak_i - d_j)}{(peak_i - low_i)} * 1.1774\right)^2$

And the evaluation e_j is:

$$g_{ij} = 2 * exp\left(-\frac{f_{ij}}{2}\right) - 1$$

Figure 8.7 illustrates these functions. Their gaussian form is appealing because it is continuous and smooth and relates well to gaussian error distributions from property estimation. Other functions meet the requirements, but stronger requirements could not be found that define the function more precisely.

A property constraint's evaluation is given by the data value that best satisfies the constraint. This is because model-to-data correspondences have not been made yet, so the evaluations are undirected. As the point of invocation is suggestion, any datum within the constraint range is contributory evidence, and correct models will have all their constraints satisfied. Hence, the final evidence value for this constraint is given by:

$$e_i = max_j(g_{ij})$$

This portion of the invocation network is illustrated in Figure 8.8.

The evaluation of binary property evidence takes into account the plausibility of the subcomponents as well as the property value itself. Thus:

$$h_{abi} = c_1 * g_i(a, b) + c_2 * p_{ar} + c_2 * p_{bs} + c_3$$

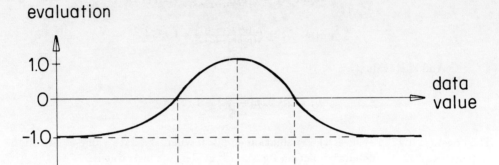

a) "central include" evaluation function

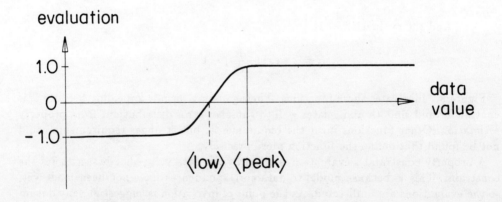

b) "above include" evaluation function

Figure 8.7: Data Evaluation Functions

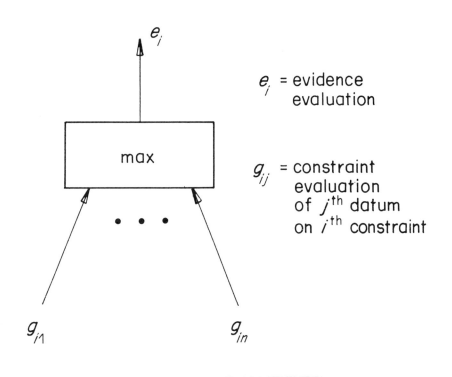

e_i = evidence
evaluation

g_{ij} = constraint
evaluation
of jth datum
on i^{th} constraint

Figure 8.8: Best Evaluation Selection Network Fragment

is the evidence evaluation function for the ith binary evidence constraint, relating model subcomponent r to model subcomponent s, when using the value of the given property between data features a and b. $g_i(a, b)$ is the same evaluation function as for the unary properties (g_{ij}), p_{ar} and p_{bs} are the plausibilities that data feature a has model identity r, data feature b has model identity s, and c_1, c_2 and c_3 are constants that express the relative importance of the different terms $(c_1 = 0.8, c_2 = 0.4, c_3 = -0.6)$. The final binary property evidence value is:

$$e_i = max_{ab}(h_{abi})$$

This picks the best evidence over all pairs of immediate subfeatures in the data context.

The evaluations for individual property requirements then need to be integrated. One function that satisfies the evidence integration constraints is a weighted harmonic mean:

Let:

e_i be the data evaluation for the ith property constraint

w_i be the weight for that evidence type

Then:

$$evd_{prop} = harmmean(\{(e_i, w_i)\})$$

where

$$A = \sum w_i$$

$$B = \sum \frac{w_i}{e_i + 2}$$

$$harmmean(\{(e_i, w_i)\}) = \frac{A}{B} - 2$$

If no property evidence is available, this computation is not applied. The modified harmonic mean is continuous, gives additional weight to negative evidence and integrates all values uniformly. Moreover, it has the property that:

$$harmmean(\{(e_1, w_1), (e_2, w_2), (e_3, w_3)\})$$
$$= harmmean(\{(e_1, w_1), (harmmean(\{(e_2, w_2), (e_3, w_3)\}), w_2 + w_3)\})$$

This means that we can add evidence incrementally without biasing the results to the earlier or later values (provided that we also keep track of the weighting of the values). The offset of 2 is used to avoid problems when the plausibility is near -1, and was chosen because it gave good results. The integrated property evidence has a weight that is the sum of the individual property weights: $w_{prop} = \sum w_i$.

This harmonic mean can be implemented in a value passing network, as shown in Figure 8.9, which integrates the evidence values e_i with weights w_i. Here, the square boxes represent unary or binary arithmetic units of the designated type, and circular units represent either constants, or the evidence values imported from the above calculation.

8.2.2   Supercomponent Associations

This relationship gives evidence for the presence of an object, given the presence of a larger object of which it may be a subpart. Though evidence typically flows from subcomponents to objects, supercomponent evidence may be available when: (1) the supercomponent has property or relationship evidence of its own, or (2) other subcomponents of the object have been found. Unfortunately, the presence of the supercomponent implies that *all* subcomponents are present (though not necessarily visible), but not that an image structure is any particular component. As the supercomponent evidence (during invocation) cannot discriminate between likely and unlikely subcomponents in its context, it supports all equally and thus implements a "priming" operation. This is because the computation is one of plausibility, not certainty. Weighting factors control the amount of support a structure gets. When support is given for the wrong identities, other evidence contradicts and cancels this evidence.

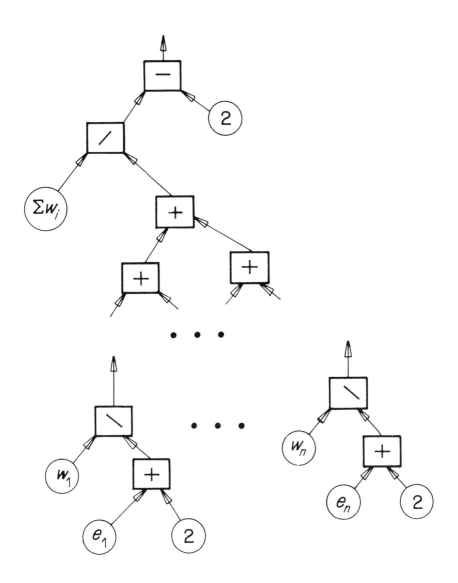

Figure 8.9: Harmonic Mean Network Fragment Integrating Property Evidence

There are several constraints derivable from the problem that help define the evidence computation. They are:

- The presence of a supercomponent makes the presence of an object plausible.

- The more plausible the presence of the supercomponent, the more plausible the presence of the object.

- There is at most one supercomponent of any object, though there may be many candidates.

- The context of the supercomponent must contain the context of the object.

The formal definition of the supercomponent relationship computation is:

> Given:
>> a model instance of type M in image context C
>>
>> a set $\{S_i\}$ of supercomponents of M
>>
>> a set $\{C_j\}$ of supercontexts of C, including C itself and
>>
>> p_{ij} is the plausibility that model M_i occurs in context C_j
>
> Then:
>> $$f_i = max_j(p_{ij})$$

chooses the best evidence for a supercomponent over all supercontexts and

$$evd_{supc} = max_i(f_i)$$

picks the best supercomponent evidence over all supercomponent types. The current context is also included because the supercomponent may not have been visually segmented from the object. If no supercomponent evidence is defined or observed, this computation is not applied.

The network created for this evidence type is simply a tree of binary "max" units linked as defined above.

8.2.3   Subcomponent Associations

This relationship gives direct evidence for the presence of an object, given the presence of its subcomponents. It is stronger than the supercomponent relationship, because the subcomponents are necessary features of the objects, but it is not a complete implication because the subcomponents may be present without the presence of the assembled object. The computation described below only requires the presence of the subcomponents and does not consider their geometric relations.

This computation is defined by several constraints:

- The more subcomponents present, the more plausible is the object's presence.

- Even if all subcomponents are present, this does not guarantee the presence of the object.

- Subcomponents are typically seen in viewpoint dependent groupings, and are seen from only one viewpoint at a time.

- The more plausible a subcomponent's presence, the more plausible is the object's presence.

- The context of all subcomponents must lie within the context of the object.

The computation is formalized below and looks for the most plausible candidate for each of the subcomponents in the given context, and averages the subcomponent's contributions towards the plausibility of the object being seen from key viewpoints. The final plausibility is the best of the viewpoint plausibilities. Each of the individual contributions is weighted. The averaging of evidence arises because each subcomponent is assumed to give an independent contribution towards the whole object plausibility. Because all subcomponents must lie within the same surface cluster as the object, the context of evidence collection is that of the hypothesis and all contained subcontexts.

The formal definition of the subcomponent relationship calculation is:

> Given:
>> a model instance of type M in image context C
>
>> a set $\{(S_i, w_i)\}$ of subcomponents of M,
>>> where w_i is the weight of subcomponent S_i
>
>> sets $G_k = \{S_{ki}\}$ of subcomponents representing groups
>>> of subcomponents visible from typical viewpoints
>
>> a set $\{C_j\}$ of subcontexts of the context C including C itself
>
>> a set of model instances of type S_i, in context C_j,
>>> with plausibility value p_{ij}

The weight factors designate significance within the group, with larger weights emphasizing more important or significant features. The subcomponent weights are the sum of the weights of the property evidence specified for the subcomponents.

The first value calculated is the best evidence for each subcomponent type in the subcontexts:

$$b_i = max_j(p_{ij})$$

This is implemented as a tree of binary "max" units. Then, the evidence for each viewpoint is calculated by integrating the evidence for the expected viewpoints using the modified harmonic mean function described above:

$$v_k = harmmean(\{(b_{i(k)}, w_{i(k)})\})$$

over all $i(k)$ subcomponents in G_k.

Finally, the evidence from the different viewpoints is integrated, by selecting the best evidence:

$$evd_{subc} = max_k(v_k)$$

The assumption is that if the object is present, then there should be exactly one visibility group corresponding to the features visible in the scene. Subcomponent evidence has a weighting that is the maximum visibility group's weight, which is the sum of the weights of the subcomponents and their properties:

$$w_{subc} = max_k\left(\sum w_{i(k)}\right)$$

Relative importances between subcomponents and properties can be modified by scaling the relevant weights. The network structure for this computation is similar to those previously shown. If no subcomponent evidence is available, this computation is not applied.

8.2.4   Description Evidence

This relationship gives direct evidence for an object, because all properties of the description type (i.e. a generic objects) are also object properties – the type is a description of the object. The object may have several description types: a "square" is both a "rectangle" and a "rhombus". Hence, evidence for a description type is also evidence for an object that uses the description, and this is expressed by a plausibility relationship.

Constraints that help specify the description evidence computation are:

- The more plausible the description, the more plausible the object.

- Each description gives additional evidence for an object.

- A weight expresses the importance of the description relative to other property evidence.

- The context of the description is that of the object.

Formally, the description evidence computation is defined:

> Given:
>> a model instance of type M in image context C
>>
>> a set $\{(D_i, w_i)\}$ of descriptions D_i of M with associated weights w_i
>>
>> a set $\{p_i\}$ of plausibilities of description D_i in context C

Then, using the modified harmonic mean, the description evidence is:

$$evd_{desc} = harmmean(\{(p_i, w_i)\})$$

The resulting weight of evidence is:

$$w_{desc} = \sum w_i$$

If no description types are defined, this computation is not applied. The portion of the network associated with this evidence is similar to those shown above.

8.2.5   Superclass Evidence

This relationship gives evidence for the presence of an object of class M, given the presence of an object of superclass S. For example, evidence for the object being a wide-bodied aircraft lends some support for the possibility of it being a DC-10. The use of superclass is not rigorous here – the notion is of a category generalization along arbitrary lines. Hence, a class may have several generalizations: an $< automobile\ wheel >$ may generalize to $< torus - like\ object >$ or $< automobile\ part >$. Class generalization does not require that all constraints on the generalization are satisfied by the specialization, which differentiates this evidence type from the description relationship. So, a superclass need not be a strictly visual generalization, that is, there may be different models for the object and its superclass.

Superclasses provide circumstantial, rather than direct, evidence as the presence of the $< torus - like\ object >$ alone does not provide serious evidence for the $< wheel >$ being present. If the object had both strong $< torus >$ and $< automobile\ part >$ evidence, the implication should be stronger. If the object had strong $< torus >$ and weak $< automobile\ part >$ evidence, then it would be less plausible for it to be a $< automobile\ wheel >$. Because the superclass is a generalization, its plausibility must always be at least as great as that of the object. Hence, the evidence for an object can be at most the minimum of the evidence for its superclasses.

Constraints that help specify the superclass evidence computation are:

- The presence of a superclass increases the plausibility of the object's presence.

- The more plausible the superclass, the more plausible the object.

- The plausibility of an object is less than that of a superclass.

- The context of the superclass is that of the object.

These constraints lead to the following formal definition of the superclass evidence computation:

Given:
      a model instance of class M in image context C

      a set $\{S_i\}$ of superclasses of M

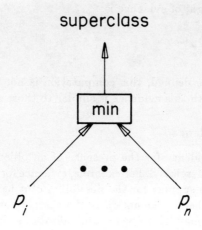

Figure 8.10: Superclass Evidence Integration Network Fragment

a set $\{p_i\}$ of plausibilities of model S_i in context C

Then, the superclass evidence is:

$$evd_{supcl} = min_i(p_i)$$

If no superclass evidence is available, this computation is not applied. The portion of the network associated with this evidence is shown in Figure 8.10, where the square unit is a "min" unit (representing a balanced tree of binary "min" units) and the inputs come from the appropriate superclass nodes.

8.2.6   Subclass Evidence

This relationship gives evidence for the presence of an object of class M, given the presence of an object of subclass S. As above, the notion of subclass is that of a specialization, and an object may have several. Here, the implication is a necessary one, because an instance of a given subclass is necessarily an instance of the class. Hence, the plausibility of the object must not be less than that of its subclasses.

The constraints that specify the subclass relationship calculation are:

- The more plausible the subclass, the more plausible the object.

- The plausibility of the object is at least that of each subclass.

- The context of the subclasses is the context of the object.

These constraints lead to the following formal definition of the subclass evidence computation:

> Given:
>
> > a model instance of class M in image context C
>
> > a set $\{S_i\}$ of subclasses of M
>
> > a set $\{p_i\}$ of plausibilities of model S_i in context C
>
> Then, the subclass relationship evidence value is:

$$evd_{subcl} = max_i(p_i)$$

If no subclass evidence is available, this computation is not applied. The invocation network fragment for this evidence type is similar to those shown previously.

8.2.7   General Associations

This relationship gives evidence for the presence of an object of type M, given the presence of an object of arbitrary type S. This is not a structure or class relationship, which have already been considered in Sections 8.2.2, 8.2.3, 8.2.5 and 8.2.6. It is an "other relationships" category. An relationship of this type might be: "the presence of a desk makes the presence of a chair plausible". This allows many forms of peripheral evidence and can be thought of as a "priming" relationship.

Association is not commutative, so individual connections need to be made, if desired, for each direction. For example, the presence of a car makes the presence of a road likely, whereas there are many roads without cars. On the other hand, the evidence supplied is weak: the certain presence of the car does not necessarily mean the object under consideration is a road. Further, the strength of association will depend on the objects involved.

The previous evidence types have clearly specified contexts from which evidence came, but this type does not. Generally associated objects could be anywhere in the scene, so all nodes of the desired type give support.

Some constraints on this type of relationship are:

- The presence of an associated object increases the plausibility of the object.

- The more plausible the associated object, the more plausible the object.

- The weight of an association expresses the expectation that the desired object is present, given that the associated object is present.

- The context of the association is the whole image.

These constraints lead to the following formal definition of the general association computation:

Given:

a model instance of type M in image context C

a set $\{(S_i, w_i)\}$ of associated models
(where w_i is the strength of association)

a set $\{C_j\}$ of all contexts

a set $\{p_{ij}\}$ of plausibilities of model S_i in context C_j

Then, the association relationship evidence is:

$$evd_{ass} = max_i(w_i * max_j(p_{ij}))$$

which chooses the best evidence for each associated type, and then the best weighted association type. If no association evidence is available, this computation is not applied. The invocation network fragment for this evidence type is shown in Figure 8.11, where the "max" units represent balanced trees of binary "max" units and the p_{ij} come from other nodes, as described above.

8.2.8   Identity Inhibition

A structure seldom has more than one likely identity, unless the identities are related (e.g. a structure that is likely to be a DC-10 can also be a wide-bodied aircraft but seldom a banana). Hence, an identity should be inhibited by other unrelated identities having high plausibilities in the same context. A second source of inhibition comes from the same identity in subcontexts, to force invocation to occur only in the smallest satisfactory context. The key questions are what types provide inhibition, how to quantify the amount of inhibition and how to integrate this inhibition with the other evidence types.

Type-related inhibition is a complicated issue. Competition does not always occur even between unrelated generic types. For example, the generic type "positive-cylindrical-surface" should not compete with the generic type "elongated-surface", whereas it should compete with the generic type "negative-cylindrical-surface". The latter comparison is between two members of a set of related types that also include: "planar", "positive-ellipsoid", "negative-ellipsoid" and "hyperboloid" surfaces. All types in this set compete with each other, but not with any other types.

Inhibition results in a plausibility value like those discussed in previous sections and is then integrated with the other evidence types, as discussed below. An advantage to

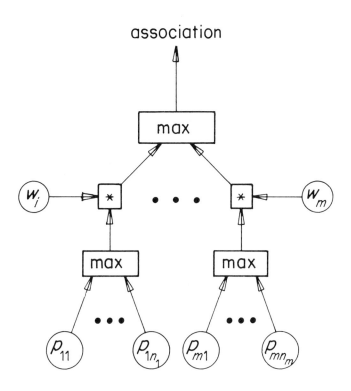

Figure 8.11: Association Evidence Network Fragment

this method is that it still allows for alternative interpretations, as in the ambiguous duck/rabbit figure (e.g. [ARB79]), when evidence for each is high enough.

Some constraints on the inhibition computation are:

- Inhibition comes from the same type in subcontexts.

- All members of specified sets of generic descriptions inhibit each other.

- All subcomponents and supercomponents of the object do not inhibit the object.

- All types of the same category (SURFACE or ASSEMBLY) that are not component, description or class related inhibit each other.

- Only positive evidence for other identities inhibits.

- The inhibition should be proportional to the plausibility of the competing identity.

- The inhibition should come from the strongest competition.

- The context of inhibition is the current context for competing identities and all subcontexts for the same identity.

These constraints lead to the inhibition computation:

Given:

a model instance of type M in image context C

a set $\{S_i\}$ of all identities competing with M

a set $\{C_j\}$ of subcontexts of context C

a set $\{p_i\}$ of plausibilities for the identities S_i in context C

a set $\{p_j\}$ of plausibilities for the identity M in the subcontexts C_j

Then, the inhibition evidence is:

$$evd_{inh} = max(max_i(p_i), max_j(p_j))$$

This computation gives no inhibition if no competing identities exist.

If several identities have roughly equal plausibilities, then inhibition will drive their plausibilities down, but still leave them roughly equal. A single strong identity would severely inhibit all other identities. Figure 8.12 shows the invocation network unit for computing the inhibition evidence, where the lower "max" units represent balanced trees of binary "max" units and the p_i come from competing identities and the p_j come from subcontexts, as described above.

8.2.9 Evidence Integration

There are eight evidence types, as discussed in the previous eight sections, and a single integrated plausibility value needs to be computed from them. All values are assumed to be on the same scale so this simplifies the considerations.

Some constraints the computation should meet are:

- Directly related evidence (property, subcomponent and description) should have greater weight.

- If there is no property, description or subcomponent evidence, then evidence integration produces no result.

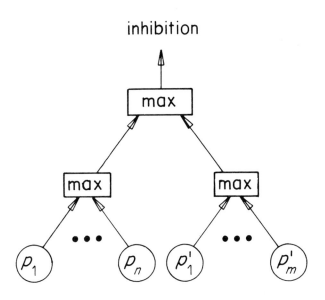

Figure 8.12: Inhibition Invocation Network Fragment

- Other relationship evidence should be incremental, but not overwhelmingly so.

- Only types with evidence are used (i.e. some of the evidence types may not exist, and so should be ignored).

- Property, description and subcomponent evidence are complementary in that they all give explicit evidence for the object and all should be integrated.

- If supercomponent evidence is strong, then this gives added support for a structure being a subcomponent. Weak supercomponent evidence has no effect, because the subcomponent could be there by itself, or not be there at all.

- If superclass evidence is strong, then this gives added support for the object.

- Strong association evidence supports the possibility of an object's presence.

- If other identities are competing, they reduce the plausibility.

- As subclasses imply objects, the plausibility of an object must be at least that of its subclasses.

Based on these constraints, the following integration computation has been designed:

Let:

$$evd_{prop}, evd_{desc}, evd_{subcl}, evd_{supcl}, evd_{subc}, evd_{supc}, evd_{ass}, evd_{inh}$$

be the eight evidence values, with weightings:

$$w_{prop}, w_{desc}, w_{subc}$$

Then:

$$v_1 = harmmean(\{(evd_{prop}, w_{prop}), (evd_{desc}, w_{desc}), (evd_{subc}, w_{subc})\})$$

if $evd_{supc} > 0$
  then $v_2 = v_1 + c_{supc} * evd_{supc}$ $(c_{supc} = 0.1)$
  else $v_2 = v_1$

if $evd_{ass} > 0$
  then $v_3 = v_2 + c_{ass} * evd_{ass}$ $(c_{ass} = 0.1)$
  else $v_3 = v_2$

if $evd_{supcl} > 0$
  then $v_4 = v_3 + c_{supcl} * evd_{supcl}$ $(c_{supcl} = 0.1)$
  else $v_4 = v_3$

if $evd_{inh} > 0$
  then $v_5 = v_4 + c_{inh} * evd_{inh}$ $(c_{inh} = -0.25)$
  else $v_5 = v_4$

Finally, the integrated plausibility is:

$$min(max(v_5, evd_{subcl}, -1.0), 1.0)$$

The -1.0 and $+1.0$ terms in the final function ensure the result is in the correct range. The weighting constants (0.1 and -0.25) used above were chosen to influence but not dominate the evidence computation and were found empirically. Small changes (e.g. by 10%) do not affect the results.

The invocation network fragment executing this function is similar to those previously shown except for the use of a "gated-weight" function unit that implements the evidence increment function for supercomponent, association, superclass and inhibition evidences.

8.2.10   Network Evaluation

The invocation network is automatically created from the model base, image surfaces and surface cluster hierarchy. One model instance node is created for each pairing of a model feature to an image feature, provided that both are compatible – image surfaces are compatible with model SURFACEs and surface clusters are compatible with model ASSEMBLYs. The model instance nodes are then connected by network fragments that compute the evidence relations defined above. The number and type of fragments used depend on the relationships defined in the model base, the surface hypotheses and the surface cluster hierarchy.

Plausibilities are calculated by value propagation in the network. Property evidence evaluations are computed for all models with property evidence requirements, and these evidence values then initiate plausibility propagation. New values are recomputed and propagated whenever the inputs to a function unit or model instance node change if the new result is more than 0.1% different from the previous result.

The ideal computation has the network computing continuously as new descriptions are computed, assuming the invocation process executes independently of the data description process. When there is enough data to cause a plausibility to go above the invocation threshold, then that model could be invoked.

However, here we used a serial implementation that computed all property evaluations initially. Then, plausibilities are propagated throughout the network, until convergence is reached. On convergence, nodes with positive plausibilities are invoked for model-directed processing (Chapter 9). Invocations are ordered from simple-to-complex to ensure that subcomponents are identified for use in making larger hypotheses.

Because an object may appear in several nested surface clusters, it makes little sense to invoke it in all of these after it has been successfully found in one. Further, a smaller surface cluster containing a few subcomponents may acquire plausibility for containing the whole object. These too should not cause invocation. The inhibition formulation partly controls this, but one active measure was also needed. After an object hypothesis is successfully verified (Chapter 10), the hypothesis is associated with the smallest surface cluster completely containing the object. Then, all surface clusters containing or contained by this cluster have their plausibility for this model set to -1.

8.3 Evaluating the Invocation Process

The properties that we would like invocation to have are:

1. Correct models are always invoked, and in the correct context.

2. No matter how large the model base, the only false hypotheses invoked are those that are "similar" to the true ones.

This section presents the evidence that the proposed theory has these properties. In evaluating this theory, it is hard to apply general mathematical or computational analysis as:

1. The performance depends on the particular network used, and there are few constraints on this.

2. The network executes a complicated, non-linear computation.

3. No valid statistics are available for the performance of structure description (Chapter 6) on general position, unobscured structures.

4. It is not possible to characterize the scenes sufficiently well to predict typical structure occlusions.

5. Little information is available to assess performance of the structure description on partially obscured structures.

Three minor analytic results have been found:

(1) If all property, subcomponent, description and superclass evidence is perfect, then the correct model is always invoked. This is equivalent to saying that the object has the correct identity and all properties are measured correctly. If we then assume the worst (i.e. that the other four evidence types are totally contradictory) then evidence integration gives:

Let:

$$evd_{prop} = 1.0, \; evd_{subcl} = -1.0, \; evd_{supcl} = 1.0, \; evd_{subc} = 1.0,$$
$$evd_{supc} = -1.0, \; evd_{desc} = 1.0, \; evd_{ass} = -1.0, \; evd_{inh} = 1.0$$

be the eight evidence values

Then, following the integration computation from Section 8.2.9:

$$v_1 = harmmean(\{(evd_{prop}, w_{prop}), (evd_{desc}, w_{desc}),$$
$$(evd_{subc}, w_{subc})\}) = 1.0$$

$$v_2 = v_1 = 1.0$$

$$v_3 = v_2 = 1.0$$

$$v_4 = v_3 + c_{supcl} * evd_{supcl} = 1.0 + 0.1 * 1.0 = 1.1$$

$$v_5 = v_4 + c_{inh} * evd_{inh} = 1.1 + (-0.25) * 1.0 = 0.85$$

and the integrated plausibility value p is:

$$p = min(max(v_5, evd_{subcl}, -1.0), 1.0) = 0.85$$

(2) Assume N independent properties are measured as property evidence for a structure, and all are equally weighted. Then, the probability that the property evidence evaluation is greater than zero is shown in Figure 8.13, assuming all constraint ranges have the widths shown, and the data values are normally distributed. The point is to estimate how many properties are needed and what the constraint ranges on a property should be, to ensure that the property evidence almost always supports the correct identity. The graph shows that if at least 5 gaussian distributed properties are used, each with constraint width of at least 1.6 standard deviations, then there is a probability of 0.98 for positive property evidence. These results were found by simulation.

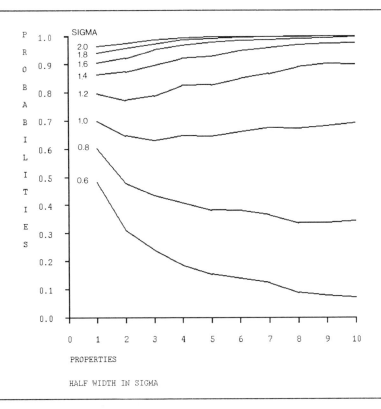

Figure 8.13: Probability of Positive Property Evidence Versus Number of Properties

(3) There is some relative ranking between the same model in different contexts: model M_i has better evidence in context C_a than in context C_b if, and only if $p(M_i, C_a) > p(M_i, C_b)$. Further, if model M_i implies model M_j (i.e. a superclass), then in the same context C:

$$p(M_j, C) \geq p(M_i, C)$$

Unfortunately, not much can be said regarding the ranking of different models in the same context, because each has different evidence requirements.

The theory proposed in this chapter accounts for and integrates many of the major visual relationship types. The surface cluster contexts focus attention to ASSEMBLY identities (and surface contexts to SURFACE identities), the object types denote natural conceptual categories, and the different relationship links structure the paths of evidence flow. The mathematical results suggest that "correct models are always invoked" if the data is well-behaved.

The "no false invocations" requirement is not easily assessed without a formal definition of "similar", and none has been found that ensures that false invocations are unlikely. So, a performance demonstration is presented, using the model base partly shown in Appendix A with the test image, and show that the invocation process was effective and robust.

Suppose interest is in the plausibility of the trash can outer surface ("tcanoutf") as an explanation for region 9 (see Figure 3.10). The description process produces the following results:

DESCRIPTION	VALUES
maximum surface curvature	0.091
minimum surface curvature	0.0
relative size	0.92
absolute size	1082
elongation	2.0
boundary relative orientation	1.64, 1.45, 1.45, 1.73
parallel boundaries	2
boundary curve length	33.6, 26.7, 30.5, 28.0
boundary curvature	0.058, 0.0, 0.085, 0.0

The property evidence computation is then performed, based on the following evidence constraint (all other properties are in the description "tcanfac"):

PROPERTY	LOW	PEAK	HIGH	WEIGHT
maximum curvature	0.058	0.078	0.098	0.5

This results in a property evidence value of 0.74 with weight 0.5. After invocation converges, there are also the relationship evidence values. No subclasses, superclasses, subcomponents or associations were defined for this model, so their evidence contribution is not included. The model has a description "tcanfac" that shares properties of the trash can inner surface ("tcaninf") except for its convexity or concavity, and its evidence value is 0.66 with a weight of 5.3. The supercomponent evidence value is 0.38 because "tcanoutf" belongs to the trash can ASSEMBLY. The maximum of the other SURFACE plausibility values for non-generically related identities is 0.41 (for the "robbodyside" model), so this causes inhibition. These evidence values are now integrated to give the final plausibility value for "tcanoutf" as 0.62. As this is positive, the trash can outer surface model will be invoked for this region.

We now consider the problem of invoking the trash can ASSEMBLY model in surface cluster 8 (from Table 5.1), which is composed of exactly the trash can's outer and inner surface regions. For each of the two surfaces, three possible identities obtain: trash can inner surface, trash can outer surface and trash can bottom. The trash can model specifies only subcomponent and inhibition relationships and defines three subcomponents:

SUBCOMPONENT	WEIGHT
tcanoutf	0.9
tcaninf	0.6
tcanbot	0.4

These are organized into three visibility groups:

```
SUBCGRP OF trashcan = tcanoutf tcaninf;
SUBCGRP OF trashcan = tcanoutf tcanbot;
SUBCGRP OF trashcan = tcaninf tcanbot tcanoutf;
```

The plausibilities of the subcomponent model SURFACE instances are:

	DATA INNER	DATA OUTER
MODEL INNER	-0.42	0.26
MODEL OUTER	-0.48	0.62
MODEL BOTTOM	-0.81	-0.88

The subcomponent evidence computation starts with the best plausibility for each model feature: inner = 0.26, outer = 0.62, bottom = -0.81. (Note that, because of occlusion, the data outer surface provides better evidence for the model inner SURFACE that the data inner surface, because all properties other than maximum curvature are shared. This does not cause a problem; it only improves the plausibility of the inner SURFACE model.) The visibility group calculation used the harmonic mean with the weightings given above to produce a subcomponent evidence value of 0.46, -0.08 and 0.01 for the three visibility groups. Finally, the best of these was selected to give the subcomponent evidence of 0.46.

The highest competing identity was from the robbody model, with a plausibility of 0.33. Integrating these evidence values gives the final plausibility for the trash can as 0.38, which was the supercomponent plausibility used in the first example.

Because there are far too many plausibility and evidence values to describe the whole network, even for this modest model base (16 ASSEMBLYs, 25 SURFACEs, and 24 generic descriptions: 22 for SURFACEs and 2 for ASSEMBLYs), we next present a photograph of the network to illustrate the general character of the computation, and then look at the invoked model instances in more detail. Figure 8.14 shows all model instance nodes of the network in its converged state. In the large region at the upper left of the picture (with the textured appearance) each small grey colored rectangle represents one model instance. The brightness of the box encodes its plausibility, from black (-1.0) to white ($+1.0$). The model instances are represented in a two dimensional grid, indexed by the image features horizontally from left-to-right with surfaces first and then the surface clusters. The vertical index lists the model features from top to bottom, with model SURFACEs and then ASSEMBLYs. The two large black areas on the upper right and lower left arise from type incompatibility (model SURFACEs with surface clusters on the upper right and ASSEMBLYs with image surfaces on the lower left). The cover jacket of the book shows the results of the network more clearly, by encoding the plausibility from blue (-1.0) to red ($+1.0$).

Several interesting features can be seen immediately. First, there is a strong horizontal grouping of black and white boxes near the middle of the upper left surface pairing nodes. These are for the generic description evidence types, such as planar, positive cylinder, etc. As they are defined by only a few properties, they achieve strong

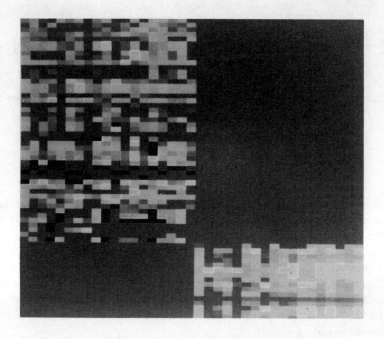

Figure 8.14: Model Instance Node Summary after Convergence

positive or negative plausibilities. The specific model SURFACEs are above, and other generic SURFACE features are below these. Only the specific model SURFACEs can be invoked, and there are only a few bright-grey to white nodes with a plausibility that is high enough for this, whereas there are many darker grey low plausibility nodes (more details below).

A similar pattern is seen in the ASSEMBLY nodes on the lower right, except for a large brightish region on the right side, with many potentially invokable model instances. This bright region occurs because: (1) there are several nested surface clusters that all contain much of the robot and (2) a surface cluster containing most of an object generally acquires a high plausibility for the whole object. This led to the explicit disabling of model instance nodes after verification, as described previously.

All invocations for this image are summarized in Tables 8.1 and 8.2 (surface clusters are listed in Table 5.1 and image regions are shown in Figure 3.10). As commented above, successful invocations in one context mask invocations in larger containing contexts. Further, generic models are not invoked – only the object-specific models. Hence, not all positive final plausibilities from Figure 8.14 cause invocation.

ASSEMBLY invocation is selective with 18 invocations of a possible 288 (16 ASSEMBLY models in 18 surface cluster contexts). Of these, all appropriate invocations

Table 8.1: Invoked ASSEMBLY Model Hypotheses

MODEL	SURFACE CLUSTER	PLAUSIBILITY	INVOCATION STATUS	NOTES
robshldbd	3	0.50	E	
robshldsobj	5	0.45	E	
robshldsobj	2	0.44	I	2
robshldsobj	11	0.44	I	2
robshould	11	0.39	E	
trashcan	8	0.38	E	
robbody	12	0.33	I	1
robbody	13	0.33	I	1
robbody	8	0.33	I	1
robbody	15	0.33	L	
lowerarm	7	0.29	E	
link	15	0.15	E	
robot	14	0.14	I	3
robot	15	0.14	E	
link	17	0.11	I	3
armasm	13	0.09	E	
upperarm	9	0.05	E	
robot	17	0.02	I	3

STATUS
  E – invocation in exact context
  L – invocation in larger than necessary context
  I – invalid invocation

NOTES
  1 – because true model is very similar
  2 – ASSEMBLY with single SURFACE has poor discrimination
  3 – not large enough context to contain all components

occur, and nine are in the smallest correct context and one is in a larger context. Of the others, three are justified by close similarity with the actual model (note 1 in the table) and five are unjustified (notes 2 and 3).

SURFACE model invocation results are similar, with 21 invocations out of 475 possible (25 SURFACE models in 19 surface contexts). Of these, ten were correct, five are justifiably incorrect because of similarity (note 1) and six are inappropriate invocations (notes 2 and 3).

Table 8.2: Invoked SURFACE Model Hypotheses

MODEL	SURFACE REGION	PLAUSIBILITY	INVOCATION STATUS	NOTES
robshldend	26	0.76	C	
tcanoutf	9	0.61	C	
robbodyside	9	0.41	I	1
robshoulds	29	0.40	C	
robshoulds	27	0.40	I	3
ledgea	18	0.36	C	
lendb	31	0.27	C	
tcaninf	9	0.26	I	1
ledgeb	18	0.25	I	1
robshould1	16	0.21	I	1
robshould2	16	0.21	C	
lsidea	12	0.20	I	1
lsideb	12	0.20	C	
robbodyside	8	0.11	C	
robshould1	12	0.10	I	3
robshould2	12	0.10	I	3
uside	19,22	0.07	C	
uedgeb	19,22	0.07	I	2
lsidea	19,22	0.04	I	2
lsideb	19,22	0.04	I	2
uends	25	0.02	C	

STATUS
C – correct invocation
I – invalid invocation

NOTES
1 – because of similarity to the correct model
2 – because the obscured correct model did not inhibit
3 – because of some shared characteristics with the model

Clearly, for this image, the invocation process works well. The chief causes for improper invocation were:

1. combinatorial surface cluster formation, resulting in similar but not directly related contexts which are thus not inhibited by the correct context, and

2. superficial similarity between features.

Possible solutions to these problems are:

- improving the depth merged surface cluster formation process and

- increasing the number of object properties.

8.4 Related Work

There is little work on model invocation in the context of three dimensional vision. The most common technique is comparing all models to the data and is useful only when few possibilities exist.

A second level used a few easily measured object (or image) properties to select a subset of potential models for complete matching. Roberts [ROB65] used configurations of approved polygons in the line image to index directly models according to viewpoint. Nevatia and Binford [NEV77] used an indexing scheme that compared the number of generalized cylinders connecting at the two ends of a distinguished cylinder.

Object properties have often been used to discriminate between potential objects in the domain using tabular and decision-tree techniques. Examples include the early SRI work (e.g. [BAR76], [TEN73], [TEN74]), which recognized objects in office scenes using constraints that held between objects. This work did not distinguish invocation from verification, and was successful because the model bases were small, the domain simple and the objects easily discriminable. If model bases are large, then there are likely to be many objects with similar properties. Further, data errors and occlusion will make the choice of initial index property difficult, or require vast duplication of index links.

Bolles et al. [BOL80] implemented a powerful method for practical indexing, in their local feature focus method (for use in a two dimensional silhouette industrial domain). The method used key features (e.g. holes and corners) as the primary indices (focus features), which were then supported by locating secondary features at given distances from the first.

Key properties are clearly needed for this task, so these were good advances. However, property-based discrimination methods are sensitive to property estimation errors. Moreover, there are other classes of evidence and object relationships. Property-based indexing often makes subfeatures unusable because of their being too complex to calculate everywhere or too object specific. Alternately, the properties are too simple and invoke everywhere and do not properly account for commonality of substructures.

When it comes to sophisticated three dimensional vision, Marr stated:

"Recognition involves two things: a collection of stored 3-D model descriptions, and various indexes into the collection that allow a newly derived description to be associated with a description in the collection." ([MAR82], page 318)

He advocated a structured object model base linked and indexed on three types of links: the specificity, adjunct and parent indices, which correspond to the subclass, subcomponent and supercomponent link types used here. He assumed that the image structures are well described and that model invocation is based on searching the model base using constraints on the relative sizes, shapes and orientations of the object axes. Recognized structures lead to new possibilities by following the indices. The ACRONYM system [BRO81] implemented a similar notion.

Direct indexing will work for the highest levels of invocation, assuming perfect data from perfectly formed objects. However, it is probably inadequate for more realistic situations. Further, there remains the problem of locating the point from which to start the search from, particularly in a large model base.

Arbib [ARB79] also proposed an invocation process that takes place in a schematic context. In his view, schemata have three components:

i. Input-matching routines which test for evidence that that which the schema represents is indeed present in the environment.

ii. Action routines – whose parameters may be tuned by parameter-fitting in the input-matching routines.

iii. Competition and cooperation routines which, for example, use context (activation levels and spatial relations of other schemas) to lower or raise the schema's activation level.

His point (i) requires each schema to be an active matching process, but is similar, in principle, to the evidence accumulation process discussed here. His point (ii) corresponds to the hypothesis construction and verification processes (Chapters 9 and 10) and point (iii) corresponds closely to the inhibition and relation evidence types used here. His schema invocation process was not defined in detail and considered mainly the highest levels of description (e.g. of objects) and only weakly on the types of visual evidence or the actual invocation computation.

Hoffman and Jain [HOF87] described an evidence-based object recognition process that is similar to the one described in this chapter. Starting from a set of surface patches segmented from range data, they estimated a set of unary and binary properties. Evidence conditions were formulated as conjunctions of property requirements. The degree to which an evidence condition supported or contradicted each model was also specified. When an unknown object was observed, a similarity measure was computed for each model. This approach can use object-specific evidence conditions, leading to more precise identification, but at the cost of evaluating the conditions for all objects. Good results were demonstrated with a modest model-base.

Binford et al. [BIN87] also described a similar (though probability based) invocation approach. The scheme uses a "Bayesian network", where probabilities accumulate from subcomponent relationships and originate from the likelihood that an observed two dimensional image feature is the projection of a three dimensional scene feature.

Reliability is enhanced by only using "quasi-invariant" features (i.e. those nearly constant over a large range of viewing positions), such as the fixed relative orientation between two axes. The network formulation used alternating layers of object and relative placement relationships ("joints"). Subcomponent *a priori* distributions were generated heuristically from occurrences in the model base.

There are obvious links between the network approach described here and the connectionist approach. In the latter, the domain knowledge is implicit in the weighted interconnections between simple identical processing units, which represents the interobject relationships. These machines can converge to a fixed output state for a given input state, and can learn network connection weights (e.g. [HOP84], [HIN83], [ACK85]). Many of the computations proposed for invocation can probably be implemented using such devices.

Hinton proposed and evaluated ([HIN81], [HIN85]) a connectionist model of invocation that assigns a reference frame as well as invoking the model. The model uses connections between retinotopic feature units, orientation mapping units, object feature (subcomponent) units and object units. This model requires duplicated connections for each visible orientation, but expresses them through a uniform mapping method. Consistent patterns of activity between the model and data features reinforce the activation of the mapping and model units. The model was proposed only for two dimensional patterns (letters) and required many heuristics for weight selection and convergence.

Feldman and Ballard [FEL83] proposed a connectionist model indexing scheme using spatial coherence (coincidence) of properties to gate integration of evidence. This helps overcome inappropriate invocation due to coincidentally related features in separate parts of the image. The properties used in their example are simple discriminators: "circle, baby-blue and fairly-fast" for a frisbee.

This proposal did not have a rich representation of the types of knowledge useful for invocation nor the integration of different types of evidence, but did propose a detailed computational model for the elements and their connections.

Feldman [FEL85] later refined this model. It starts with spatially co-located conjunctions of pairs of properties connected in parallel with the feature plane (descriptions of image properties). Complete objects are activated for the whole image based on conjunctions of activations of these spatially coincident pairs. The advantage of complete image activation is that with this method it is not necessary to connect new objects in each image location. The disadvantage is in increased likelihood of spurious invocations arising from cross-talk (i.e. unrelated, spatially separated features invoking the model). Top-down priming of the model holds when other knowledge (e.g. world knowledge) is available. Structured objects are represented by linkage to the subcomponents in the distinct object viewpoints. Multiple instances of the objects use "instance" nodes, but little information is given to suggest how the whole image model can activate separate instances.

These approaches are similar to those of this chapter: direct property evidence triggers structurally decomposed objects seen from given viewpoints. The network formulation for invocation proposed here has a parallel structure for two reasons: (1) the need for fast retrieval and (2) it is a convenient formalism for expressing the computational relationships between evidence types.

A key difference between the connectionist work reviewed above and the work described in this book is the use of dedicated network structures, as specified by the evidence type's constraints, etc. There is also an implementation difference, in that many of the connectionist networks express their results as states or configurations of activity of the network, rather than as the activity at a single node, which is the approach here.

Other Potential Techniques

There has been little Artificial Intelligence research done that treated model invocation as a specific issue. Work (e.g. [MIN75], [SCH75]) has focused more on the contents and use of models or schemas than on how a schema is selected.

The NETL formalism of Fahlman ([FAH80], [FAH81]) is a general indexing approach to invocation. This approach creates a large net-like database, with generalization/specialization type links. One function of this structure is to allow fast parallel search for concepts based on intersections of properties. For example, an elephant node is invoked by intersection of the "large", "grey" and "mammal" properties. The accessing is done by way of passing markers about the network (implemented in parallel), which is a discrete form of evidence passing. The few links used in this approach make it difficult to implement suggestiveness, as all propagated values must be based on certain properties.

General pattern recognition/classification techniques are also of some use in suggesting potential models. A multi-variate classifier (e.g. [DUD73]) could be used to assign initial direct evidence plausibility to structures based on observed evidence. Unfortunately, this mechanism works well with property evidence, but not with integrating evidence from other sources, such as from subcomponent or generic relationships. Further, it is hard to provide the *a priori* occurrence and property statistics needed for the better classifiers.

The relaxation-based vision processes are also similar to the plausibility computation. Each image structure has a set of possible labels that must be consistent with the input data and related structure labels. Applications have tended to use the process for either image modification [ROS78], pixel classification [HAN78a], structure detection, or discrete consistency maintenance [WAL75]. Most of the applications modify the input data to force interpretations that are consistent with some criterion rather than to suggest interpretations that are verified in another manner. Unfortunately, invocation must allow multiple labels (generics) and has a non-linear and non-probabilistic formulation that makes it difficult to apply previous results about relaxation computations.

8.5   Discussion

The purpose of invocation is to reduce the computation involved in the model-to-data matching process. This has been partially achieved by basing invocation on propagated plausibility values, so the computation has been reduced from a detailed object comparison to evidence accumulation. Unfortunately, virtually every object model still needs to be considered for each image structure, albeit in a simplified manner. On the other hand, the model-to-data comparison computation has now been simplified. As a result, it is now amenable to large scale parallel processing.

One deficiency in this method is the absence of a justified formal criterion that determines when to invoke a model. Invoking when the plausibility was positive worked well in practice, but most seriously incorrect hypotheses are near -1.0. Hence, a threshold somewhat lower than 0.0 could be considered. This might lead to each object having a different threshold.

This work leaves several open "learning" problems:

1. How is the structure of the model network created and modified?

2. How are the features used for invocation selected?

3. How are the property and relationship weights chosen?

Other unsolved problems include resolving the problem of multiple invocations within the extended surface cluster hierarchy (as discussed above), preventing data feature evidence from being used for more than one model subcomponent and deciding when to invoke generic models (as well as the object-specific ones). The theory could also be extended for non-shape properties (e.g. color, texture, etc.) and quantified descriptors (e.g. "larger", "much larger") proposed by Marr [MAR82] as an attempt to achieving scale invariance. Finally, though the class hierarchy and evidence computations were defined, no significant testing of this feature was undertaken.

For each evidence computation, some natural constraints were proposed as specification criteria. But, there were never enough constraints to uniquely determine the computation. The hope is that the variations in algorithms that this allows result only in slightly different performance levels. This has been partially tested using substantially different property evidence evaluation and evidence integration functions, without significant differences in the invocation results.

This chapter has only concerned visual recognition, but this invocation approach may have more general applicability. Any form of symbolic inference requires accessing the correct symbol. So, the model invocation problem is also a general cognitive problem, with the following aspects:

- low level symbolic assertions are produced for the current input whether from an external (e.g. raw sense data) or internal (e.g. self-monitoring) source,

- higher level concepts/symbols tend to be semi-distinctly characterizable based on "configurations" of lower level symbolic descriptions,

- there are many potential higher level symbols, but only a small subset should be selected for closer consideration when matching a symbol,

- the importance of a particular concept in invoking another is dependent on many factors, including structure, generics, experience and context, and

- symbols "recognized" at one description level (either primitive or through matching) become usable for the invocation of more complex symbols.

Examples of this in a non-vision context might be something like an invocation of a Schankian fast-food restaurant schema [SCH75] or recognizing words in speech.

Final Comments

This chapter formalized the associative basis of a model invocation process with the major elements as object types, property evidence inputs and associative links based on generic and component relations. The theory was based on sets of constraints describing how different evidence affects plausibility, and the use of surfaces and surface clusters as the contexts in which to accumulate evidence.

CHAPTER 9

Hypothesis Construction

At this point the recognition process has isolated a set of data, described its features and invoked a model as its potential identity. To claim that the object is genuinely recognized requires the pairing of model features to image data. Without these correspondences object recognition is only suggestive – like saying a collection of gears and springs is a watch. Hence, the hypothesis construction process has the goal of fully instantiating correctly invoked models, estimating object position and accounting for the appearance of the object, including occlusion. These tasks are the first stage in substantiating the existence and identity of the object, as described in this chapter.

The chapter also describes some more recent work that uses a value-propagating network for geometric reasoning.

9.1 Thoughts on Hypothesis Construction

The hypothesis construction process described below attempts to find evidence for all model features. This is somewhat controversial and it is worthwhile to briefly discuss the motivations for this decision.

If we are working in a restricted domain (such as on an industrial assembly line) the numbers and types of objects in the scene are usually limited. Here, many details would be object-specific, and a goal-directed argument suggests that only the key differentiating features need be found. When the domain is sufficiently restricted, specific features will be unique signifiers. However, this would not be an appropriate strategy for a general vision system because, without additional descriptions or non-visual knowledge of the restricted domain, it would not ordinarily be possible to reach the stage where only a few identities were under consideration.

However, identifying individuals or subclasses requires finer details (e.g. distinguishing between two people, or even between two "identical" twins). Many individual objects differ only slightly or share identical features. Consider how often one recognizes a facial feature or a smile of a friend in the face of a complete stranger. Though the stranger is unique through the configuration of his/her features, some details are held in common with the friend. If recognition were predicated on only a few features, which may sometimes be sufficient for unique identification in a limited domain, then we would be continually misrecognizing objects. While only a few may be necessary for model invocation, many others are necessary for confirmation.

185

These problems suggest that the hypothesis construction process should try to find direct image evidence for all model features.

On the other hand, partial evidence is often sufficient. We usually have no trouble identifying a friend even when a mustache has been shaved off, and often do not even notice that there is a change, let alone know what the change is. Or we can often recognize them, having seen only a portion of their face.

Moreover, finding evidence for all features is usually impossible, as resolution changes might make the information too large or too small to directly detect, and occlusion will hide some of it.

Yet, we tend to expect recognition to be perfect. So, on idealistic grounds, a general vision system should acquire as much information as possible. This is also supported by the usual role of a general vision system – that it should be a largely autonomous, data-driven analysis system, providing environmental descriptions to a higher-level action module, which may then instigate additional goal-directed visual analysis.

In summary, our desire for full model instantiation derives from:

- a philosophical requirement – that true image understanding requires consistent interpretation of all visible features relative to a model and contingent explanation of missing features,

- an environmental requirement – that many details are needed to distinguish similar objects, especially as objects share common features and some details will be absent for environmental reasons (e.g. occlusion), and

- a practical requirement – that objects should be recognized to the degree they need to be distinguished.

Why Use Surfaces as Evidence

What is desired is image evidence that supports the existence of each model feature. In edge-based recognition systems, an image edge was the key evidence for a model feature, because surface orientation discontinuity boundaries were observed as edges. This was even more important in polyhedral domains (without reflectance boundaries), where extremal boundaries were also orientation discontinuity boundaries. Unfortunately, more naturally shaped and colored objects led to a veritable plethora of problems: there were fewer traditional orientation edges, extremal boundaries no longer corresponded to orientation discontinuities and reflectance and illumination variations created new edges. So, these made the search for simple and directly corresponding edge evidence much more difficult.

Two of the advantages of using surfaces given in Chapter 3 are mentioned here again:

- using surfaces as the primary representational unit of both the raw data and the object model makes the transformation distance between the two almost non-existent, and

- the interpretation of a surface data unit is unambiguous (unlike image edges, which may correspond to a variety of scene phenomena).

With surface representations, it is again possible to find image evidence that directly matches with model features. Assuming that there is a consistent segmentation regimen for both the surface image and model SURFACEs, the model feature instantiation problem can be reduced to finding which model SURFACE corresponds to each data surface.

Finding all model features first requires understanding how three dimensional objects appear in images – to locate image evidence for oriented model instances. Here the recognition process must understand, or at least be able to predict how a surface patch's appearance varies with changes in the surface's position relative to the viewer. The segmentation process attempts to produce surface patches with a uniform curvature characterization, so it is easy to approximate the visible shape to first-order, given the model patch and its relative position. Also, given recent advances in computer graphics, it is possible to deduce the visibility status of most surface patches.

Another result of using the surface segmentation is a discrete symbolic partitioning of the complete object surface. This simplifies the surface matching computation tremendously. An infinitesimal element of a surface could have many possible identities and this shows up in practice as the need to rotate incrementally and shift surfaces when matching (e.g. [IKE81], [POT83]). A segmented surface immediately simplifies the matching by choosing a higher level structure for comparison. Topology further decreases the amount of matching as adjacent model SURFACEs must pair with adjacent data surfaces, reducing the problem to subgraph isomorphism. If the invocation process gives strong suggestions to the identity of the various surfaces, then combinatorial matching is almost completely unnecessary.

9.2   Deducing Object Position

Part of competent object recognition is knowing where an object is – hence its three dimensional location and orientation must be determined. This information is also needed internally, as identity verification requires finding that all visible object features are correctly placed. Moreover, an estimate of an object's position enables prediction of image locations for missing features.

Invocation suggests a few model-to-data feature (e.g. surface) correspondences to form an initial "island of stability". From this, the reference frame of the object relative to the viewer can be deduced by analyzing the geometric relationships between the features. For example, a single surface correspondence constrains the object to a single rotational degree-of-freedom about a nominal surface normal (assuming that the model and data normals can be paired). A second rotation axis, whether from a second surface or from an axis of curvature on the first surface, usually completely constrains the object's orientation (though possibly up to a mirror image).

9.2.1   Geometric Reasoning

Recently, Orr [ORR87] analyzed several prominent three dimensional scene analysis systems, including the **IMAGINE I** system described here, and concluded that five generic functions provided the geometric reasoning needed for most computer vision tasks. The functions were:

LOCATE – producing position estimates from model-to-data feature correspondences,

PREDICT – predicting a data feature for a given model feature, given an estimate of the object's position,

MERGE – integrating two position estimates to produce a better estimate, or to signal inconsistency between the estimates,

TRANSFORM – expressing a position in another reference frame and

INVERSE – inverting the transformation between two reference frames.

Central to these functions was a position data type, that represented the rotation and translation between two geometric reference frames. This relationship may be exact (as in a model), complete but inexact (as when accounting for measurement uncertainty), or partial (as represented by, for example, an underdetermined rotation constraint).

At the time of the research undertaken here, two of the best approaches to representing position estimates were based on either an explicit complete position, perhaps with some error estimates (i.e. from a least-squared error technique, such as Faugeras and Hebert [FAU83]) or by parameter ranges, linked to algebraic inequality constraints over the parameters (as in the ACRONYM system [BRO81]).

The first approach integrated a set of uniform data (e.g. model-to-data vector pairings) to give a single-valued estimate, but at some computational cost. On the other hand, ACRONYM's advantage was that it could easily integrate new evidence by adding new constraints, the range of possible values was made explicit and inconsistency was detectable when parameter ranges became non-existent. Its disadvantage was that the current estimate for a parameter was implicit in the set of constraints and could only be obtained explicitly by substantial algebraic constraint manipulation of non-linear inequalities, which result only in a range of values with no measure of "best".

More recent work by Durrant-Whyte [DUR87] represented position estimates statistically, computing the transformations of positions by a composition technique. This has the advantage of propagating uncertainties concisely and gives a "best" estimate, but does not easily provide the means to determine when inconsistency occurs (other than low probability). Further, approximations are needed when the reference frame transformations themselves involve uncertainty, or when uncertainty is other than statistical (e.g. a degree-of-freedom about a joint axis).

The techniques used in **IMAGINE I** are now described, and related to the five function primitives described above.

Each individual parameter estimate is expected to have some error, so it is represented by a range of values. (The initial size of the range was based on experience with parameter estimation.) An object's position is then represented by a six dimensional parameter volume, within which the true parameter vector should lie. Thus, the position representation is a simplified, explicit version of that used by ACRONYM (but less precise, because constraint boundaries are now planes perpendicular to the coordinate axes). This leads to more efficient use, while still representing error ranges and detecting inconsistency.

Integrating parameter estimates (i.e. MERGE) is done by intersecting the individual parameter volumes. All the six dimensional parameter volumes are "rectangular solids" with all "faces" parallel, so that the intersection is easily calculated and results in a similar solid. Because the true value is contained in each individual volume, it must also lie in the intersection. The effect of multiple estimates is to refine the tolerance zone by progressively intersecting off portions of the parameter volume, while still tolerating errors. If a final single estimate is needed, the average of each pair of limits is used.

As described so far, the transformation of coordinate reference systems (TRANS-FORM) has been done by multiplication of the homogeneous coordinate matrices representing the transforms. Since we are now using a parameter estimate range, the transformation computation must be modified. In the most general case, each transformation would have its own range, but, as implemented here, only the transformation from the camera coordinate system to the object global reference frame is allowed statistical variations. (Although, transformations may have parameterized degrees-of-freedom – see Chapter 7.) These variations propagate through the calculation of the global or image locations for any feature specified in any level of reference frame. The variation affects two calculations:

1. how to calculate a combined transformation given that one transformation is a range, and

2. how to calculate the range of positions for a point given a transformation range.

The technique used for both of these problems is similar, and is only an approximation to a complete solution:

1. For a subset of values in the parameter range,

    (a) Calculate a transformation

    (b) Transform the second parameter vector (or point)

2. Bound the set of transformed vectors (or points).

This process is illustrated in Figure 9.1. In part (a), a two dimensional parameter range with the subset of points is designated. In part (b), the original range is rotated to a new range, and part (c) shows the parameter bounds for the new range.

The figure illustrates one problem with the method – parameter bounds are aligned parallel with the coordinate axes, so that the parameter volume (actually six dimensional) increases with each transformation. A second problem is that the rotation parameter space is not rigid in this coordinate system, so that the shape of the parameter space can change greatly. If it expands in a direction not parallel with a coordinate axis, the combination of the first problem with this one can result in a greatly expanded parameter space. Further, the transformation is not unique, as zero slant allows any tilt, so any transformations that include this can grow quickly.

One general problem with the method is that consistent data does not vary the parameter bounds much, so that intersecting several estimates does not always tighten the bounding greatly. Hence, there is still a problem with getting a "best" estimate

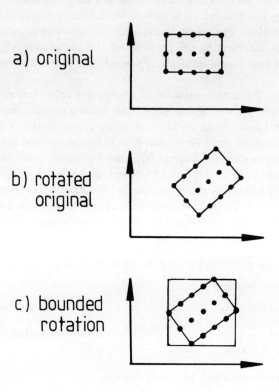

Figure 9.1: Two Dimensional Rotation of Parameter Ranges

from the range. Another problem with the general case is that each model variable increases the dimensionality of the parameter space, requiring increased computation and compounding bounding problems.

The conclusion is that this simplified method of representing and manipulating parameter estimates is not adequate, which led to the work by Fisher and Orr [FIS88] described in Section 9.2.4.

The INVERSE function occurs in two forms. Inverting an exact transformation (represented by a homogeneous coordinate matrix) is simply matrix inversion. Inverting an estimate range is given by bounding the inversions of a subset of the original range (similar to TRANSFORM).

The PREDICT function uses either an exact transformation from the model or the mean value of a data-derived parameter range to predict either three dimensional vector directions, three dimensional points or two dimensional points (by projection of the three dimensional points).

The LOCATE function is specific to the data and model feature pairings, and is described in more detail in the next two sections.

9.2.2 Estimating Individual Surface Reference Frames

Estimating Surface Rotation

A SURFACE's spatial position is represented by the transformation from the camera coordinate frame to that of the SURFACE. Several constraints are available to help deduce the transformation.

Fisher [FIS83] showed how the transformation could be deduced using the two dimensional boundary shape. Estimation of the orientation parameters (rotation, slant and tilt) used the cross-section width as a function of the image angle, which deforms in a characterizable way.

In the research presented here, surface normals are directly available. If a planar data patch is paired with a model patch, their normal vectors must be parallel so only one rotational degree-of-freedom needs to be resolved. The final rotation degree-of-freedom is estimated by correlating the angular cross-section width as a function of rotation angle. Figure 9.2 illustrates this. For non-planar surfaces, an approximate solution is obtained by using the normals at the centroids of the surfaces. A more complete solution using the curvature axis is presented below.

The complete method is:

> Rotate the image surface until the central point normal is aligned with the -Z camera axis (R_1).
> Rotate the model SURFACE until the central point normal is aligned with the -Z camera axis (R_2).
> Calculate data surface cross-section widths.
> Calculate model SURFACE cross-section widths.
> For each rotation angle (α) about the model normal axis:
>> calculate model rotation $(R_3(\alpha))$
>> correlate cross-section widths
> Set a threshold = 0.9 * peak correlation.
> Pick peak correlations (α_i).
> (If more than 30% above threshold, declare circularly symmetric: $\alpha_i = 0.0$).
> Solve for reference frames: $R_1^{-1} R_3(\alpha_i) R_2$.

Some of the estimated and nominal rotation values for the modeled SURFACEs successfully invoked in the test image are given in Table 9.1. The full set of results are in [FIS86a], and those shown here include the best, worst and typical results. All values given in the tables below are in the camera reference frame. The estimates shown here are only the mean values of the estimate intervals, whose size depends on the input data error and the amount of parameter space intersection.

The rotation estimates are good, even on small SURFACEs (robshoulds) or partially obscured SURFACEs (uside, uends, lsideb, ledgea).

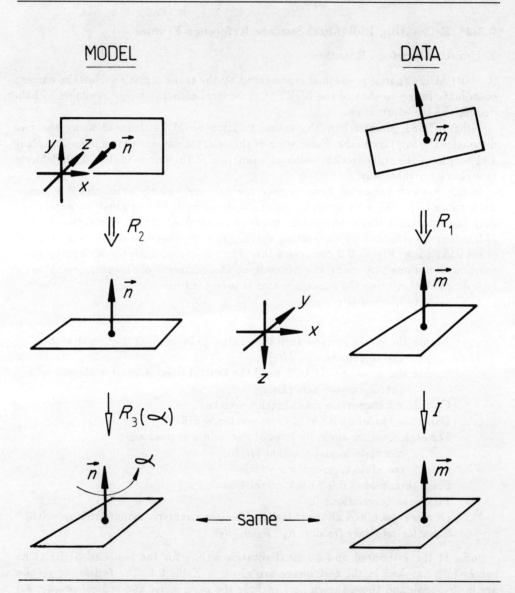

Figure 9.2: Estimation of Rotation for Isolated Surface Patches

Table 9.1: Rotation Parameters For Single SURFACEs

SURFACE	Image Region	Measured (rad)			Estimated (rad)		
		ROT	SLANT	TILT	ROT	SLANT	TILT
robbodyside	8	0.00	0.13	4.71	0.02	0.13	4.76
robshoulds	29	0.05	0.70	6.08	0.02	0.84	6.15
uside	19,22	6.04	0.88	3.48	5.20	0.88	4.32
uends	25	3.12	0.75	2.75	3.16	0.66	3.21
lsideb	12	1.51	0.88	1.73	1.70	0.88	1.54
tcanoutf	9	0.00	0.13	4.71	0.02	0.11	4.56

Table 9.2: Rotations for Single SURFACEs Using the Curvature Axis

SURFACE	Image Region	Measured (rad)			Estimated (rad)		
		ROT	SLANT	TILT	ROT	SLANT	TILT
robbodyside	8	0.00	0.13	4.71	6.28	0.13	4.77
robshoulds	29	0.05	0.70	6.08	0.10	0.83	6.07
uends	25	3.12	0.75	2.75	3.12	0.66	3.24
tcanoutf	9	0.00	0.13	4.71	0.01	0.18	4.61

SURFACE orientation can be estimated without using the boundary if there is significant surface curvature in one direction. Here, the three dimensional orientation of the major curvature axis constrains the remaining angular degree-of-freedom to two possible orientations. The transformation from the model normal and curvature axis vectors to those of the data gives the orientation estimate. Data errors complicate the calculation, which is described in detail in Section 9.2.3. Figure 9.3 illustrates the process of rotation estimation using the normal and curvature axis. Table 9.2 lists the results for this case.

Table 9.3 shows the results obtained by integrating the above results with those from Table 9.1 (by parameter space intersection). As the curvature based estimation process gives nearly the same results as the boundary based process, the intersection hardly improves the results. This suggests that the initial estimation techniques are both generally accurate.

Estimating SURFACE Translations

Given the rotations, the translations are estimated. Fisher [FIS83] estimated these directly from the boundary data. Depth was estimated by comparing model and data areas and cross-section widths. The three dimensional translation was estimated using the two dimensional translation that best fitted the data and then inverting the projection relationship using the estimated depth.

Here, depth estimates are directly available, and the xy translation is estimated by relating the rotated model SURFACE centroid to the two dimensional image centroid

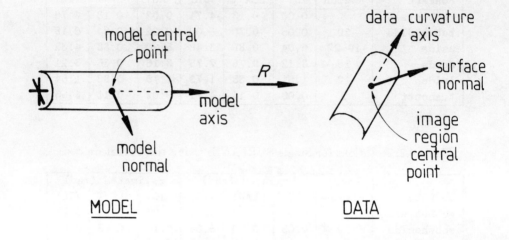

Figure 9.3: Rotation Estimation from Normal and Curvature Axis

Table 9.3: Combined Rotation Parameters For Single SURFACEs

SURFACE	Image Region	Measured (rad)			Estimated (rad)		
		ROT	SLANT	TILT	ROT	SLANT	TILT
robbodyside	8	0.00	0.13	4.71	0.01	0.13	4.76
robshoulds	29	0.05	0.70	6.08	0.02	0.83	6.15
uends	25	3.12	0.75	2.75	3.16	0.66	3.21
tcanoutf	9	0.00	0.13	4.71	0.01	0.18	4.56

and inverting the projection relationship. Typical estimated and nominal translation values for the modeled SURFACEs successfully invoked in the test image are given in Table 9.4.

The translation estimates are reasonable, though not as accurate as the rotation estimates. This is true even though SURFACEs lsideb, ledgea and uside were substantially obscured. For the unobscured SURFACEs, the average translation error for the test image is (-6.0,1.6,-1.6), and is believed to arise from errors in estimating the camera coordinate system. Other sources of error include measurement error (estimated as 1.0 cm and 0.1 radian), image quantization (estimated as 0.6 cm at 5m and 0.002 radian) and errors arising from the approximate nature of the parameter estimations.

Table 9.4: Translation Parameters For Single SURFACEs

SURFACE	Image Region	Measured (cm)			Estimated (cm)		
		X	Y	Z	X	Y	Z
robbodyside	8	-13.9	-32.4	565	-13.5	-35.9	562
robshoulds	29	-20.9	17.8	556	-16.2	9.8	564
uside	19,22	-21.0	13.4	585	-13.6	31.0	578
uends	25	27.2	16.6	547	35.6	16.5	551
lsideb	12	23.7	16.9	533	21.9	28.4	539
tcanoutf	9	22.3	-44.1	536	29.1	-44.2	541

In any case, the error is about 1.5% of the distance to the object, so the relative position error is small.

To illustrate the position results for the test image better, several pictures are shown with the SURFACEs drawn in their estimated positions on top of the original scene. Figure 9.4 shows the robot body side SURFACE (robbodyside), the robot upper arm side SURFACE (uside) and the trash can outer SURFACE (tcanoutf). Figure 9.5 shows the robot shoulder end SURFACE (robshldend), the robot lower arm side SURFACE (lsideb) and the robot upper arm small end SURFACE (uends). The lower arm side SURFACE y translation estimate is high because of occlusion.

9.2.3   Estimating ASSEMBLY Reference Frames

If a set of model vectors (e.g. surface normals) can be paired with corresponding data vectors, then a least-squared error estimate of the transformation could be estimated using methods like that of Faugeras and Hebert [FAU83]. This integrates all evidence uniformly. The method described below estimates reference frame parameters from smaller amounts of evidence, which is then integrated using the parameter space intersection method described above. The justification for this approach was that it is incremental and shows the intermediate results more clearly. It can also integrate evidence hierarchically from previously located subcomponents.

Each data surface has a normal that, given correspondence with a particular model SURFACE, constrains the orientation of the ASSEMBLY to a single rotational degree-of-freedom about the normal. A second, non-parallel, surface normal then fixes the object's rotation. The calculation given here is based on transforming a pair of model SURFACE normals onto a data pair. The model normals have a particular fixed angle between them. Given that the data normals must meet the same constraint, the rotation that transforms the model vectors onto the data vectors can be algebraically determined. Figure 9.6 illustrates the relationships.

Use of surface normals is reasonable only for nearly planar surfaces. For cylindrical or ellipsoidal surfaces, normals at the central points on the data and model surfaces can be computed and compared, but: (1) small displacements of the measurement point on surfaces with moderate curvature lead to significant changes in orientation, and (2) occlusion makes it impossible to accurately locate corresponding points. Fortunately,

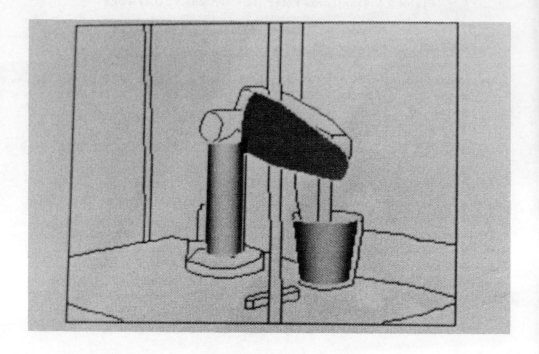

Figure 9.4: Test Scene with some Estimated SURFACE Positions

highly curved surfaces often have a curvature axis that is more accurately estimated and is not dependent on precise point positions nor is it affected by occlusion. Figure 9.7 illustrates these points.

A third approach uses the vector through the central points in the surfaces, which is most useful when the surfaces are widely separated. Then, variations in point placement (e.g. due to occlusion) will cause less significant effects in this vector's orientation.

Given these techniques, two surface patches give rise to eight orientation estimation cases:

1. Two planes with surface normals not parallel: use the data normals paired to the model normals.

2. Two planes with surface normals nearly parallel: use one data normal paired to the model normal and the second vector from paired central points.

3. Any shape and a generic surface (i.e. with two non-zero curvatures), normals not parallel: use the data normals paired to the model normals.

4. Any shape and a generic surface, normals nearly parallel: use one data normal paired to the model normal and the second vector from paired central points.

Figure 9.5: Test Scene with Other Estimated SURFACE Positions

5. Plane and cylinder, cylinder axis not parallel to plane normal: use paired plane
   data and model normals, paired cylinder data and model axes.

6. Plane and cylinder, cylinder axis nearly parallel to plane normal: use the data
   normals paired to the model normals.

7. Two cylinders, axes not parallel: use data axes paired with model axes.

8. Two cylinders, axes nearly parallel: use one data axis paired to the model axis
   and the second vector from paired central points.

After feature pairing, the rotation angles are estimated. Unfortunately, noise and
point position errors mean that the interior angles between the pairs of vectors are
only approximately the same, which makes exact algebraic solution impossible. So, a
variation on the rotation method was used. A third pair of vectors, the cross product
of each original pair, are calculated and have the property of being at right angles to
each of the original pairs:

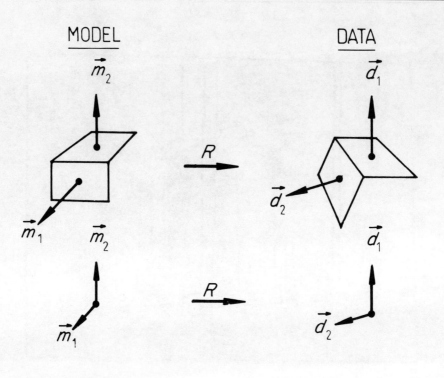

Figure 9.6: Rotating Model Normals to Derive the Reference Frame

Let:

$\vec{d}_1$, $\vec{d}_2$ be the data normals
$\vec{m}_1$, $\vec{m}_2$ be the model normals

Then, the cross products are:

$$\vec{c_d} = \vec{d}_1 \times \vec{d}_2$$
$$\vec{c_m} = \vec{m}_1 \times \vec{m}_2$$

From $\vec{d}_1$ and $\vec{c_d}$ paired to $\vec{m}_1$ and $\vec{c_m}$ an angular parameter estimate can be algebraically calculated. Similarly, $\vec{d}_2$ and $\vec{c_d}$ paired to $\vec{m}_2$ and $\vec{c_m}$ gives another estimate, which is then integrated using the parameter space intersection technique.

Fan et al. [FAN88] used a somewhat similar paired vector reference frame estimation technique for larger sets of model-to-data vector pairings, except that they picked the single rotation estimate that minimized an error function, rather than integrated all together. This often selects a correct rotation from a set of pairings that contains a

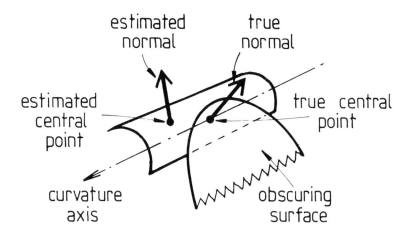

Figure 9.7: Axis Stability on Cylindrical Surfaces

bad pairing, thus allowing object recognition to proceed.

Before the rotation is estimated from a pair of surfaces, a fast compatibility test is performed, which ensures that the angle between the data vectors is similar to that between the model vectors. (This was similar to the angular pruning of Faugeras and Hebert [FAU83]). The test is:

Let:

$\vec{d}_1$, $\vec{d}_2$ be the data normals
$\vec{m}_1$, $\vec{m}_2$ be the model normals

If:

$$| (\vec{d}_1 \circ \vec{d}_2) - (\vec{m}_1 \circ \vec{m}_2) | < \tau_c \qquad (\tau_c = 0.3)$$

Then, the vector pairs are compatible.

The global translation estimates come from individual surfaces and substructures.

For surfaces, the estimates come from calculating the translation of the nominal central point of the rotated model SURFACE to the estimated central point of the observed surface. Occlusion affects this calculation by causing the image central point to not correspond to the projected model point, but the errors introduced by this technique were within the level of error caused by mis-estimating the rotational parameters. The implemented algorithm for SURFACEs is:

Let:
> G be the transformation from the ASSEMBLY's coordinate system to that of the camera

> A be the transformation from the SURFACE's coordinate system to that of the ASSEMBLY

Then:

1. Get the estimated global rotation for that SURFACE: (GA)
2. Rotate the central point $(\vec{p})$ of the model SURFACE: $(\vec{v}_1 = GA\vec{p})$
3. Calculate the three dimensional location $(\vec{v}_2)$ of the image region centroid, inverting its image coordinates using the depth value given in the data
4. Estimate the translation as $\vec{v}_2 - \vec{v}_1$

ASSEMBLY Reference Frame Calculation Results

The estimation of an ASSEMBLY's reference frame is demonstrated for the robot lower arm.

As the rigidly attached hand subcomponent is not visible, it contributes no information. Each of the SURFACEs paired and transformed according to the above theory contributes to these estimates (in the camera coordinate system):

OBJECT		ROT	SLANT	TILT
lsideb & lendb	MIN	3.966	1.158	4.252
	MAX	0.633	0.204	3.949
lendb & ledgea	MIN	3.487	1.190	4.693
	MAX	0.192	0.216	4.405
ledgea & lsideb	MIN	3.853	1.361	4.599
	MAX	0.430	0.226	4.257

The rotation estimates are integrated by intersection to give the following result:

	ROT	SLANT	TILT
MIN	3.966	1.361	4.693
MAX	0.192	0.204	3.949

and the average value is:

ROT	SLANT	TILT
5.220	2.353	1.180

which compares well with the measured value of:

ROT	SLANT	TILT
5.060	2.236	1.319

Translation is estimated after rotation, and starts with an estimate from each individual SURFACE. These estimates are:

		X	Y	Z
lsideb	MIN	-1.891	-10.347	503.
	MAX	57.262	48.807	592.
lendb	MIN	-1.206	-26.849	500.
	MAX	58.259	32.616	589.
ledgea	MIN	-1.058	-20.298	503.
	MAX	58.116	38.875	592.

The translation estimates are integrated by intersection to give the following result:

	X	Y	Z
MIN	-1.058	-10.347	503.
MAX	57.262	32.616	589.

and the average value is:

X	Y	Z
28.1	11.1	546.

which compares well with the measured value of:

X	Y	Z
26.6	8.79	538.

Tables 9.5 and 9.6 summarize the results for the primitive ASSEMBLYs in the test image whose estimates resulted from using more than one SURFACE. The other primitive ASSEMBLYs have reference frames identical to that of the single SURFACE (rotated into the ASSEMBLY's reference frame if necessary). All results are given in the camera coordinate system. The parameter estimates are good, even though both the upper and lower arm are substantially obscured.

Estimating Reference Frames from Previously Recognized Subcomponents

Each previously recognized subcomponent contributes a position estimate. Suppose, the subcomponent has an estimated global reference frame G_s and the transformation

Table 9.5: Translation Parameters For Primitive ASSEMBLYs

ASSEMBLY	Measured (cm)			Estimated (cm)		
	X	Y	Z	X	Y	Z
robshldbd	-13.9	17.0	558.	-15.7	11.5	562.
upperarm	0.95	26.4	568.	0.60	17.1	570.
lowerarm	26.6	8.79	538.	28.1	11.1	546.

Table 9.6: Rotation Parameters For Primitive ASSEMBLYs

ASSEMBLY	Measured (rad)			Estimated (rad)		
	ROT	SLANT	TILT	ROT	SLANT	TILT
robshldbd	0.257	2.23	6.12	0.135	2.30	6.28
upperarm	3.72	2.23	2.66	3.22	2.24	3.14
lowerarm	5.06	2.23	1.32	5.22	2.35	1.18

from the subcomponent to the main object is A (given in the model). (If the subcomponent is connected with degrees-of-freedom, then any variables in A will be bound before this step. This is discussed in Section 9.4.4.) Then, the estimated new global frame is $G_s A^{-1}$. Figure 9.8 illustrates how the subcomponent's reference frame relates to that of the object.

In the test image, these ASSEMBLYs had their positions estimated by integrating estimates from subcomponents:

ASSEMBLY	SUBCOMPONENTS
armasm	lowerarm, upperarm
robshould	robshldbd, robshldsobj
link	robshould, armasm
robot	link, robbody

The reference frame estimates for these ASSEMBLYs are summarized in Tables 9.7 and 9.8. Integrating the different position estimates sometimes gives better results and sometimes worse (e.g. robbodyside *versus* robot rotation). Often, there was little effect (e.g. upperarm *versus* armasm rotation). A key problem is that transforming the subcomponent's reference frame expands the position estimates so much that it only weakly constrained the ASSEMBLY's reference frame.

The numerical results for the whole robot in the test scene are summarized in Table 9.9. Here, the values are given in the global reference frame rather than in the camera reference frame.

Better results could probably have been obtained using another geometric estimate integration method (e.g. [FAU83], [DUR87]). However, the results here are generally accurate, mainly because of the richness of information in the surface image and geometric object models.

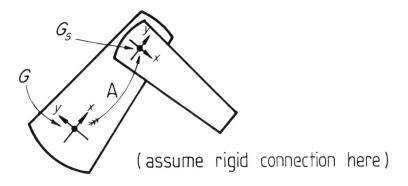

Figure 9.8: Object and Subcomponent Reference Frame Relationship

Table 9.7: Translation Parameters For Structured ASSEMBLYs

ASSEMBLY	Measured (cm)			Estimated (cm)		
	X	Y	Z	X	Y	Z
armasm	0.95	26.4	568.	0.60	17.1	553.
robshould	-13.9	17.0	558.	-15.7	10.3	562.
link	-13.9	17.0	558.	-9.7	16.3	554.
robot	-13.8	-32.6	564.	-13.5	-35.9	562.

Table 9.8: Rotation Parameters For Structured ASSEMBLYs

ASSEMBLY	Measured (rad)			Estimated (rad)		
	ROT	SLANT	TILT	ROT	SLANT	TILT
armasm	3.72	2.23	2.66	3.20	2.29	3.11
robshould	0.257	2.23	6.12	0.135	2.29	6.28
link	0.257	2.23	6.12	0.055	2.29	0.05
robot	0.0	0.125	4.73	0.0	0.689	4.75

Table 9.9: Measured And Estimated Spatial Parameters

PARAMETER	MEASURED	ESTIMATED
X	488 (cm)	486 (cm)
Y	89 (cm)	85 (cm)
Z	554 (cm)	554 (cm)
Rotation	0.0 (rad)	0.07 (rad)
Slant	0.793 (rad)	0.46 (rad)
Tilt	3.14 (rad)	3.53 (rad)
Joint 1	2.24 (rad)	2.18 (rad)
Joint 2	2.82 (rad)	2.79 (rad)
Joint 3	4.94 (rad)	4.56 (rad)

9.2.4   Network Based Geometric Reasoning

Position errors result from two causes - errors in the input data and deficiencies in the position estimation algorithms. To help remove the second source, Fisher and Orr [FIS88] developed a network technique based on the algebraic method used in ACRONYM. The technique implements the constraint relationships as a value-passing network that results in tighter bounds and improved efficiency. Moreover, we observed that the forms of the algebraic constraints tended to be few and repeated often, and hence standard subnetwork modules could be developed, with instances allocated as new position constraints were identified. Examples of these network modules are: "a model vector is transformed to a data vector" and "a data point must lie near a transformed model point".

There are three aspects to the new network-based geometric reasoner:

1. specifying the geometric problem as algebraic constraints,

2. evaluating the constraints in a value-passing network and

3. partitioning the network into prototypical modules.

These are now described in more detail.

The key data type is the position, which represents the relative spatial relationship between two features (e.g. world-to-camera, camera-to-model, or model-to-subcomponent). A position consists of a 3-vector representing relative translation and a unit 4-vector quaternion representing relative orientation (of the form $(cos(\theta/2), sin(\theta/2)\vec{w})$ for a rotation of θ about the axis $\vec{w}$).

The key geometric relationships concern relative position and have two forms: exact and partially constrained. An example of an exact form is: let object A be at global position $(\vec{r}_A, \vec{t}_A)$, (translation $\vec{t}_A$ and rotation $\vec{r}_A$) and object B be at $(\vec{r}_{AB}, \vec{t}_{AB})$ relative to A. Then, the global position of B is:

$$(r_{AB} * r_A, r_{AB} * t_A * r'_{AB} + t_{AB})$$

where ∗ is the quaternion multiplication operator:

$$(q_0, q_1, q_2, q_3) * (p_0, p_1, p_2, p_3)$$
$$= (q_0p_0 - q_1p_1 - q_2p_2 - q_3p_3, q_2p_3 - q_3p_2 + q_0p_1 + q_1p_0,$$
$$q_3p_1 - q_1p_3 + q_0p_2 + q_2p_0, q_1p_2 - q_2p_1 + q_0p_3 + q_3p_0)$$

and the quaternion inverse operator " ′ " is:

$$(r_0, r_1, r_2, r_3)' = (r_0, -r_1, -r_2, -r_3)$$

A partially constrained position is given by an inequality constraint, such as:

$$t_{Az} \geq 50$$

This means that the z component of A's global position is at least 50. Such a constraint might arise from some *a priori* scene knowledge, or observing a fragment of a surface.

Other relationships concern vectors or points linked by a common transformation, as in $T\vec{v}_1 = \vec{v}_2$, or the proximity of points or vectors:

$$| \vec{p}_1 - \vec{p}_2 | < \epsilon$$

Instances of these constraints are generated as recognition proceeds. Then, with a set of constraints, it is possible to estimate the values of the constrained quantities (e.g. object position) from the known model, the data values and their relationships. Alternatively, it may be possible to determine that the set of constraints is inconsistent (i.e. the set of constraints has no solution), and then the hypothesis is rejected.

A key complication is that each data measurement may have some error or uncertainty, and hence the estimated values may also have these. Alternatively, a variable may be only partially constrained in the model or *a priori* scene information. Hence, each numerical quantity is represented by an interval [ALE83]. Then, following ACRONYM with some extensions, all constraints are represented as inequalities, providing either upper or lower bounds on all quantities.

We now look at how the constraints are evaluated.

ACRONYM used a symbolic algebra technique to estimate upper (SUP) and lower (INF) bounds on all quantities. When bounds cross, i.e. $SUP(x) < INF(x)$, then inconsistency was declared and the hypothesis rejected. This symbolic algebra method was slow and did not always give tight bounds.

The basis of the network approach is the propagation of updated bounds, through functional units linked according to the algebraic problem specification. A simple example is based on the inequality:

$$A \leq B - C$$

By the SUP/INF calculus ([BLE75], [SHO77], [BRO81]), the upper bound of A is constrained by:

$$SUP(A) \leq SUP(B) - INF(C)$$

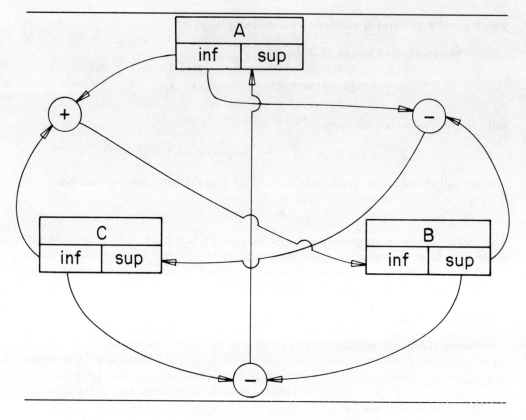

Figure 9.9: Small Constraint Network

as are the lower bounds of B and C:

$$INF(B) \geq INF(A) + INF(C)$$

$$SUP(C) \leq SUP(B) - INF(A)$$

Thus, one can use the value of $SUP(B) - INF(C)$ as an estimated upper bound for A, etc. These relationships are used to create the network for this single inequality, which is shown in Figure 9.9. As new bounds on (for example) B are computed, perhaps from other relationships, they propagate through the network to help compute new bounds on A and C.

There are two advantages to the network structure. First, because values propagate, local improvements in estimates propagate to help constrain other values elsewhere. Hence, even though we still have rectangular interval parameter space bounds, the constraints are non-rectangular and thus can link changes in one variable to others. Even for just local problems, continued propagation until convergence produces better results than the symbolic methods of ACRONYM. Second, these networks have a natural wide-scale parallel structure (e.g. 1000+) that might eventually lead to extremely fast network evaluation in VLSI (e.g. 10-100 microseconds). One disadvantage of the network approach is that standard bounding relationships must be pre-computed as the network is compiled, whereas the symbolic approach can be opportunistic when a fortuitous set of constraints is encountered.

For a given problem, the networks can be complicated, particularly since there may be both exact and heuristic bounding relationships. For example, the network express-ing the reference frame transformation between three positions contains about 2000 function nodes (of types "+", "-", "*", "/", "sqrt", "max", "greaterthan", "if" etc.). The evaluation of a network is fast, even in serial, because small changes are truncated to prevent trivial propagations, unlike other constraint propagation approaches (see [DAV87]). Convergence is guaranteed (or inconsistency detected) because bounds can only tighten (or cross), since only sufficiently large changes are propagated.

The creation of the networks is time-consuming, requiring a symbolic analysis of the algebraic inequalities. Fortunately, there is a natural modular structure arising from the types of problems encountered during scene analysis, where most geometric constraints are of a few common types. Hence, it is possible to pre-compile network modules for each relationship, and merely allocate a new instance of the module into the network as scene analysis proceeds. To date, we have identified and implemented network modules for:

SS - two scalars are close in value

PP - two points are close in location

VV - two vectors point in nearly the same direction

TP - a transformation links a pair of points

TV - a transformation links a pair of vectors

TV2 - a transformation links two pairs of vectors

TT - a transformation links from one position to a second by a third position

P2V - a vector can be defined by two points

QWT - a quaternion is equivalent to an axis of rotation and an angle

One important feature of these modules is that they are bi-directional, in that each variable partially constrains all other related variables. Hence, this method is usable for expressing partial constraints (such as "the object is above the table" or $Z \geq 0$). The constraints on other related variables can then help fully constrain unbound or partially constrained variables.

We now include a simple and a complicated example of network use. Suppose sub-components B and C are rigidly connected to form object A. With the estimated positions of the subcomponents in the global coordinate system, P_{g-B} and P_{g-C}, and the transformations between the object and local coordinate systems, P_{A-B} and P_{A-C}, then these can be used to estimate the global object position, P_{g-A}, by using two instances of the "TT" module listed above. Figure 9.10 shows this network. Notice that each subcomponent gives an independent estimate of P_{g-A}, so that the network keeps the tightest bounds on each component of the position. Any tighter resulting

Rigid Subcomponent Hierarchy   Corresponding Geometric Network

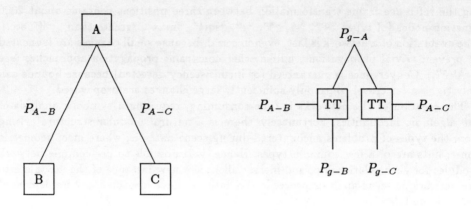

Figure 9.10: A Simple Geometric Reasoning Network

bounds then propagate back through the modules to refine the subcomponent position estimates.

Figure 9.11 shows the full network generated for analyzing the robot in the test scene. As before, the boxes represent transformations, but there are more types used here. The "TPn" boxes stand for n instances of a "TP" module. The circular "J_n" boxes represent three identical instances of subnetworks allocated for transformations involving joint angles, which are omitted to simplify the diagram (each contains 7 network modules). The relative positions of objects are given by the P structures, such as P_{g-R}, which represents the position of the robot in the global reference frame. These are linked by the various transformations. Links to model or data vectors or points are represented by the unconnected segments exiting from some boxes.

The top position P_{g-C} is the position of the camera in the global coordinate system, and the subnetwork to the left and below relates features in the camera frame to corresponding ones in the global coordinate system. Below that is the position P_{g-R} of the robot in the global coordinate system and the position P_{C-R} of the robot in the camera coordinate system, all linked by a TT position transformation module. Next, to the bottom left is the subnetwork for the cylindrical robot body P_{g-B}. The "J_1" node connects the robot position to the rest ("link") on the right, whose position is P_{g-LK}. Its left subcomponent is the rigid shoulder ASSEMBLY (SH) with its subcomponents, the shoulder body (SB) and the small shoulder patch (SO). To the right, the "J_2" node connects to the "armasm" ASSEMBLY (A), linking the upper arm (U) to the lower

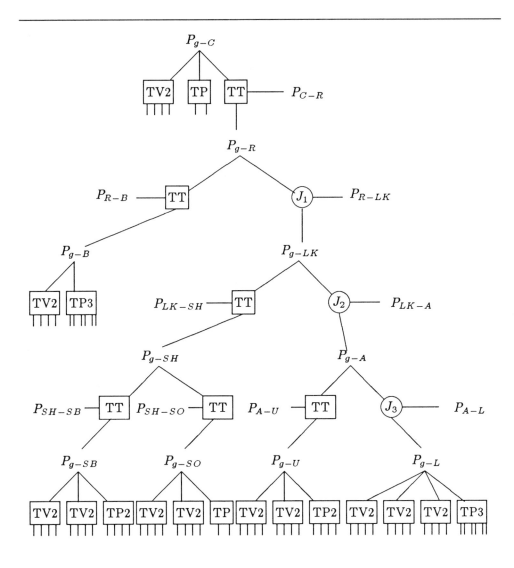

Figure 9.11: Robot Scene Geometric Reasoning Network

arm (L), again via another joint angle (*"J_3"*). At the bottom are the modules that link model vectors and points to observed surface normals, cylindrical axis vectors, and central points, etc. Altogether, there are 61 network modules containing about 96,000 function nodes.

The network structure closely resembles the model subcomponent hierarchy, and only the bottom level is data-dependent. There, new nodes are added whenever new model-to-data pairings are made, producing new constraints on feature positions.

Evaluating the complete network from the raw data requires about 1,000,000 node evaluations in 800 "clock-periods" (thus implying over 1000-way parallelism). Given the simplicity of operations in a node evaluation, a future machine should be able to support easily a 1 microsecond cycle time. This suggests that an approximate answer to this complicated problem could be achieved in about 1 millisecond.

As the tolerances on the data errors propagate through the network modules, they do not always produce tight result intervals, though some interval reduction is achieved by integrating separate estimates. For example, if each orientation component of a random position P_{a-b} has interval width (i.e. error) δ and each orientation component of a random position P_{b-c} has interval width ϵ, then each component of the resulting position $P_{a-c} = P_{a-b} * P_{b-c}$ has interval width:

$$\frac{16(\delta + \epsilon)}{3\pi}$$

However, this interval width is less or non-existent for most of the actual rigid transformations used here.

Because the resulting intervals are not tight, confidence that the mean interval value is the best estimate is reduced, though the bounds are correct and the mean interval values provide useful position estimates. To tighten estimates, a post-processing phase iteratively shrinks the bounds on a selected interval and lets the new bounds propagate through the network. For the robot example, this required an additional 12,000 cycles, implying a total solution time of about 13 milliseconds on our hypothetical parallel machine.

Using the new geometric reasoning network, the numerical results for the whole robot in the test scene are summarized in Table 9.10. Here, the values are given in the global reference frame rather than in the camera reference frame.

The results of the position estimation can been seen more clearly if we look at some figures showing the estimated object positions overlaying the original scene. Figure 9.12 shows the estimated position of the trash can is nearly correct. The robot upper arm (Figure 9.13) and lower arm (Figure 9.14) are also close. When we join these two to form the armasm ASSEMBLY (Figure 1.10), the results are still reasonable, but by the time we get to the whole robot (Figure 9.15), the accumulated errors in the position and joint angle estimates cause the predicted position of the gripper to drift somewhat from the true position (when using the single pass at network convergence). The iterative bounds tightening procedure described above then produces the slightly better result shown in Figure 1.11. Note, however, that both network methods produced improved position results over that of the original **IMAGINE I** method, which is shown in Figure 9.16.

Table 9.10: Measured And Estimated Spatial Parameters

PARAMETER	MEASURED	ESTIMATED
X	488 (cm)	487 (cm)
Y	89 (cm)	87 (cm)
Z	554 (cm)	550 (cm)
Rotation	0.0 (rad)	0.038 (rad)
Slant	0.793 (rad)	0.702(rad)
Tilt	3.14 (rad)	2.97 (rad)
Joint 1	2.24 (rad)	2.21 (rad)
Joint 2	2.82 (rad)	2.88 (rad)
Joint 3	4.94 (rad)	4.57 (rad)

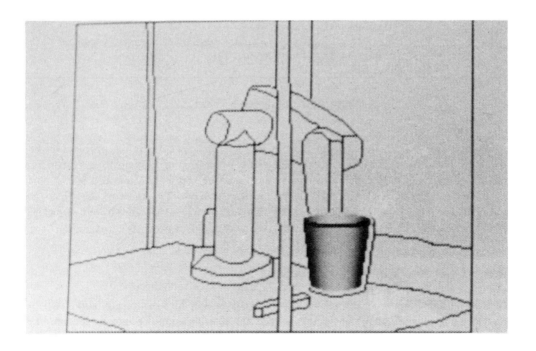

Figure 9.12: Recognized Trash Can

Figure 9.13: Recognized Upper Arm

Though research on the efficient use of these networks is continuing, problems overcome by the new technique include the weak bounding of transformed parameter estimates and partially constrained variables, and the representation and use of constraints not aligned with the parameter coordinate axes. The network also has the potential for large scale parallel evaluation. This is important because about one-third of the processing time in these scene analyses was spent in geometric reasoning.

9.3 Feature Visibility Analysis

In three dimensional scenes, not all object features will be visible (e.g. some will be on the back side of an object), and a true three dimensional scene understanding program should account for this. There are three distinct cases of feature invisibility. The first case always occurs: there are features on the back side of every object and these cannot ordinarily be detected from a single viewpoint (except by using mirrors or shadows). At the same time, it is easy to predict what cannot be seen, using the estimated orientation of hypotheses to predict back-facing SURFACEs.

The next case is forward-facing self-obscured features. Here, an object feature is

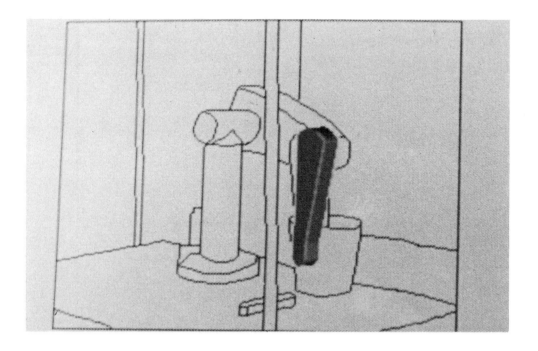

Figure 9.14: Recognized Lower Arm

obscured by one or more closer surfaces from the same object. Given knowledge of the object's shape and position relative to the viewer, the relative surface positions and their visibility can be predicted.

Finally, there is structure obscured by unrelated objects. Here, the details of occlusion cannot be predicted, nor is it easy to deduce the invisible structure (though context and historical information could help – as in the top of a desk). Perhaps the best that can be done is to show that what remains is consistent with the hypothesis of obscured structure. Consequently, indirect evidence for some features must be found. This requires three actions – predicting feature visibility, finding evidence for closer structures and verifying that the available features up to the point of occlusion are consistent with the model.

After feature visibility analysis, the results are used in three ways:

1. SURFACEs predicted to be invisible are not searched for,

2. SURFACEs predicted to be partially self-obscured are verified as having one or more boundaries that show this (e.g. back-side obscuring between this and other object SURFACEs), and

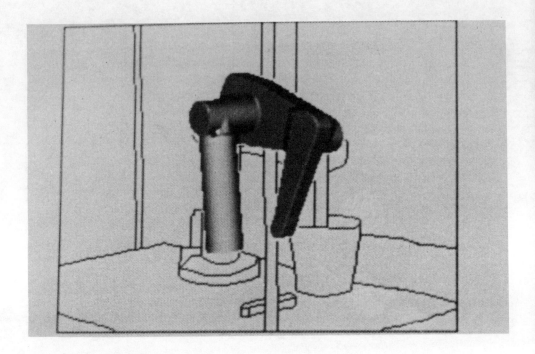

Figure 9.15: Recognized Complete Robot Using One-Pass Network Method

3. SURFACEs predicted to be completely visible are verified as having no back-side obscuring boundaries (unless obscured by unrelated objects).

Because of parameter estimation errors, test 3 is not reliable and is not performed (more discussion below).

These three cases of feature visibility are only applied to individual SURFACEs, as any ASSEMBLY can be decomposed into SURFACEs.

9.3.1 Deducing Back-Facing SURFACEs

Deducing whether planar SURFACEs are back-facing or not is simple: if the predicted surface normal points away from the camera, then the SURFACE is not visible.

Let:

$\vec{n}$ be the model SURFACE normal ($(0, 0, -1)$ by definition)

A be the coordinate transformation from the SURFACE's
   local system to that of the whole object

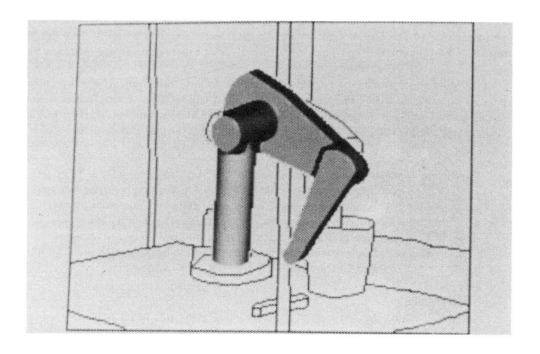

Figure 9.16: Original **IMAGINE I** *Recognized Complete Robot*

G be the transformation from the object's
local system to that of the camera
$\vec{p} =$ a nominal point on the SURFACE in local coordinates

Then:

$\vec{m} = GA\vec{n}$ is the predicted normal orientation
$\vec{v} = GA\vec{p}$ is the view vector from the camera to the point
on the SURFACE

Test:

if $\vec{v} \circ \vec{m} > 0$, then the SURFACE is back-facing

For curved SURFACEs, we test the normal at each point on the boundary. By the segmentation assumptions (Chapter 3), the surface varies smoothly within the boundaries, so if all points on the boundary and the nominal central point are back-facing, then the interior of the surface almost always is as well.

A problem occurs with the combination of nearly tangential SURFACEs and parameter misestimation. Here, SURFACEs predicted as visible may not always be so, and *vice versa*. This case can be detected, by detecting surface normals oriented nearly perpendicular to the line of sight at the surface boundary. If a SURFACE is determined to be tangential, hypothesis construction does not require image evidence for it.

Classifying the visibility of curved SURFACEs follows this logic: If a substantial portion of a curved SURFACE is front-facing, then call it "front-facing". If it is not "front-facing" and a substantial portion of the SURFACE is tangential, then call it "tangential". Otherwise, call it "back-facing". The ideal form of this test is:

Let:

T = set of points whose surface normals are nearly perpendicular to the three dimensional line of sight (i.e. the tangential points)

F = set of points whose surface normals face the viewer, but are not in T (i.e. the front-facing points)

B = set of points whose surface normals face away from the viewer, but are not in T (i.e. the back-facing points)

Then:

If empty(F) and empty(T), then back-facing (i.e. never seen)

If empty(F) and not(empty(T)), then tangential (i.e. possibly seen)

If not(empty(F)), then front-facing (i.e. always seen)

Because of parameter estimation errors, some compromises in the above ideal algorithm are made:

- thresholds are added to decide the visibility class of each vector

- thresholds are added to decide the visibility class of the whole SURFACE

The algorithm to classify individual vectors is:

Let:

$\vec{v_i}$ be the line of sight to point i

$\vec{m_i}$ be the predicted surface normal vector at i

$d_i = \vec{v_i} \circ \vec{m_i}$

Then:

if $d_i > \tau_1$, then $i \in B$ $(\tau_1 = 0.1)$

if $d_i < -\tau_1$, then $i \in F$

$i \in T$ otherwise

Table 9.11: Predicted SURFACE Visibility

Object	SURFACE Visibility	
robbody	front-facing = {robbodyside(1)}	
	tangential = {robbodyside(2)}	*1
robshldbd	front-facing = {robshldend,robshould2}	
	tangential = {robshould1}	*1
robshldsobj	front-facing = {robshoulds(1)}	
	tangential = {robshoulds(2)}	*1
upperarm	front-facing = {uside(2),uends,uedgel(1)}	
	back-facing = {uside(1),uendb,uedgel(2)}	
	tangential = {uedges(1),uedges(2)}	
lowerarm	front-facing = {lsideb,ledgea,lendb}	
	back-facing = {lsidea,ledgeb}	
trashcan	front-facing = {tcanoutf(1),tcaninf(1),	
	tcanbot(1)}	
	back-facing = {tcanbot(2)}	
	tangential = {tcanoutf(2),tcaninf(2)}	*1

*1 – largely back-facing curved SURFACE has tangential sides

The classification of the whole SURFACE is obtained by:

Let:
$$b = \text{size}(B)$$
$$f = \text{size}(F)$$
$$t = \text{size}(T)$$
$$s = b + f + t$$

Then:

if $f/s > \tau_2$, then front-facing $(\tau_2 = 0.1)$
else if $t/s > \tau_3$, then tangential $(\tau_3 = 0.1)$
else back-facing

When this classification was applied to the objects with their estimated reference frames in the test image, surface visibility was correctly deduced. The results are shown in Table 9.11.

9.3.2 Deducing Self-Obscured SURFACEs

Given the deductions of the previous subsection, all remaining SURFACEs must be at least partially front-facing, but some may be partially or wholly self-obscured by other closer SURFACEs from the same object.

Self-occlusion analysis uses the object model and position estimates to predict an image of the object, which is then analyzed for visibility. The process occurs in three stages:

1. prediction of visible SURFACEs,

2. deduction of missing SURFACEs and

3. deduction of partially self-obscured SURFACEs.

The first step is implemented using a raycasting depth image generator. Here, a ray from the viewer is intersected with the model SURFACEs placed according to the object's estimated position. The raycaster produces an array of pixels valued with the depth and identity of the closest (i.e. visible) SURFACE.

The detection of completely obscured structure is now trivial and consists of finding those front-facing SURFACEs (from the analysis of the preceding subsection) not visible in the predicted image.

The detection of partially obscured SURFACEs is also simple. During image generation, whenever a predicted visible surface pixel was replaced or not included because of a closer pixel, then self-occlusion occurred. The identities of all SURFACEs that suffered this are recorded during the generation of the synthetic image. Any such SURFACE not completely self-obscured is then partially self-obscured.

Parameter estimation errors may cause nearly obscured SURFACEs to disappear and barely obscured SURFACEs to reappear. A similar effect occurs with unobscured SURFACEs becoming partially obscured (i.e. because a closer SURFACE moves slightly in front of it) and *vice versa*. So, the following algorithm was implemented to decide the visibility classes:

> Let:
> > v = number of visible pixels (predicted by raycasting)
> > n = number of obscured pixels (predicted by raycasting)
> > $p = v/(v + n)$ (percentage of visible pixels)
>
> Then:
> > if $p > \tau_1$, then the SURFACE is fully visible ($\tau_1 = 0.9$)
> > if $\tau_1 \geq p > \tau_2$, then the SURFACE is partially obscured ($\tau_2 = 0.05$)
> > Otherwise, the SURFACE is fully obscured

Table 9.12 records the predicted occlusion status for all front-facing SURFACEs of all primitive ASSEMBLYs in the test image. This corresponds exactly to the observed visibility of all SURFACEs (disregarding external occlusion, which is discussed below). For structured ASSEMBLYs, the process is similar, only some previous cases of external occlusion now become self-occlusion as components are connected together.

9.3.3 Detecting External Occlusion

Structure obscured by unrelated objects cannot be anticipated in coincidental scene arrangements, unless closer objects can be identified. What remains possible is to show that the absence of a feature is consistent with the assumption of occlusion, that is,

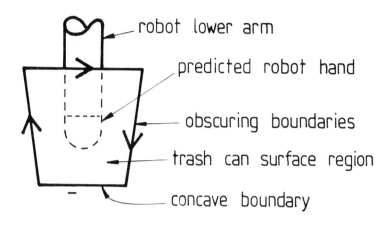

robot lower arm

predicted robot hand

obscuring boundaries

trash can surface region

concave boundary

Figure 9.17: Boundaries Surround Completely Obscured Surface

Table 9.12: Predicted Self-Occlusions

Object	Occlusion Status
robbody	fully-visible = {robbodyside(1)}
robshldbd	fully-visible = {robshldend,robshould2}
robshldsobj	fully-visible = {robshoulds(1)}
upperarm	fully-visible = {uside(2),uends}
lowerarm	fully-visible = {lsideb,ledgea}
	partially-self-obscured = {lendb}
trashcan	fully-visible = {tcanoutf(1)}
	partially-self-obscured = {tcaninf(1)}
	fully-self-obscured = {tcanbot(1)}

there are closer, unrelated surfaces completely covering the portion of the image where it is expected. This unrelatedness can be verified by detecting front-surface-obscuring or concave boundaries completely surrounding the closer surfaces, as in Figure 9.17.

The other case considered occurs when non-self-obscured SURFACEs are observed as partially obscured. These must meet all shape and adjacency constraints required by the model and the invisible portions must be totally behind other unrelated surfaces (as before). The boundary between the partial object and obscuring surfaces must be obscuring.

Verifying fully obscured structure is the simplest case. Here, every portion of the predicted model SURFACE must be behind an unrelated data surface. Minor errors in absolute distance prediction make it difficult to directly verify that an object surface pixel is further away than the corresponding observed pixel, such as when a piece of paper lies on a table surface. Fortunately, relative surface depth differences have already been accounted for in the labeling of obscuring boundaries and the formation of depth ordered surface clusters (Chapter 5). The ordering test can then be reformulated to verify that the entire missing SURFACE lies within the image region belonging to an unrelated, closer, surface cluster. In practice, the test can be performed using a raycasting technique:

1. Find the set of closer, unrelated surfaces.

2. Predict the image locations for the missing SURFACE.

3. For each pixel, verify that the observed surface image region has been assigned to one of the closer surfaces.

Again, this ideal algorithm was altered to tolerate parameter misestimation:

Let:

P = set of predicted image positions for the SURFACE
I = subset of P lying on identified object surfaces
   (should be empty)
O = subset of P lying on closer unrelated obscuring
   surfaces (should be P)
E = subset of P lying elsewhere (should be empty)

If:

$\text{size}(I) \ / \ \text{size}(P) < \tau_1$ and $\text{size}(E) \ / \ \text{size}(O) < \tau_2$
$(\tau_1 = 0.2, \tau_2 = 0.2)$

Then: declare the surface to be externally obscured

Figure 9.18 illustrates the test.

Because of the depth ordering ambiguities of concave surface boundaries (i.e. which surface, if either, is in front of the other), this approach will fail to detect some cases of external occlusion. Difficulties also occur with surfaces that lie both in front of and behind objects. In the absence of more accurate depth predictions, the only correct test may be to observe an obscuring boundary between the visible portions of the object and the missing portions.

The only fully externally obscured structure was the robot hand, which was correctly detected. Because the reference frame estimates for the lowerarm had a slightly larger rotation angle, part of the hand was predicted not to be obscured by the trash can. This motivated the threshold based test described above.

Figure 9.19 shows the predicted position of the robot hand on top of the scene.

Determining the visibility status of the model features was computationally expensive – particularly the raycasting image generation for self-occlusion analysis. About

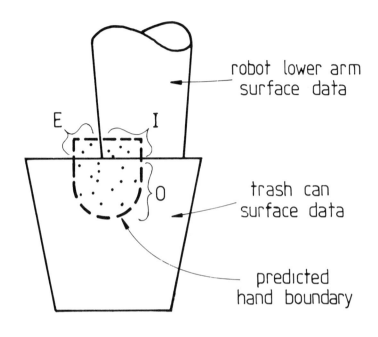

Figure 9.18: Predicted Boundary of Externally Obscured Surface

one-third of the processing time was spent in this process. In response to this, the SMS modeling approach [FIS87a] was developed. These models explicitly record the visibility of all model features for the SMS equivalent of each ASSEMBLY, for the key viewpoints. The model does not specify the visibility relationship of all recursively accessible features, merely those represented at the current level of the hierarchy, which considerably reduces the number of occlusion relationships considered for each object. Feature visibility is associated with a partitioning of the view sphere, and the relative position between the viewer and the object determines which partition applies at a given time. From this index, the visibility is directly accessed.

9.4 Direct Evidence Collection

The visibility analysis deduced the set of SURFACEs for which image evidence should be available and we now discuss how such evidence is detected and matched to the model.

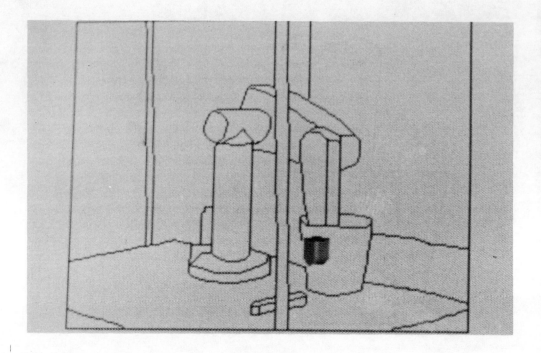

Figure 9.19: Predicted Gripper Position

9.4.1   Initial (Invocation) Feature Evidence

Model SURFACEs have no substructure, so the evidence for a hypothesized model SURFACE is the associated surface image region. ASSEMBLYs are then formed by hierarchical synthesis [TUR74], so previously verified subcomponents or SURFACE hypotheses are evidence for a hypothesized ASSEMBLY.

If invocation occurs, at least one subcomponent grouping (Section 8.2.3) must have positive plausibility, which suggests that some subcomponents are visible and are likely to have been previously recognized. (If none were invoked, then it is unlikely that the object will be invoked.) Then, verified subcomponent hypotheses become the initial evidence for the structure.

For each image structure associated with the invocation subcomponent group, all verified hypotheses of the correct types in the current image context (surface cluster) are located. Then, groups of these verified subcomponent hypotheses are combinatorially paired with the invoked model's features to create a new hypothesis, provided that:

1. Each model feature gets at most one hypothesis, which must have the correct type.

2. No image structure is used more than once.

3. Only maximal pairings are considered.

4. There is a consistent reference frame that unifies all subcomponents.

The combinatorial matching is potentially explosive, but each image substructure generally has only a few verified hypotheses, usually arising from symmetry or ambiguity. Objects with these problems or duplicated features generate more initially consistent hypotheses, but most of these are eliminated by constraints (2) and (4).

The worst combinatorial explosion occurs with the robot lower arm, where each of the visible planar surfaces could be one of two model SURFACEs, each in two possible orientations. The curved end SURFACE has one model in two possible orientations. Altogether, there are initially 32 possible pairings using previously recognized subcomponents. Fortunately, the constraints eliminate all but two, which are indistinguishable in this scene. The upper arm is the next worst case, with eight initial pairings of which two are left after the constraints. All other initial hypothesis generations had four or fewer cases. Most invalid cases were eliminated by constraint (4).

9.4.2 Additional SURFACE Feature Location

Given the initial location estimates and the geometric model, it is easy to predict where a visible surface should appear. This prediction simplifies direct search for image evidence for the feature. This is, in style, like the work of Freuder [FRE77], except that three dimensional scenes are considered here.

To select good image evidence for an uninstantiated model feature, the oriented model is used to predict roughly where the surface data should appear. Figure 9.20 shows the predicted location for the robot upper arm *uedgel* panel superimposed on the original image using the initial parameter estimates for *upperarm*.

Other constraints can then be applied to eliminate most inappropriate surfaces from the predicted area. The constraints that a potential surface must meet are:

1. It must not be previously used.

2. It must be in the surface cluster for the ASSEMBLY.

3. It must be in the correct image location.

4. It must have the correct three dimensional surface orientation.

5. It must have the correct three dimensional location.

6. It must have the correct size.

7. Its visible portions must have the correct shape.

The implemented algorithm used the constraints 1 to 5, with some parameter tolerances on 3, 4 and 5. The 7th was not used because likely causes for not finding the surface during invocation were: it was partially obscured, it was incompletely segmented or it was merged during the surface reconstruction process (Chapter 4). The

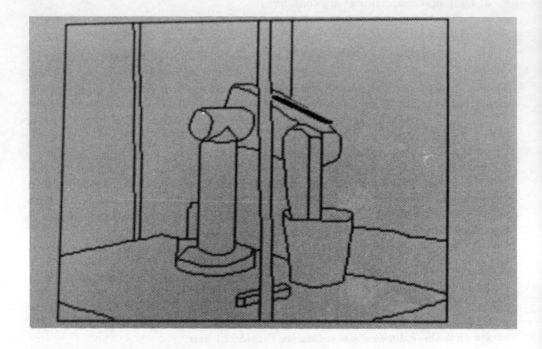

Figure 9.20: Predicted Uedgel Panel on Image

result of these would be incorrect shapes. These factors also affect the area constraint
(6), so this was used only to select a single surface if more than one met the first five
constraints (but this did not occur in the test scene).

The implemented algorithm is:

Let:

$S = \{$all surfaces in the surface cluster not previously used
          in the hypothesis$\} = \{s_d\}$
$\vec{c}_p = $ predicted image central point for the missing SURFACE
$\vec{c}_d = $ observed image central point for s_d
$\vec{n}_p = $ predicted three dimensional surface normal at $\vec{c}_p$
$\vec{n}_d = $ observed three dimensional surface normal at $\vec{c}_d$
$z_p = $ predicted depth at $\vec{c}_p$
$z_d = $ observed depth at $\vec{c}_d$
$A_p = $ model area for missing SURFACE
$A_d = $ estimated area for s_d

If:

(constraint 3)

$$| \vec{c}_d - \vec{c}_p | < \tau_1 \qquad\qquad (\tau_1 = 20 \text{ pixels})$$

(constraint 4)

$$\vec{n}_p \circ \vec{n}_d > \tau_2 \qquad\qquad (\tau_2 = 0.8)$$

(constraint 5)

$$| z_p - z_d | < \tau_3 \qquad\qquad (\tau_3 = 50 \text{ cm})$$

Then: s_d is an acceptable surface

The surface selected is the acceptable s_d whose area is closest to that predicted, by minimizing:

$$| 1 - \frac{A_d}{A_p} |$$

In the test image, the only missing SURFACEs were the two side surfaces on the upper arm and the inside surface at the back of the trash can. For the trash can, the only potential image surfaces for the trash can back surface were the two visible surfaces in the surface cluster. The front surface was already used in both cases, and the rear surface met all the other constraints, so was selected. A similar process applied to the upper arm side panels.

9.4.3   Rigid Subcomponent Aggregation

Surfaces are not the only evidence accepted for model features – previously recognized subcomponents are also used. For example, a nose would be such a subcomponent in the context of a face. The structures can be rigidly connected to the parent object (e.g. nose to face) or non-rigidly connected (e.g. arm to body). The collections should correspond to model features because of the model segmentation assumptions (Chapter 7) and the surface cluster formation process (Chapter 5).

Any analysis associated with these structures can be reduced to analysis of the sub-component SURFACEs, but it would be desirable to use the larger units. First, the substructures might have been previously identified, and so processing should not be duplicated, and second, the use of larger structural units helps reduce the combinatorial matching. Finally, parsimony dictates that matching should proceed at the level of descriptions, and complex objects would be described using subcomponents.

Because of the hierarchical synthesis [TUR74] nature of the recognition process, previously recognized subcomponents can be directly integrated as evidence, without having to return to the surface analysis [FIS83]. As the subcomponent's type is already a strong constraint on its usability, the remaining constraints are:

1. being in the surface cluster,

2. having the correct adjacent structure and

3. having correct placement.

The placement test is:

Let:

G_s be the global transformation for the subcomponent
A be the transformation from the subcomponent's
to the object's reference frame

Then:

if $G_s A^{-1}$ (by INVERSE and TRANSFORM) is consistent with the
object's reference frame (by MERGE) then allow attachment.

No structure adjacency criterion was implemented, but subcomponent SURFACEs should be adjacent to other object SURFACEs, as conditioned by any external or self-occlusion. Figure 9.8 illustrates the subcomponent aggregation process.

Only one instance of a recognizable rigidly connected subcomponent occurred in the test image. Here, the cylindrical robot shoulder body and the small triangular shoulder patch were joined to form the complete robot shoulder. The combination passed the placement test, so proceeded to verification.

9.4.4 Binding Subcomponents with Degrees of Freedom

Subcomponents whose attachment is only partially constrainted (such as the lowerarm ASSEMBLY of a PUMA robot) also need to be aggregated. As the subcomponent has been recognized previously, its coordinate frame must be consistent with the object's, given the degrees-of-freedom inherent in the modeled relationship between their respective coordinate frames. At the same time, the test also binds the values for the remaining degrees-of-freedom in the coordinate relationship. This results in numerical values being bound in the particular hypothesis context for the symbolic variables used in the model definition (Chapter 7). Figure 9.21 illustrates the partially constrained subcomponent attachment process.

The matching and binding is by a "numerical" unification process:

Let:

G be the global reference frame transformation for the object
S be the global reference frame transformation for the subcomponent
$A(\vec{x})$ be the transformation from the subcomponent's reference frame
to the object's reference frame with $\vec{x}$ as the unbound variables

Then:

Compare $G^{-1}S$ to $A(\vec{x})$
Where $A(\vec{x})$ has bound variables, then the values must match
(i.e. parameter estimate ranges overlap)
Where $A(\vec{x})$ has unbound variables, then the variables are set
to the corresponding parameter ranges from $G^{-1}S$

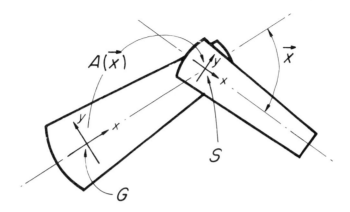

Figure 9.21: Partially Constrained Subcomponent Aggregation (in 2D)

Table 9.13: Correct Partially Constrained Subcomponent Attachments

Object	Subcomponents	Modeled Parameter	Measured Value	Estimated Value
robot	link, robbody	jnt1	2.24	2.18
link	armasm, robshould	jnt2	2.82	2.79
armasm	upperarm, lowerarm	jnt3	4.94	4.56

The results for the correct partially constrained subcomponent aggregations are summarized in Table 9.13. All correct bindings were made, and the table shows that the connection parameters were estimated well. Most of the incorrect combinatorial subcomponent groupings were eliminated during the binding process because of inconsistent reference frames, so this was also a benefit.

In the test scene, one binding occurred between inappropriate hypotheses, when constructing the armasm ASSEMBLY. Because of symmetry, each of its two subcomponents (upperarm and lowerarm) had two hypotheses. Hypothesis pairing produced four pairs, of which two passed the above test. Only one should have passed, but because of the tolerances on reference frame estimates, it was not possible to eliminate the grouping that placed the lower arm behind the upper arm solely by using geometric constraints. Self-occlusion analysis during verification (Chapter 10) did eliminate the extra hypothesis, however.

9.5   Relation to Other Research

Though pattern recognition techniques are widespread, and may give rough information about the object's image position, they do not usually provide precise placement, description and feature correspondences. Another technique, graph matching (e.g. [BAR71]), typifies topological matching methods that make correspondences between image and model features, but again do not give scene placement nor precise image description. The graph arcs can include rough spatial relations (e.g. above, left, near) between image features and an image model (e.g. [HAN78b], [NAG79], [OHT79], [ABE83]). They can also include environmental relations like the sky being at the top of an image and above roofs [OHT79], or most scene lines being vertical [KEN83], which allow for rough correspondences and object placement in the image. These classes of techniques do not strongly exploit the geometric structure of objects and scenes (which often provide the best constraints on the identity and position of objects) though the algorithms do offer simplicity and well-defined decision procedures.

Geometric scene understanding systems can be classified by the dimensionality of their model features (i.e. point, curve, region or volume) and their image data (i.e. two or three dimensional). All of the key research discussed below used three dimensional geometric models.

Early scene understanding systems (e.g. [ROB65], [FAL72]) used two dimensional point or corner correspondences to solve for object location and projection relationships. Later, Turner [TUR74] located objects by using three dimensional points found from stereo triangulation of paired two dimensional image points.

Three influential edge-based recognition systems are:

- Brooks' ACRONYM system [BRO81] matched pairs of nearly parallel two dimensional lines ("ribbons") to the extremal boundaries of generalized cylinders, thus instantiating model primitives. Larger objects were found by a graph matching technique, where the arcs in the graphs represented two dimensional projections of three dimensional geometric relationships between the generalized cylinders (e.g. relative orientation). Three dimensional object position was found by using the two dimensional image measurements (feature sizes and positions, etc.) to back-constrain the range of position parameters.

- Lowe's SCERPO system [LOW85] used groupings of straight two dimensional line features to suggest and orient model instances - which were sets of three dimensional lines. To help avoid combinatorial matching problems, he used a "perceptual organization" technique that grouped edges by colinearity, parallelism and endpoint connectivity and then formed larger features, like parallelograms. A measure of significance related to the probability of random occurrence of the segment groupings was calculated for both model and data segments, which was then used to help order search. With a pairing of three or more segments, three dimensional position was found by using an iterative least-squared error algorithm. Hypotheses were then verified and refined by collecting additional line evidence, using direct feature predictions from the initial position estimates.

- The University of Sheffield TINA system [POR87] matched three dimensional lines derived from binocular stereo to a three dimensional wire frame object model (which was itself derived empirically from observed instances of the objects). The use of edge information implied the objects needed to be largely polyhedral. A least-squared error matching process deduced the position of the object from the three dimensional feature correspondences.

Lowe's work was analyzed by McIvor [MCI88], with the main criticisms being over weak initial position estimates, ignoring edge fragmentation, incorrect probability analysis for larger groups, unnecessary projection relationship simplifications and insufficient discriminatory powers. However, McIvor also demonstrated the approach was successful in 10 of 16 views of a test part.

There has been little geometric matching of two dimensional image regions to three dimensional model surfaces. Fisher [FIS83] used heuristics based on the deformations of the three dimensional model surface patches when seen in two dimensions to estimate three dimensional surface patch position. This supported a hierarchical synthesis matching process that recognized larger objects. Ballard and Sabbah [BAL81b] used a variety of Hough transformation techniques to estimate the six positional parameters sequentially. This uniform mechanism is more stable to noise, but is likely to suffer when the object's shape varies dramatically with the viewpoint. Turner [TUR74] attempted a more symbolically descriptive matching technique by using surface patches classified according to the patterns of iso-intensity curves. The elementary recognition operation used property and relation matching. More complicated objects were recognized by aggregating subcomponents in a hierarchical synthesis process.

Three dimensional surfaces have been used for recognition since the early 1970's. Several researchers (e.g. [SHI71], [POP75]) collected surface data from a structured light system, where configurations of light stripes characterized regular surface shapes. This method of data collection has again become popular (e.g. [OSH81], [BOL83]). A particularly significant result was obtained by Faugeras and Hebert [FAU83], who recognized an irregular part using locally planar patches, by matching to an empirically derived model (although the matcher only found a few correspondences). Grimson and Lozano-Perez [GRI84] extended this work by developing a set of heuristics that eliminate many spurious initial hypotheses. Their features were three dimensional image points with attached vectors (such as surface normals). Grimson [GRI87] later extended this work to recognizing families of scaled, stretched or jointed two dimensional piecewise linear objects, by propagating and refining estimates of the scale or stretch factor down the model-to-data segment pairing search tree.

In a "continuous" version of surface matching, Ikeuchi [IKE81] used an extended gaussian image method to reduce object description to a sphere with quills representing the sizes of areas with the corresponding orientations. Matching used three dimensional data and was largely a constrained correlation. His method was successful with some curved objects, but ignored the object's structural features, and might fail for complicated or non-convex objects.

In general, recognition results have been limited to complete image understanding of simple geometric objects (e.g. [ROB65]) or partial understanding of complex assemblies of simple objects, such as airplanes [BRO81]. Irregular objects are not well understood at this level, in part because of problems with object modeling and in part because of the difficulty in obtaining useful image data.

Once an initial object position has been estimated, object models can be used to predict the location and appearance of the remaining image features. Falk [FAL72] predicted lines in a blocks world domain, and Freuder [FRE77] predicted image region locations in two dimensions with procedural models of hammers. More recently, Brooks [BRO81] showed how a range of image positions could be predicted using partial constraints on object location. Hogg [HOG84] used edge point information to verify the positional parameters of a generalized cylinder human model over time in a natural scene. Individual evidence was weak, but requiring evidence for the whole complex model led to good results. Aylett et al. [AYL88] used constraints similar to Grimson and Lozano-Perez [GRI84] to match stereo-derived three dimensional edges to predicted model edges. The model edges were predicted from a constructive solid geometry object model in a known position and the goal was to eliminate known features from a scene.

Understanding occlusion in three dimensions has had few results to date. Blocks world scenes have been successfully analyzed by Guzman's heuristics [GUZ67]. These included the paired-TEE occlusion identification and image region pairing heuristics. Fisher [FIS83] and Adorni and Trucco [ADO86] have extended and applied these ideas to three dimensional scene analysis. Koenderink and van Doorn [KOE82] characterized occlusion on curved surfaces by their local surface relationships, and showed how the occlusion signatures progressively vary as viewpoints change. This micro-level occlusion understanding could help predict local surface shape for the verification of hypothesized occlusion.

Most model-based three dimensional vision systems are slow. Goad [GOA86] described a very efficient three dimensional model edge to two dimensional data straight edge matching algorithm (achieving several second recognition). He represented a discrete set of object orientations (tessellations of a viewsphere) as a boolean bit string, thus allowing fast geometric operations. Matching used a tree search, and Goad pre-expanded the tree branching on the outcome of visibility prediction and feature detection. Impossible branches were pruned at compile time using a combination of geometric, reliability and plausibility analysis. Relative feature positions could be pre-computed for the tessellations, allowing fast run-time absolute feature prediction.

9.6 Discussion

There is an "idealism" embedded in the matching assumptions, with the goal of accounting for all model features. This most stringent criterion is ultimately not practical because position estimate errors will make location of smaller features difficult and segmentation may not isolate the desired structures, or isolate them at a different level of analytic scale. Other phenomena that cause the loss of data include occlusion, faulty objects, sensor noise and generic object variations. The result is that bad or unexpected evidence will cause failure, such as when a surface is too fragmented.

In general, numerical techniques (e.g. least-squared error) could probably improve the methods used here, provided the problems could be reformulated to allow the degrees-of-freedom needed for partially constrained relationships, such as joint angles. This seems like a suitable extension for a final geometric reasoning refinement phase, after all evidence has been accumulated.

The programs account for several expected difficulties, such as when two surfaces are not properly segmented (as in the upper arm edge surfaces), or when thin cylindrical features (e.g. chair legs) are too distant to be considered cylinders. Further, variation in segmentation is allowed by not examining boundary placement when matching surfaces.

Some special case reasoning seems acceptable, but incompleteness of evidence should also be permitted. Unfortunately, this leads to heuristic match evaluation criteria, or explicit designation of required versus auxiliary evidence. More generally, a full model of an object should also have descriptions at several scales and the construction process should match the data across the levels.

Another major criticism is that the recognition process only uses surfaces. The traditional "edge" is still useful, especially as surface data does not represent reflectance variations (e.g. surface markings). Volumetric evidence could also be included. Relationships between structures, such as line parallelisms and perpendicularities can provide strong evidence on orientation, particularly when occlusion leaves little visible evidence.

Object knowledge could help the recognition of subcomponents. Each subcomponent is currently recognized independently and then aggregated in a strictly bottom-up process. However, one subcomponent may invoke the object, which could partially constrain the identity and location of the other subcomponents. Since these objects often obscure each other in unpredictable ways, there may not be enough evidence to invoke and identify a subcomponent independently, whereas additional active top-down object knowledge might overcome this.

The level of detail in a model affects the quantity of evidence required. Hierarchical models that represent finer details in lower levels of the model lead to hypothesis construction processes that add the details once the coarser description is satisfied (if the details are needed). This symbolic coarse-to-fine recognition approach has not been well explored yet, but some modeling systems (e.g. ACRONYM [BRO81], SMS [FIS87a]) have experimented with scale dependent models.

Final Comments

This chapter has investigated model matching mechanisms that use surfaces as the primary recognition evidence. Previous work has demonstrated how to use surfaces, but their approaches, while using real data, did not use all available data (including surface curvature), understand the visibility of model features or richly exploit hierarchical models. This chapter showed how to use models, surfaces and associated positional information to:

- estimate the reference frame for objects,

- deduce the visibility of all model features,

- predict where to find all visible features,

- explain missing data as instances of occlusion, and

- ensure consistent data.

CHAPTER 10

Hypothesis Verification

The model invocation and hypothesis construction processes are largely based on processing symbolic structural descriptions and do not closely examine the input data. Further, tolerances are allowed in the matching process to overcome noise, segmentation variations and imperfect descriptive processes. Consequently, it is possible for coincidental scene arrangements to lead to spurious object hypotheses. Many of these false hypotheses will have been eliminated by the geometric constraints examined during hypothesis construction, but some may remain. This chapter discusses additional constraints on solid physical objects that help guarantee object existence and identity.

10.1 What Should Verification Do?

Models are invoked by attributes suggesting objects; thus invocation is necessarily coincidental. Hypothesis construction is more constraining, requiring geometric coordination among features as dictated by the model, but can still leave spurious, well advanced, hypotheses that need to be eliminated. Hence:

> verification aims to ensure that what is recognized is only what is contained in the scene.

In a philosophical sense, verification should try to maximally confirm the validity of the hypothesized identity of an image structure, to the limits of the object representation. The point is to ensure that the object both physically exists and has the requisite properties, by extending the depth of the subordinate concept structure beyond merely superficial attributes. In a sense, this is a true "seeing" of the object. Previous stages of analysis only considered subsets of the features in a "suggestive" sense, whereas verification should now look for all features and can report what it finds.

More practically, verification should also eliminate hypotheses that arise from coincidental arrangements of image features. This approach leads to defining a set of constraints that an object must satisfy to be said to exist and have a given identity. These, in turn, entail knowing both what is important in an object and its representation, and what makes it appear as it does.

We would like reasonable criteria for ensuring correct object hypotheses, with "reasonable" encompassing both richness of detail and conceptual appropriateness. Unfortunately, "ensuring" is impossible because all interpretations of sensory data are

233

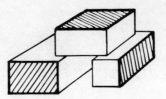

Figure 10.1: Unrelated Planes Invoke Cube

necessarily imperfect and because no real object can be completely and uniquely characterized. Practical problems are related and stem from impoverished models and descriptive terms and lack of resolution in the data. However, some verification is both necessary and of value and should remove the most obvious cases of misidentification.

Existence Verification

Little work has addressed the question of: "Does the object exist, or are the features merely coincidental?". Geometric constraints increase the certainty by showing that the image features are consistent with a particular object instance, but they do not guarantee that the features are causally related. Figure 10.1 shows three orthogonal planes that invoke a cube model, but fail to meet the general physical requirements of connectedness. Hence, we can help ensure existence by requiring the objects to be completely bounded by a connected set of surfaces.

Because of philosophical and practical difficulties, the work will only consider how to eliminate ASSEMBLYs whose features are *definitely* unrelated.

Identity Verification

Identity verification is needed because similar models could be invoked and successfully constructed. This suggestive "recognition" is appropriate for artistic vision systems, but inappropriate for precise object recognition, which is the intent of this research.

Verification could be achieved by synthesizing an image from the model and then doing detailed surface comparisons, but this is both computationally expensive and unnecessary. Considering all object features would be ideal for verifying identity. Unfortunately, practicality and finite termination requires using only a limited subset of all possible properties. Verification should be carried out at a conceptual level that is efficacious, representationally appropriate, and efficient. As this research has concentrated on object shape, our verifying properties are based on shape and structural relationships. Further, as the data is already segmented, we will use the segments themselves (as compared to the raw data).

Our segmentation assumptions imply that surface class, curvature parameters and boundary location define the surfaces (though they do not distinguish subtle differences in shape). Comparison requires knowing the surface's three dimensional position and which observed boundaries correspond to model boundaries (as distinct from obscuring or extremal boundaries). However, as position estimates may be slightly erroneous and segmentation boundaries may not be precisely placed (as at curvature discontinuities), detailed boundary and surface comparison is inappropriate.

For ASSEMBLYs, identity is maximally verified if all the predicted visible features are found in the correct places. The subcomponent identities and their relative geometric positions were verified previously by the hypothesis construction process. Hence, to increase our certainty, we must check that their observed interrelationships (e.g. adjacencies, self-occlusions) correspond to those predicted by the model.

The hypothesis construction process understands occlusion and records missing structures whose locations were predicted, but which were declared obscured based on other evidence. Verification of partially obscured structures must show that the remaining visible portions of the object are consistent with what is predicted given the model, its spatial location, the occlusion annotations and the image evidence.

As certainty of identity is impossible, the goal of identity verification is to falsify hypotheses that do not satisfy all identity constraints.

In summary, verification must:

1. consider SURFACEs and ASSEMBLYs,

2. question both existence and identity and

3. verify both shape and configuration.

10.2   Constraining Object Existence and Identity

The input to verification is a fully instantiated object hypothesis.

SURFACEs necessarily exist as they are inputs to recognition, so only ASSEMBLY existence needs to be verified. The goal is to reject hypotheses that are coincidental, which means showing that the surfaces associated with the hypothesis cannot be organized into a solid. Solidity is based on complete connection of all visible surfaces, which requires a topological examination of the evidence.

Identity is based on object-specific properties. The level of detail for most previous three dimensional object recognition systems was superficial and so an object meeting the criteria was identified as far as the computation was concerned, but, unfortunately, not for us as observers. Here, identification is complete to the level of description embodied in the model, so increasing the level of verification entails increasing the level and structure of the evidence. Hence, associated with each model is a set of constraints that the data must satisfy, and any structure that meets these is accepted as a model instance.

The main goal of verification is to reject false hypotheses, and this ultimately requires comparison between the object and model shapes. This can be done efficiently
by comparing the symbolic characterizations of the surfaces (the boundaries, the curvature axes and the curvature magnitudes) and the relationships of these features in
the object reference frame.

Following ACRONYM [BRO81], it seems sensible to specify property requirements
using numerical constraints on the values of an object's properties. Each satisfied
property gives some measure of certainty and together they help ensure correct identification.

10.2.1   SURFACE Verification

Invocation of SURFACEs is largely based on summary characteristics (e.g. areas),
rather than detailed shape. As surface regions are characterized by their boundaries
and internal shapes, verification could then ensure that:

- The observed surface has the same shape as that of the forward-facing portions
  of the oriented model SURFACE.

- The surface image boundaries are the same as those predicted by the oriented
  model.

Several problems complicate this approach: unmodeled extremal boundaries on
curved surfaces, inexact boundary placement at surface curvature discontinuities, and
information lost because of occlusion.

As extremal boundaries are not modeled, they should not be considered, except
perhaps for verifying that the surface has the appropriate curvature directions.

The second problem causes variable sized surface regions and hence makes it difficult to compare surfaces and boundaries exactly. But, some possibilities remain.
In particular, all model boundaries are either orientation or curvature discontinuity
boundaries. The former should remain stable and appear as either predictable shape
segmentation or front-side-obscuring boundaries. Detailed shape analysis may distinguish front-side-obscuring boundaries arising from orientation discontinuities from
extremal boundaries. Curvature discontinuity boundaries should probably be ignored.

Occlusion causes data loss, but is detectable as the back-side-obscuring boundaries
associated with the surface indicate the initial point of occlusion. As the visible data
must be a subset of the predicted data, the back-side-obscuring boundary must be
internal to the predicted surface. Concave boundaries are also ambiguous regarding
surface ordering, so may not be true surface boundaries.

Figure 10.2 illustrates these points, which are summarized as:

[S_1] All data boundaries labeled as front-side-obscuring and surface orientation discontinuity should closely correspond to portions of the boundaries predicted by
the model. The back-side-obscuring and concave boundaries must lie on or be
internal to the predicted region.

[S_2] The data surface should have the same shape as a subset of the oriented model
SURFACE, except where near curvature discontinuities. This entails having similar areas, surface curvatures and axis orientations.

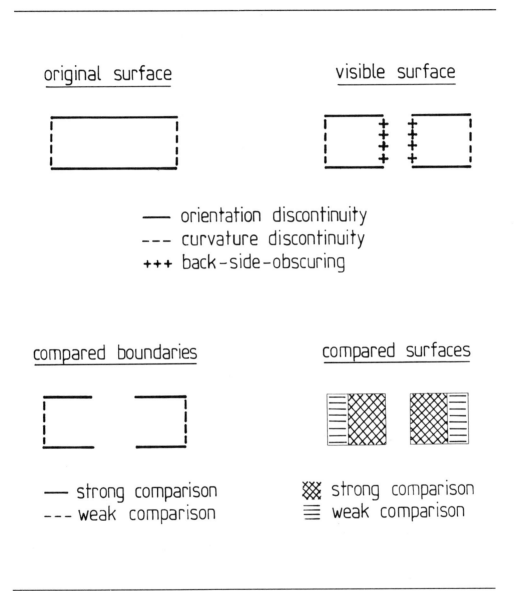

Figure 10.2: Boundary and Surface Comparison

Because of errors in estimating SURFACE reference frames, it was difficult to predict surface orientation and boundary locations accurately enough for direct comparison. As a result, only test S_2 was implemented:

[S_2] Surface Shape Verification Test

Let:

S and $\hat{S}$ be the predicted and observed surface shape class

M and $\hat{M}$ be the predicted and observed major curvatures

m and $\hat{m}$ be the predicted and observed minor curvatures

$\vec{a}$ and $\vec{\hat{a}}$ be the predicted and observed major curvature axes

τ_c, τ_a be thresholds

If:

S is the same as $\hat{S}$,

$\mid M - \hat{M} \mid < \tau_c,$ $(\tau_c = 0.05)$

$\mid m - \hat{m} \mid < \tau_c,$ and

$\mid \vec{a} \circ \vec{\hat{a}} \mid > \tau_a$ $(\tau_a = 0.80)$
(planar surfaces do not use this last test)

Then: the proposed identity of the surface is accepted.

10.2.2 Rigid ASSEMBLY Verification

Rigid ASSEMBLYs should meet both existence and identity requirements.

Most real objects are compact solids and one manifestation of this is connectedness of all object surfaces. Hence, surfaces composing the object must somehow be directly or transitively connected to each other without using unrelated surfaces.

Unfortunately, it is difficult to always determine if two surfaces are directly or indirectly connected. Convex surface orientation discontinuity boundaries definitely mean connectedness, but concave boundaries are ambiguous regarding surface connectivity. Because of self-occlusion, direct connections may not be visible, as when one subcomponent overlaps another. Finally, obscuring objects can prevent observation of adjacency, though surface reconstruction (Chapter 4) eliminates some cases of this. Other cases, like that in Figure 10.3 are not solved by this.

Because of these difficulties, hypotheses will be rejected if it is certain that they cannot be fully connected, i.e., if there are subcomponents between which no connection exists. (Of course, two isolated objects could be connected by hidden structure to

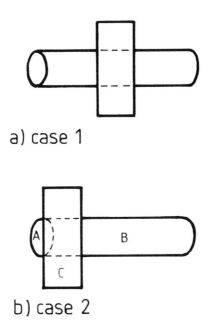

a) case 1

b) case 2

Figure 10.3: Indeterminate Surface Connectivity Behind Obscuring Structure

a common background, but here we assume objects are seen in general position.)
The implemented test is:

[E_1] All Surfaces Must Be Potentially Connecting

Let:
  {D_i} be the subcomponents used in the hypothesis

  $PC(D_a, D_b)$ means that D_a and D_b are potentially directly
      connecting and holds if:

      a) D_a and D_b share any type of boundary or

      b) there is a surface cluster having a front-side-obscuring
          or concave relation to both D_a and D_b

  $TC(D_a, D_b)$ be the transitive closure of $PC(D_a, D_b)$

If:

> for some D_a and D_b, $TC(D_a, D_b)$ does not hold

Then: the hypothesis is incorrectly formed.

This test rejects the false cube seen in Figure 10.1.

For rigid objects, the essence of identity is shape, and surface images make this information directly available. Given the surface image, the observed shape could be compared to that of each object from each viewpoint, but this approach is computationally infeasible. A more parsimonious solution follows, which also considers weak segmentation boundaries and occlusion.

Intuitively, correct object identification is assumed if all the right structures are found in the right places. Given the connectivity guaranteed by the above test, merely having the correct components is likely to be adequate, because the subcomponents of most objects only fit together rigidly and completely in one way (disregarding highly regular objects, like blocks). But, because there are likely to be a few counter-examples, especially with symmetric objects and misidentifications of similar surfaces, geometric, as well as topological, consistency is required. The requirement of consistent reference frames will eliminate many arbitrary groupings (and was demonstrated in the previous chapter).

Surfaces that are connected according to the model should be connected in the scene. This does not always imply adjacency is observable, because object boundaries are not visible from all viewpoints.

Occlusion affects verification because some surfaces may be partially or completely missing or a surface may be broken up by closer surfaces. Moreover, true surface boundaries may be obscured. The remaining true surface boundaries will be connected to back-side-obscuring boundaries in different locations. Since these are not model features, they are ignored.

Based on these ideas, the rigid object identity constraints are:

[R_1] – Each data subcomponent can have at most one visible forward-facing model subcomponent paired with it. (The converse may not hold because of fragmentation or occlusion).

[R_2] – The position of observed subcomponents relative to each other is as predicted for the corresponding model subcomponents.

[R_3] – Model subcomponent adjacency implies data subcomponent adjacency and *vice versa*.

These constraints were implemented as the following tests:

Let:

> $\{F_i\}$ be the visible forward-facing model SURFACEs

> $\{I_i\}$ be the image surfaces

$\vec{P_i}$ and $\vec{P_j}$ be the predicted and observed center-of-mass for
the corresponding model and image surfaces F_i and I_j

$\vec{N_i}$ and $\vec{N_j}$ be the predicted and observed surface orientations
at the centers-of-mass for the corresponding
model and image surfaces F_i and I_j

τ_t and τ_r be thresholds

Then:

$[R_1]$ For each I_i there is at most one corresponding F_j.

$[R_2]$ For each corresponding I_i and F_j:

$$| \vec{P_i} - \vec{P_j} | < \tau_t \qquad (\tau_t = 20.0)$$

$$| \vec{N_i} \circ \vec{N_j} | > \tau_r \qquad (\tau_r = 0.8)$$

$[R_3]$ Let:

I_a, I_b be two non-tangential data surfaces
F_a, F_b be the corresponding model SURFACEs

If:

F_a and F_b are observably adjacent, I_a and I_b are not
observably adjacent, and there is no surface cluster
partially obscuring both I_a and I_b,

or

F_a and F_b are not observably adjacent and I_a and I_b
are observably adjacent

Then: the hypothesis is incorrectly formed

Occlusion also has distinctive characteristics, and thus the hypothesis that an object is partially or fully obscured should be subject to some verification. Back-side-obscuring boundaries usually signal this occurrence, though not always. When a curved surface goes from facing the viewer to facing away, self-occlusion occurs without back-side-obscuring boundaries. When back-side-obscuring boundaries are present, though, three new constraints can be added:

$[O_1]$ – the back-side-obscuring boundary should lie inside the image region predicted for the SURFACE. Alternatively, the predicted image boundary should lie on or outside the observed image region. Figure 10.4 illustrates this.

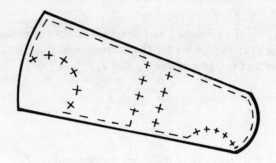

— predicted model boundary
- - - observed true data boundary
+ + + observed back-side-obscuring boundary

Figure 10.4: Occlusion Boundaries Lie Inside Predicted Model Boundaries

$[O_2]$ – Back-side-obscuring boundary segments that bound the surface image region must end as the crossbar of a "TEE" junction. This implies that there must be at least three image regions at the junction. Figure 10.5 illustrates this.

$[O_3]$ – A non-tangential image surface should be predicted as partially self-obscured during visibility analysis (Chapter 9) if and only if the corresponding data surface has at least one back-side-obscuring boundary whose closer surface is also an object surface.

Constraint O_1 was not applied because parameter estimation errors made it difficult to check this condition reliably (e.g. predicted model and data surfaces did not overlap adequately). Constraint O_2 was guaranteed assuming image labeling was correct, which was the case here.

Because of parameter estimation errors, it is likely that there are self-occlusions predicted during raycasting that are not observed (because of surfaces becoming slightly obscured). Hence, the test of verifying predicted self-occlusions was not performed. While it is also possible for slightly obscured data surfaces to be predicted as not obscured, if a self-occlusion was significant enough to be observed, then prediction was likely to show it even with parameter estimation errors. Hence, only the reverse test was implemented:

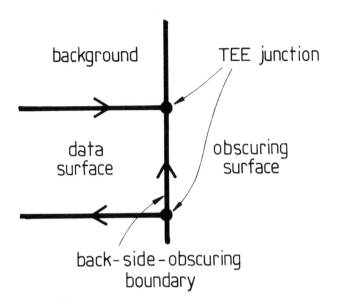

Figure 10.5: Occlusion Boundaries End on TEEs at Surfaces

[O_3] Observed Self-obscured SURFACEs Are Predicted

Let:

    $\{D_i\}$ be the non-tangential partially obscured data surfaces

    $\{C_{ij}\}$ be the closer data surfaces across obscuring
        boundaries around D_i

    S_i be the model SURFACE corresponding to D_i

    $\{M_k\}$ be the other model SURFACEs

    front(X, Y) holds if model SURFACE X is directly or indirectly in
        front of Y. This is found by raycasting and taking the
        transitive closure.

If:

> For each D_i and each C_{ij}
>> If there is a M_k corresponding to C_{ij},
>>> then front(M_k, S_i)

Then: the self-occlusion is as predicted by the model.

One application of O_3 was particularly significant. The robot upper and lower arms are nearly symmetric, so there are two values for the upperarm position and joint angle where the lowerarm can be nearly in the position shown in the test scene. The difference between the two cases is whether the lowerarm is in front of or behind the upperarm. Though the depths of the component reference frames are different in the two cases, parameter tolerances did not completely reject the second alternative. Happily, test O_3 did discriminate.

10.2.3 Non-rigidly Connected Object Verification

Non-rigidly connected object verification is trivial in comparison to the previous structures. By virtue of the hypothesis construction process, all subcomponents have been previously verified. Further, because of the coordinate frame matching process, the reference frames of the subcomponents must have the appropriate alignment relationships with the whole ASSEMBLY. Occlusion relationships were verified by the test O_3 given above. What remains is to verify that the variable joint parameters meet any given constraints. These are constrained using the general method given in the next subsection.

10.2.4 Numerical Constraint Evaluation

Many numerical values are associated with hypotheses. The most important of these are the property values described in Chapter 6, but there could also be other values such as the object position or joint angles. Constraints can be specified on these values and they must hold for the verification to succeed.

The constraints were mainly used for eliminating spurious SURFACE hypotheses and usually tested absolute surface area.

The constraints are specified as part of the model definition process, as a set of statements of the form:

$$\text{CONSTRAINT} < name > < constraint >$$

The $< constraint >$ must apply in the context of structure $< name >$. Here:

$$
\begin{aligned}
< constraint > \; ::= \; & < pconstraint > \\
& | < constraint > \text{ AND } < constraint > \\
& | < constraint > \text{ OR } < constraint > \\
& | (< constraint >)
\end{aligned}
$$

$< pconstraint > ::= < value >< relation >< number >$

$< relation > ::= <|>|=|<=|>=| !=$

$< value > ::= < variable >|< property >(< name >)$

The $< value >$ refers to a variable or a property (possibly of a substructure) in the context of the structure being constrained. Other constraint expressions could have been easily added. The verification of these constraints is trivial.

An example of such a constraint for the elbow joint angle jnt3 in the robot armasm ASSEMBLY is:

CONSTRAINT armasm (jnt3 < 2.5) OR (jnt3 > 3.78);

which constrains the joint angle to 0.0 – 2.5 or 3.78 – 6.28. Another constraint is:

CONSTRAINT uside ABSSIZE(uside) < 1900.0

which constrains the absolute surface area of uside to be less than 1900 square centimeters. The choice of the verification bounds is up to the modeler.

10.3 Verification Performance and Discussion

The goals of verification are:

1. no true hypotheses are rejected, and

2. among false hypotheses, only low level (e.g. SURFACEs), symmetric or ambiguous hypotheses are accepted.

However, as tolerances are needed to allow for segmentation variations, position parameter misestimation, and obscured surface reconstruction, some invalid verifications are expected. Some invalid SURFACEs are verified because of variability in surface shape matching and having no other constraints on their identity at this point. The effect of these hypotheses is reduced performance rates and increased chances of invocation of higher level false objects. However, verified higher false hypotheses are not likely to occur as the surfaces must then meet grouping, relative orientation and location constraints in hypothesis construction, and the verification constraints discussed in this chapter.

Table 10.1 summarizes the causes for rejection of SURFACE hypotheses, and Table 10.2 summarizes the causes for rejection of ASSEMBLY hypotheses. The tables record the rejection criterion as given in Section 10.2, except for those designated by "N", which means rejection by a modeled numerical constraint (Section 10.2.4), by "H", which means failure to establish a reference frame (Chapter 9), or by "A" which means all slots that should have been filled were not.

Some rejected curved SURFACE hypotheses had the correct identity but an inconsistent reference frame. Some false ASSEMBLY hypotheses were rejected in hypothesis

Table 10.1: SURFACE Hypothesis Rejection Summary

SURFACE	IMAGE REGIONS	REJECTION RULE	INSTANCES
uedgeb	19,22	N	2
lsidea	19,22	N	1
lsideb	19,22	N	1
robbodyside	9	N	4
robbodyside	8	S_2	2
robshould1	12	S_2	1
robshould2	12	S_2	1
robshoulds	27	S_2	2
tcaninf	9	S_2	2

Table 10.2: ASSEMBLY Hypothesis Rejection Summary

ASSEMBLY	IMAGE REGIONS	REJECTION RULE	INSTANCES	NOTE
lowerarm	12,18,31	H	30	
lowerarm	17,19,22, 25,32	A	1	
lowerarm	17,19,22, 25,32	H	1	
upperarm	17,19,22, 25,32	H	6	
armasm	12,17,18, 19,22,25 31,32	R_3	2	
armasm	12,17,18, 19,22,25 31,32	O_3	1	
robshldbd	16,26	H	3	
robshldsobj	29	H	1	*1
robbody	all appt.	H	3	*1
robot	all appt.	H	5	

*1 – valid hypothesis rejection because of geometric reasoning error

Table 10.3: Incorrectly Verified Hypotheses Analyzed

MODEL USED	TRUE MODEL	IMAGE REGIONS	NOTE
uside	uside	19,22	*3
uends	uends	25	*2
lsidea	lsideb	12	*1
lsideb	lsideb	12	*2
ledgea	ledgea	18	*2
ledgeb	ledgea	18	*1
lendb	lendb	25	*2
robbodyside	robbodyside	8	*2
robshould1	robshould2	16	*1
robshould2	robshould2	16	*2
lowerarm	lowerarm	12,18,31	*2
upperarm	upperarm	17,19,22, 25,32	*2
robbody	robbody	8	*2
trashcan	trashcan	9,28,38	*2

*1 – true model similar to invoked model
*2 – symmetric model gives match with another reference frame
*3 – error because substantially obscured

construction because no consistent reference frame could be found for them. These hypotheses are included in the analysis of rejected hypotheses given below.

Table 10.3 lists and analyzes all remaining verified hypotheses that were not "correct". The most common causes of incorrectly verified hypotheses were symmetric models, leading to multiple reference frames, and nearly identical models. The incorrect models normally were not used in larger ASSEMBLYs, because of reference frame inconsistencies.

These results show that verification worked well. Two true ASSEMBLY hypotheses were rejected because of deficiencies in geometric reasoning. All verified false hypotheses were reasonable, usually arising from either a similar or symmetric object model. Most rejected SURFACE hypotheses failed the value constraint (usually surface area – see Appendix A). Curved SURFACEs were rejected when their curvature axis was inconsistent with other orientation estimates. Most ASSEMBLYs were rejected because no consistent reference frame could be found. (Many of these hypotheses arose because hypothesis construction has a combinatorial aspect during initial hypothesis construction.)

10.4   Related Work

Historically, verification has meant several different things in the context of vision. The fundamental notion is that of confirming the existence of an oriented object, but this is often reduced to merely confirming the presence of a few object features.

Typical verification methods predict image features (e.g. lines) given the model and current state of analysis, which then strengthen or weaken the hypothesis according to the presence or absence of confirming evidence (e.g. [FAL72]). Additionally, the discrepancy between the observed and predicted position can be used to refine the position estimates [YIN84].

The best verification work has been applied in the context of two dimensional industrial scenes, as in parts location systems (e.g. [BOL80], [LUX83]). Object silhouettes are most often used, because they make the object contours explicit; however, edge detected grey level images also produce similar information. The most common verification feature is the edge, and usually just the straight edge is used, though small slots and holes at given distances from test features have also been used [BOL80]. The main advantages of these features are that their shape, location and orientation are easy to predict. Prediction also allows more sensitive edge detection ([SHI75], [YAC79]), when searching for confirming evidence.

In two dimensional scenes, overlapping parts weaken the utility of contours, because only part of each object's outline is visible, and it is also joined with those of the other objects in the pile. Since most two dimensional recognition systems are dependent on contours, this produces a serious loss of information. Yin [YIN81] hypothesized objects based on visible corners and linear features and verified them by ensuring that all unlocated corners were within the contours of the collected mass.

Verification in three dimensional scenes has not received much attention. Some work similar to the two dimensional line verification has been done in the context of three dimensional blocks world scenes by Falk [FAL72] and Shirai [SHI75]. ACRONYM's [BRO81] prediction graph informed on the observable features, their appearance and their interrelationships in the context of more complicated objects (e.g. wide-bodied airplanes). Hogg [HOG84] verified three dimensional generalized cylinder model positions by counting oriented edge points within image boxes. The boxes were predicted using the projected outlines of generalized cylinders.

Occlusion is an even greater problem in three dimensions, as scenes have natural depth and hence objects will often self-obscure as well as obscure each other. Brooks [BRO81] suggested that a model-based geometric reasoning vision system could predict what features will be self-obscured from a given viewpoint. In the context of the blocks world scene analysis, occlusion hypotheses were verified by detecting single TEE junctions to signal the start of occlusion (e.g. [WAL75]) and pairs of TEEs indicated which edges should be associated (e.g. [GUZ67]).

10.5   Discussion

The most important deficiency of verification is its approach to identity. For verification, objects are probably more suitably represented by listing desirable and undesirable properties, rather than an exact geometric model, especially as verification thoroughness is probably proportional to the individuality of the object and the degree of generic identification desired. Human faces need detailed shape comparisons for precise identification, but just to say it was human requires less. On the other hand, chairs have a tremendous variety of shapes, but there is no prototype chair model, even given division into functional groupings. If the only common factors were support for back and seat at given heights, sizes and orientations, then a pile of boxes would also be satisfactory, and this may not always be an appropriate identification.

One key benefit of the approach described in this chapter is that the specific verification criteria are linked to the geometric model, which promotes more general applicability.

There is some overlap between the functions of hypothesis construction (Chapter 9) and verification. The construction and verification sequence follows the classical Artificial Intelligence "generate and test" paradigm. The goal of the construction process is to: (1) find evidence for all model features and (2) assign a reference frame. To prevent (1) from causing a combinatorial explosion, some constraints were applied when searching for image evidence. On the other hand, verification ensures that the whole object satisfies all constraints, including some previously applied. Hence, there could be some shifting of constraint analysis to verification, particularly if hypothesis construction and verification became more of a parallel process (i.e. akin to a Waltz filtering process [WAL75]).

Verification of partially obscured or partially back-facing SURFACEs is weak. For these SURFACEs, only individual summary characteristics were checked, leaving other tests until the SURFACE was combined with others in an ASSEMBLY. More detailed symbolic comparisons could be made, as in Figure 10.6. Here, a square is somewhat obscured. Verification could easily show that it was not a circle, and that it is likely to be a square, by comparing descriptions of the boundary. This technique could also be used for the full and partial boundary comparisons, as proposed above, because comparing symbolic descriptions is faster and easier than creating the predicted boundary path.

More practical constraints will be needed for richer object domains, particularly for natural objects, where within-class variation presents problems. This is apparent with faces, whose shape changes between people and expressions. This research allowed some variation by using only approximate curvature and position in constraints (S_2 and R_2), but this is weak and may not generalize properly. Further, flexible surfaces will also have variable segmentation, which will lead to difficulties with constraints based on curvature or correspondence.

Final Comments

To summarize, this chapter extended verification to cover fully visible and partially obscured SURFACEs and ASSEMBLYs in three dimensional scenes. This required understanding how object location, external occlusion and self-occlusion affect appearance. Constraints that helped guarantee the existence and identity of the modeled objects were formulated and demonstrated.

Figure 10.6: Partially Obscured Square Verification

CHAPTER 11

Discussion and Conclusions

This book has described an Artificial Intelligence approach to the problem of three dimensional object recognition, based on methods that lead to general purpose vision systems rather than to limited single application systems. While efficiency is ultimately important, competence must come first. Only a few researchers have used $2\frac{1}{2}$D sketch-like surface data, and the work described here has attempted to explore the whole path from surfaces to objects. The structure of the approach mirrors classical edge-based recognition processes, but the use of surface data required new definitions of the processes and their interconnections.

Some of the interesting aspects of the individual recognition processes were:

1. object modeling

   - a surface modeling method based on distinct curvature class patches.
   - criteria for how to group model SURFACEs into ASSEMBLYs.

2. surface data

   - proposed criteria for segmentation of surface image data into surface patches useful for object recognition.

3. surface hypothesizing

   - analysis of surface occlusion cases to show what cases occur, how to detect them and how to hypothetically reconstruct the missing data. Because the research used three dimensional surface image data, the reconstruction is more robust than that based on only two dimensional image data.

4. surface cluster formation

   - the use of the surface cluster as an intermediate representation between the surface image and the object hypotheses.
   - rules for aggregating the surface patches into the surface clusters corresponding to distinct objects.

251

5. description

- a collection of data description modules that exploited the three dimensional character of the raw data.

6. model invocation

- a network formulation that incorporated both image property evidence and relationship evidence from class and structural associations. The formulation was incremental, used operations that were based on general reasoning rather than strictly visual requirements and supported a low-level, object independent generic vocabulary.

7. hypothesis construction

- new methods for estimating the three dimensional placement of objects from data associated with surface patches and the intersurface relationships specified by the object model.
- methods for predicting and verifying the visibility of SURFACEs, including back-facing, tangential and partially or fully self-obscured front-facing structure.
- rules for explaining missing structure as instances of occlusion by external, unrelated structure.
- methods for joining non-rigidly connected structures and simultaneously estimating the connection degrees-of-freedom.
- methods for completely instantiating hypotheses for both solid and laminar structures.

8. verification

- criteria for verifying the physical existence of a hypothesis.
- criteria for verifying the identity of an object based on surface evidence.

The research also emphasized the strong distinction between, but equally strong dependence on, the suggestive "seeing" of model invocation and the model-directed hypothesis construction and verification. Finally, the effect of occlusion was considered throughout the visual process, and methods were developed that helped overcome data loss at each stage.

When applying the recognition processes described in this book to the (hand) segmented range image shown in Figure 3.10, the **IMAGINE I** system correctly recognized all modeled objects in the test scene (the robot and trash can, and their subcomponents). No misidentifications of solids occurred, though several individual surfaces were misidentified. Since the model base included 16 ASSEMBLYs, all of about the same size, including several objects not in this scene (a chair and its subcomponents), this was a good result. The original geometric reasoning module gave decent, but not ideal position and joint angle estimation (seen in Figure 9.16) and a new network-based geometric reasoning method improved on this (see Figure 1.11).

Three test scenes were analyzed. The one used in this book was the most interesting, because it contained articulated objects with some curved surfaces, laminar
surfaced objects, partially constrained degrees-of-freedom (joints) and considerable
self-occlusion.

The success of the recognition process was largely because of the richness of the $2\frac{1}{2}$D
sketch data, but the use of the surface-based hierarchical models, shape segmented
surface patches and hierarchical surface cluster data representation made the results
easier to obtain.

This recognition process was clearly successful on the test image. However, much
research is still needed, and the following section tries to make explicit some of the
problems that remain. I welcome others to add to the list and to solve them all.

11.1 Summary of Outstanding Problems

Input Data

The data used in this research were unrealistic in several respects. Because the depth
and orientation values and the segmentation boundaries were hand-derived, they had
few of the errors likely to be present in real data. The segmentations also made nearly
perfect correspondence with the models, and thus ignored problems of data variation
and scale. Data variations, particularly for objects with curved surfaces, cause shape
segmentation boundaries to shift. Further, as the analytic scale changes, segmentation
boundaries also move, and segments may appear or disappear.

Object Modeling

The object representation was too literal and should not always be based on exact
sizes and feature placement. The object surfaces could be more notional, designating
surface class, curvature, orientation and placement and largely ignore extent. Object
representation could also have a more conceptual character that emphasizes key distinguishing features and rough geometric placement, without a literal CAD-like model
(as used here). Finally, the models could allow alternative, overlapping representations,
such as having two surfaces used individually and as part of a connecting orientation
discontinuity.

As data occurs at unpredictable scales, the models might record the features at a variety of scales. The models should also include other data elements such as references to
solids (e.g. generalized cylinders), reflectance, surface shape texture and distinguished
axes (e.g. symmetry and elongation), etc. The representation could have used a more
constraint-like formulation, as in ACRONYM [BRO81], which would allow inequality
relationships among features, and also allow easier use of model variables. Many of
these inadequacies were subsequently overcome in the SMS representation approach
[FIS87a] described in Chapter 7.

Surface Reconstruction

An open question about the surface reconstruction process is whether to replace the
representation of two partially obscured surfaces by a single merged surface (as was

done) or to keep both alternatives. Keeping the extra hypotheses causes redundant processing and may lead to duplicated invocation and hypothesis construction, but allows correct processing if the merging was inappropriate. Keeping only the merged surface may cause invocation and matching failures, or require a more intelligent hypothesis construction process that uses the model to decide if the two surfaces were incorrectly merged.

Surface Cluster Formation

The surface cluster formation process has a similar problem. When one surface cluster overlaps another, then a third surface cluster merging the two is created as well. This was to provide a context within which all components of a self-obscured object would appear. The problem is how to control the surface cluster merging process when multiple surface clusters overlap (as is likely in a real scene), which causes a combinatorial growth of surface clusters.

Data Description

While shape is very informative, many additional description types could be added to help characterize objects: reflectance and shape texture (both random and patterned), reflectance itself, translucency, surface finish, etc.

Model Invocation

Invocation evaluated a copy of the network in every image context. This is computationally expensive, considering the likely number of contexts (e.g. 100) and the number of models (e.g. 50,000) in a realistic scene. Parallel processing may completely eliminate the computational problem, but there remains the problem of investigating just the relevant contexts. There should probably be a partitioning of the models according to the size of the context, and also some attention focusing mechanism should limit the context within which invocation takes place. This mechanism might apply a rough high-level description of the entire scene and then a coarse-to-fine scale analysis focusing attention to particular regions of interest.

Redundant processing might arise because an object will invoke all of its generalizations. The invocations are correct, but the duplication of effort seems wasteful when a direct method could then pursue models up and down the generalization hierarchy.

As currently formulated, the invocation network must be created symbolically for each new scene analyzed, as a function of the scene, model base and evidence computations. It would be interesting to investigate how the network might re-organize itself as the image changed, maintaining the fixed model dependent relationships, but varying the image dependent ones.

The variety of objects in the natural word suggests that there may not be a "rich" description hierarchy, nor a deep subcomponent hierarchy for most objects, nor a general subclass hierarchy. Though these factors contribute substantially, it appears that there are relatively few object types in our everyday experience. Instead, there are many individuals and considerable variation between individuals. Thus, the most important aspect of object representation may be the direct property and primitive description evidences, which would then differentiate individuals.

Hypothesis Construction

The major criticism of the hypothesis construction process is its literality. In particular, it tried to find evidence for all features, which is probably neither fully necessary, nor always possible.

Literality also appeared in the dependence on the metrical relationships in the geometric model (e.g. the surface sizes and boundary placements). These were used for predicting self-occlusion and for spatially registering the object. While these tasks are important, and are part of a general vision system, they should have a more conceptual and less analytic formulation. This would provide a stronger symbolic aspect to the computation and should also make the process more capable of handling imperfect or generic objects.

The Recognition Approach as a Whole

One significant limitation of the recognition approach is the absence of scale analysis. Objects should have different conceptual descriptions according to the relevance of a feature at a given scale, and recognition then has to match data within a scale-dependent range of models.

A more relational formulation would help, but there does not seem to be a matching method that neatly combines the tidiness and theoretical strengths of graph matching with the efficiency and prediction capability of model-based geometric matching.

The proposed recognition model ignored the question of when enough evidence was accumulated. Recognition need not require complete evidence or satisfaction of all constraints, provided none actually fail, and the few observed features are adequate for unique identification in a particular context. However, the implementation here plodded along trying to find as much evidence as possible. An object should be recognizable using a minimal set of discriminating features and, provided the set of descriptions is powerful enough to discriminate in a large domain, the recognition process will avoid excessive simplification. Recognition (here) has no concept of context, and so cannot make these simplifications. On the other hand, the additional evidence provides the redundancy needed to overcome data and segmentation errors.

The evaluation on hand-collected and segmented data did not adequately test the methods, but research using this approach is continuing and some simpler genuine range data scenes have been successfully analyzed.

11.2   The IMAGINE II System

Experience with the **IMAGINE I** program has led to a redesign embodied in the **IMAGINE II** system. Though the re-implementation is not complete, the design of the system and its key representations and processes are summarized here. Figure 11.1 shows a block diagram of the main modules of the **IMAGINE II** system. The system is intended to interpret data deriving from scenes containing self and externally obscured complex, non-polyhedral man-made objects including possible degrees-of-freedom (e.g. robot joints).

As in **IMAGINE I**, data comes from a segmented $2\frac{1}{2}$D sketch, except that curve and volumetric scene features may be part of the input, too. The data may be fragmented or incomplete. The input data structure is a REV (Region, Edge, Vertex) graph. The system output is, as before, a list of object hypotheses with position and parameter estimates and a set of image evidence and justifications supporting the object hypothesis.

Building the VSCP Structure

The first new representation is the VSCP structure (Volume, Surface, Curve, Point), which is constructed from the REV by knowledge-based structure completion processes. The goal of this process is to group curve and surface features from the REV to overcome fragmentation and occlusion effects and to remove non-structural artifacts (e.g. reflectance edges). The original raw data might be interrogated to help verify deductions.

An example of an occlusion rule is:

- If two valid TEE junctions lying on the boundary of the same surface can be extended (using the local boundary shape) until they intersect, and the curve extensions lie behind closer surfaces, then hypothesize that the original shape of the partially obscured surface is that of the extended surface.

An example of a fragmentation rule is:

- If two surface patches are "adjacent", have similar shape, depth and orientation and there are not intervening space curves (e.g. from patch edges or closer surfaces), then merge the two patches.

Here "adjacent" is a heuristic concept because the surface characterization is assumed to be neither complete nor dense (i.e. there may be missing surfaces and there might be substantial gaps between nearby patches).

Building the Contexts Structure

Invocation and matching occur in data contexts, only now contexts exist for curves and volumes as well as surfaces and surface clusters. Contexts improve matching efficiency by grouping related data and thereby isolating irrelevant data, and create a structure that can accumulate plausibility for model invocation.

The context structures are hierarchical in that contexts can be grouped to form larger contexts. Contexts are designed to support recognition of curves, surfaces, volumes and larger groupings of features. For example, the information contained in a surface context might link to both curve fragments and surface patches, because either might help define a complete surface.

Examples of context-forming rules are:

- If a set of adjacent surface patches are completely isolated by depth discontinuity boundaries and there are no such boundaries internal to the group, then these surfaces form a context for recognizing an ASSEMBLY.

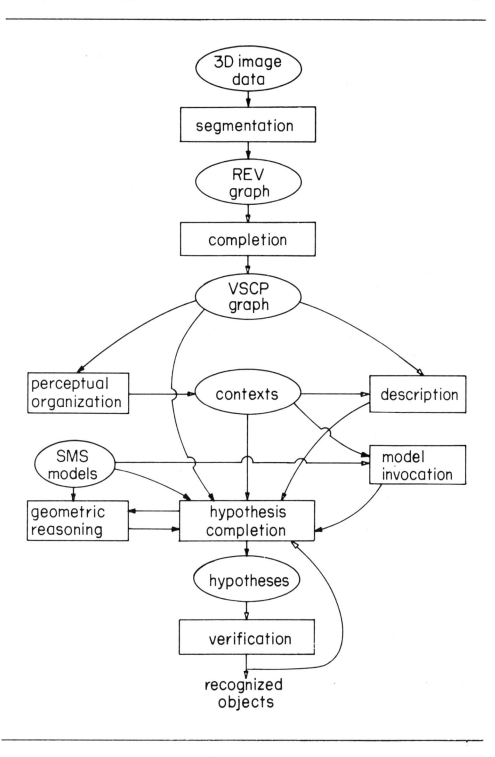

Figure 11.1: IMAGINE II Modules and Data Structures

- If a set of space curves roughly surrounds a region of two dimensional image space and the curves are not radically different in depth, then hypothesize that a surface context lies within the curves.

Structure Description

Model invocation and hypothesis construction require property estimates for image features, and because we are using 2 1/2D sketch data, three dimensional properties can be directly measured. These properties are similar to those used for **IMAGINE I** (Chapter 6), and include:

- curve fragment properties: length, curvature, ...

- surface fragment properties: area, curvature, elongation, ...

- curve fragment pairs: relative orientation, relative size, ...

- surface fragment pairs: relative orientation, relative size, ...

Model Invocation

Model invocation is nearly the same as in **IMAGINE I** (Chapter 8). A network implements the computation in a manner suitable for parallel evaluation. Nodes represent the pairing between individual model and data features, and are connected to other nodes according to the type of relation. Relations include: structural (e.g. "subcomponent of"), generic (e.g. "visual specialization of"), class (e.g. "non-visual specialization of"), inhibiting and general association. Direct evidence comes from a measure of the fit between data and model properties.

Object Models

The SMS models are used, as described in Chapter 7. They are primarily structural with model primitives designed to match with either curve, surface or volumetric data as alternatives. The models are hierarchical, building larger models from previously defined substructures. All model dimensions and reference frame transformations may involve variables and expressions, and algebraic constraints can bound the range of the variables.

The models have viewpoint dependent feature groups, which record the fundamentally distinct viewpoints of the object. They also identify (1) model features visible from the viewpoint and (2) new viewpoint dependent features (such as occlusion relationships, TEE junctions or extremal boundaries).

Hypothesis Construction

Initial selection of the model may come bottom-up from invocation or top-down as part of another hypothesis being constructed. Hypothesis construction then attempts to find evidence for all model features.

Feature visibility information comes from a viewpoint dependent feature group, which is selected according to the estimated orientation of the object.

Construction is largely hierarchical, grouping recognized subcomponents to form larger hypotheses. The most primitive features are designed to be recognized using either curve, surface or volumetric data, depending on what is available. At all stages, geometric consistency is required, which also results in more precise position estimates and estimates for embedded variables (such as a variable rotation angle about an axis).

Construction is a heuristic process whereby various approaches are tried to find evidence for a feature. For example, some heuristics for surface finding are:

1. Use an image patch if it has the predicted position, orientation, shape and size.

2. Use a smaller image patch if it has the predicted position, orientation and shape and no patch of the correct size is found (i.e. accept fragmented patches).

3. Do not look for the surface if it is small and far away.

Application of the heuristics is controlled through routines that know what approaches are available for finding features (and when to try them) and has somewhat of an "expert system" character.

Geometric Reasoning

The network-based geometric reasoning was described in Section 9.2.4. The geometric relationships between model features, model and data pairings and *a priori* scene knowledge are represented algebraically and are implemented as networks expressing the computational relationships between the variables.

Analysis of the types of geometric relationships occurring in scene analysis showed that most relationships could be expressed using only a small set of standard relationships (e.g. "a model point is paired with a data point"). The standard relationships are then be used to create standard network modules, which are allocated and connected as model matching produces new model-to-data pairings.

Agenda Management

To facilitate experimentation with different control regimes, the hypothesis construction processes are activated from a priority-ordered agenda. The processes take inputs from and return results to a global blackboard. An agenda item embodies a request for applying a specified hypothesis construction process on a given datum or hypothesis. The activated process may then enter other requests into the agenda. We use the agenda to implement a mixed control regime involving both top-down and bottom-up hypothesis construction.

Hypothesis Verification

Because data can be fragmented or erroneous, object hypotheses may be incomplete. Further, spurious hypotheses may be created from coincidental alignments between scene features. Hypothesis construction and geometric reasoning eliminate some spurious hypotheses, but other instances of global inconsistency may remain.

This module considers two problems: (1) global consistency of evidence (e.g. connectedness and proper depth ordering of all components) and (2) heuristic criteria for when to accept incomplete models.

11.3   Conclusion

This concludes our description of the **IMAGINE I** vision system. Starting from surface depth and orientation information for the visible surfaces in the scene, it could:

- produce an identity-independent segmentation of the objects in the scene,

- describe their three dimensional properties,

- select models to explain the image data,

- methodically pair the data to model features (while extracting the object's spatial position and explaining missing features arising from occlusion or object position) and

- verify the existence and identity of the instantiated hypotheses

for non-polyhedral solids, laminar structures and non-rigidly connected structures, without sacrificing a detailed understanding of the objects or their relationships to the scene.

Three dimensional object recognition is obviously a complex problem, and this research has attempted to address many issues. A skeletal exploration seemed appropriate because the use of surface data for recognition was and still is relatively untried. Thus, examining the whole problem exposed many areas for future research, some of which are being investigated as **IMAGINE II** is being developed. Consequently, the results presented have not solved the problem of three dimensional scene understanding, but they are a few more steps on the way.

APPENDIX A

A Portion of the Model Base

The following is an annotated portion of the full model used for the recognitions. Because the full model base is somewhat tedious, only the portion related to the robot is reproduced here. Chapter 7 describes the geometric model and other descriptions in more detail, and Chapter 8 describes the model invocation definitions. The full model contains about 900 lines for 25 specific surface models, 22 generic surface types, and 16 solid object models.

The model file starts with a declaration of the model names and types. The specific surfaces come first:

```
TITLE = "combined model file";
SRFTYPE uside;
SRFTYPE uedges;
SRFTYPE uedgeb;
SRFTYPE uends;
SRFTYPE uendb;
SRFTYPE lsidea;
SRFTYPE lsideb;
SRFTYPE ledgea;
SRFTYPE ledgeb;
SRFTYPE lendb;
SRFTYPE handend;
SRFTYPE handsidel;
SRFTYPE handsides;
SRFTYPE robbodyside;
SRFTYPE robshould1;
SRFTYPE robshould2;
SRFTYPE robshldend;
SRFTYPE robshoulds;
```

The declaration of the generic surfaces:

```
GSRFTYPE quad;
GSRFTYPE trapezium;
```

```
GSRFTYPE llgram;
GSRFTYPE rectangle;
GSRFTYPE circle;
GSRFTYPE plane;
GSRFTYPE cylpatch;
GSRFTYPE torus;
GSRFTYPE cylinder;
GSRFTYPE lside;
GSRFTYPE ledge;
GSRFTYPE robshouldg;
GSRFTYPE sapiby2a;
GSRFTYPE sapiby2b;
GSRFTYPE sapiby2c;
GSRFTYPE sapia;
GSRFTYPE sapib;
GSRFTYPE sa3piby2;
GSRFTYPE sapiby2andpi;
```

The declaration of the solid assemblies:

```
OBJTYPE hand;
OBJTYPE lowerarm;
OBJTYPE upperarm;
OBJTYPE armasm;
OBJTYPE robshldbd;
OBJTYPE robshldsobj;
OBJTYPE robshould;
OBJTYPE link;
OBJTYPE robbody;
OBJTYPE robot;
```

The variables used for joints:

```
VARTYPE jnt1 DEFAULT 0.0;
VARTYPE jnt2 DEFAULT 0.0;
VARTYPE jnt3 DEFAULT 0.0;
ENDDEC
```

After the declarations comes a listing of the interobject relationships, as needed for model invocation. The first listed are the description relationships:

```
DESCRIPTION OF uedges IS rectangle 1.0;
DESCRIPTION OF uedgeb IS rectangle 1.0;
DESCRIPTION OF uside IS plane 2.0;
```

```
DESCRIPTION OF quad IS plane 1.0;
DESCRIPTION OF trapezium IS quad 2.0;
DESCRIPTION OF llgram IS trapezium 2.0;
DESCRIPTION OF rectangle IS llgram 2.5;
DESCRIPTION OF lside IS plane 3.0;
DESCRIPTION OF robshouldg IS cylinder 2.0;
DESCRIPTION OF lendb IS cylinder 2.0;
DESCRIPTION OF ledgea IS ledge 5.0;
DESCRIPTION OF ledgeb IS ledge 5.0;
DESCRIPTION OF ledge IS rectangle 1.0;
DESCRIPTION OF robshldend IS circle 3.0;
DESCRIPTION OF circle IS plane 1.0;
DESCRIPTION OF handsidel IS plane 1.0;
DESCRIPTION OF handsides IS rectangle 1.0;
DESCRIPTION OF robbodyside IS cylinder 2.0;
DESCRIPTION OF lsidea IS lside 5.5;
DESCRIPTION OF lsideb IS lside 5.5;
DESCRIPTION OF robshould1 IS robshouldg 7.0;
DESCRIPTION OF robshould2 IS robshouldg 7.0;
DESCRIPTION OF uside IS sapiby2b 2.0;
DESCRIPTION OF uends IS sapiby2c 1.0;
DESCRIPTION OF uendb IS sapiby2a 1.0;
DESCRIPTION OF lside IS sapiby2b 1.0;
DESCRIPTION OF lendb IS sapiby2c 1.0;
DESCRIPTION OF ledge IS sapiby2c 1.0;
DESCRIPTION OF handsides IS sapiby2andpi 1.0;
DESCRIPTION OF handsidel IS sapiby2andpi 1.0;
DESCRIPTION OF handend IS sapiby2andpi 1.0;
DESCRIPTION OF robshldend IS sapiby2b 1.0;
DESCRIPTION OF robshouldg IS sapiby2a 0.5;
DESCRIPTION OF robshoulds IS sapib 0.5;
DESCRIPTION OF cylinder IS cylpatch 2.0;
DESCRIPTION OF uendb IS cylinder 2.0;
DESCRIPTION OF uends IS cylinder 2.0;
```

The subcomponent relationships:

```
SUBCOMPONENT OF hand IS handend 0.90;
SUBCOMPONENT OF hand IS handsidel 0.90;
SUBCOMPONENT OF hand IS handsides 0.90;
SUBCOMPONENT OF link IS robshould 1.00;
SUBCOMPONENT OF link IS armasm 1.00;
SUBCOMPONENT OF lowerarm IS hand 0.90;
SUBCOMPONENT OF lowerarm IS ledgea 0.90;
SUBCOMPONENT OF lowerarm IS ledgeb 0.90;
SUBCOMPONENT OF lowerarm IS lendb 0.90;
```

```
SUBCOMPONENT OF lowerarm IS lsidea 0.90;
SUBCOMPONENT OF lowerarm IS lsideb 0.90;
SUBCOMPONENT OF robbody IS robbodyside 0.90;
SUBCOMPONENT OF robot IS link 1.00;
SUBCOMPONENT OF robot IS robbody 1.00;
SUBCOMPONENT OF robshldbd IS robshldend 0.90;
SUBCOMPONENT OF robshldbd IS robshould1 0.90;
SUBCOMPONENT OF robshldbd IS robshould2 0.90;
SUBCOMPONENT OF robshldsobj IS robshoulds 0.90;
SUBCOMPONENT OF robshould IS robshldbd 0.90;
SUBCOMPONENT OF robshould IS robshldsobj 0.90;
SUBCOMPONENT OF upperarm IS uedgeb 0.90;
SUBCOMPONENT OF upperarm IS uedges 0.90;
SUBCOMPONENT OF upperarm IS uendb 0.90;
SUBCOMPONENT OF upperarm IS uends 0.90;
SUBCOMPONENT OF upperarm IS uside 0.90;
SUBCOMPONENT OF armasm IS lowerarm 0.80;
SUBCOMPONENT OF armasm IS upperarm 0.80;
```

The supercomponent relationships:

```
SUPERCOMPONENT OF hand IS lowerarm 0.10;
SUPERCOMPONENT OF handend IS hand 0.10;
SUPERCOMPONENT OF handsidel IS hand 0.10;
SUPERCOMPONENT OF handsides IS hand 0.10;
SUPERCOMPONENT OF ledgea IS lowerarm 0.10;
SUPERCOMPONENT OF ledgeb IS lowerarm 0.10;
SUPERCOMPONENT OF lendb IS lowerarm 0.10;
SUPERCOMPONENT OF link IS robot 0.10;
SUPERCOMPONENT OF lowerarm IS armasm 0.10;
SUPERCOMPONENT OF lsidea IS lowerarm 0.10;
SUPERCOMPONENT OF lsideb IS lowerarm 0.10;
SUPERCOMPONENT OF robbody IS robot 0.10;
SUPERCOMPONENT OF robbodyside IS robbody 0.10;
SUPERCOMPONENT OF robshldbd IS robshould 0.10;
SUPERCOMPONENT OF robshldend IS robshldbd 0.10;
SUPERCOMPONENT OF robshldsobj IS robshould 0.10;
SUPERCOMPONENT OF robshould IS link 0.10;
SUPERCOMPONENT OF robshould1 IS robshldbd 0.10;
SUPERCOMPONENT OF robshould2 IS robshldbd 0.10;
SUPERCOMPONENT OF robshoulds IS robshldsobj 0.10;
SUPERCOMPONENT OF uedgeb IS upperarm 0.10;
SUPERCOMPONENT OF uedges IS upperarm 0.10;
SUPERCOMPONENT OF uendb IS upperarm 0.10;
SUPERCOMPONENT OF uends IS upperarm 0.10;
SUPERCOMPONENT OF upperarm IS armasm 0.10;
```

```
SUPERCOMPONENT OF armasm IS link 0.10;
SUPERCOMPONENT OF uside IS upperarm 0.10;
```

The general association relationships:

```
ASSOCIATION OF upperarm IS lowerarm 1.0;
ASSOCIATION OF lowerarm IS upperarm 1.0;
```

The competitor relationships amongst generic types:

```
COMPETITOR OF plane IS cylpatch 1.0;
COMPETITOR OF cylpatch IS plane 1.0;
COMPETITOR OF torus IS plane 1.0;
COMPETITOR OF plane IS torus 1.0;
COMPETITOR OF cylpatch IS torus 1.0;
COMPETITOR OF torus IS cylpatch 1.0;
COMPETITOR OF lside IS ledge 1.0;
COMPETITOR OF lside IS robshouldg 1.0;
COMPETITOR OF ledge IS lside 1.0;
COMPETITOR OF ledge IS robshouldg 1.0;
COMPETITOR OF robshouldg IS lside 1.0;
COMPETITOR OF robshouldg IS ledge 1.0;
ENDNET
```

After the relationships comes the listing of the visibility groups and what features are seen in each. This information is used to help create the invocation network.

```
SUBCGRP OF robot = robbody link;
SUBCGRP OF link = robshould armasm;
SUBCGRP OF armasm = upperarm lowerarm;
SUBCGRP OF upperarm = uside uends uedgeb uedges;
SUBCGRP OF upperarm = uside uendb uedgeb uedges;
SUBCGRP OF lowerarm = lendb lsidea ledgea;
SUBCGRP OF lowerarm = lendb lsideb ledgea;
SUBCGRP OF lowerarm = lendb lsideb ledgeb;
SUBCGRP OF lowerarm = lendb lsidea ledgeb;
SUBCGRP OF hand = handend handsides handsidel;
SUBCGRP OF robbody = robbodyside;
SUBCGRP OF robshould = robshldbd robshldsobj;
SUBCGRP OF robshldbd = robshould1 robshldend;
SUBCGRP OF robshldbd = robshould2 robshldend;
SUBCGRP OF robshldsobj = robshoulds;
ENDGRP
```

The next section lists the unary property evidence constraints, which are used for property evaluations during model invocation. Binary evidence constraints were not explicit in **IMAGINE I**. There may not always be many properties listed for an object, because (1) it may be a generic object, (2) the other properties are represented in a description or (3) the property is irrelevant.

```
UNARYEVID 2 < NUMLINB(quad) < 5 PEAK 4 WEIGHT 0.5;
UNARYEVID NUMARCB(quad) < 1 PEAK O WEIGHT 0.5;
UNARYEVID 1 < NUMARCB(circle) < 3 WEIGHT 0.5;
UNARYEVID NUMLINB(circle) < 1 PEAK O WEIGHT 0.5;
UNARYEVID 0 < DBPARO(trapezium) PEAK 1 WEIGHT 0.5;
UNARYEVID 1 < DBPARO(llgram) PEAK 2 WEIGHT 0.5;
UNARYEVID 2 < NUM90B(rectangle) < 5 PEAK 4 WEIGHT 0.5;
UNARYEVID -0.001 < MINSCURV(plane) < 0.001 WEIGHT 0.5;
UNARYEVID -0.001 < MAXSCURV(plane) < 0.001 WEIGHT 0.5;
UNARYEVID -0.001 < MINSCURV(cylpatch) < 0.001 WEIGHT 0.5;
UNARYEVID -0.001 < MAXSCURV(cylpatch) < 0.001 ABSENT WEIGHT 0.5;
UNARYEVID -0.001 < MINSCURV(torus) < 0.001 ABSENT WEIGHT 0.5;
UNARYEVID -0.001 < MAXSCURV(torus) < 0.001 ABSENT WEIGHT 0.5;
UNARYEVID 1 < NUMARCB(cylinder) < 4 PEAK 2 WEIGHT 0.5;
UNARYEVID 0 < NUMLINB(cylinder) < 4 PEAK 2 WEIGHT 0.5;
UNARYEVID 1.5 < NUM90B(cylinder) < 4.5 PEAK 4 WEIGHT 0.5;
UNARYEVID 0 < NUMEQLB(cylinder) < 3 PEAK 2 WEIGHT 0.5;
UNARYEVID 1.4 < SURSDA(sapiby2b) < 1.8 PEAK 1.57 WEIGHT 1.0;
UNARYEVID 1.5 < SURSDA(sapiby2a) < 1.65 PEAK 1.57 WEIGHT 1.0;
UNARYEVID 1.35 < SURSDA(sapiby2c) < 2.3 PEAK 1.57 WEIGHT 1.0;
UNARYEVID 3.04 < SURSDA(sapia) < 3.24 WEIGHT 1.0;
UNARYEVID 2.5 < SURSDA(sapib) < 3.7 PEAK 3.14 WEIGHT 1.0;
UNARYEVID 4.64 < SURSDA(sa3piby2) < 4.78 WEIGHT 1.0;
UNARYEVID 3.04 < SURSDA(sapiby2andpi) < 3.24 WEIGHT 1.0;
UNARYEVID 1.5 < SURSDA(sapiby2andpi) < 1.64 WEIGHT 1.0;
UNARYEVID 0.4 < RELSIZE(uside) < 0.72 WEIGHT 0.5;
UNARYEVID 1000 < ABSSIZE(uside) < 2200 WEIGHT 0.5;
UNARYEVID 2 < SURECC(uside) < 3.2 WEIGHT 0.5;
UNARYEVID 0.025 < DCURV(uside) < 0.065 WEIGHT 0.5;
UNARYEVID 0.11 < DCURV(uside) < 0.15 WEIGHT 0.5;
UNARYEVID 10 < DCRVL(uside) < 25 WEIGHT 0.5;
UNARYEVID 27 < DCRVL(uside) < 47 WEIGHT 0.5;
UNARYEVID 0.07 < DBRORT(uside) < 0.27 WEIGHT 0.5;
UNARYEVID 1.29 < DBRORT(uside) < 1.67 WEIGHT 0.5;
UNARYEVID 0.09 < DCURV(uends) < 0.17 WEIGHT 0.5;
UNARYEVID -0.003 < DCURV(uends) < 0.003 WEIGHT 0.5;
UNARYEVID 5 < DCRVL(uends) < 25 WEIGHT 0.5;
UNARYEVID 1.4 < DBRORT(uends) < 1.8 WEIGHT 0.5;
UNARYEVID 1.8 < SURECC(uends) < 2.6 WEIGHT 0.5;
UNARYEVID 130 < ABSSIZE(uends) < 250 WEIGHT 0.5;
```

```
UNARYEVID 0.04 < RELSIZE(uends) < 0.11 WEIGHT 0.5;
UNARYEVID 0.11 < MAXSCURV(uends) < 0.15 WEIGHT 0.5;
UNARYEVID 0.08 < RELSIZE(uendb) < 0.16 WEIGHT 0.5;
UNARYEVID 210 < ABSSIZE(uendb) < 430 WEIGHT 0.5;
UNARYEVID 2.8 < SURECC(uendb) < 4 WEIGHT 0.5;
UNARYEVID 1.47 < DBRORT(uendb) < 1.67 WEIGHT 0.5;
UNARYEVID 5 < DCRVL(uendb) < 15 WEIGHT 0.5;
UNARYEVID 27 < DCRVL(uendb) < 37 WEIGHT 0.5;
UNARYEVID 0.025 < DCURV(uendb) < 0.065 WEIGHT 0.5;
UNARYEVID 2.8 < SURSDA(uedges) < 3.4 WEIGHT 1.0;
UNARYEVID 1.4 < SURSDA(uedges) < 1.8 WEIGHT 0.5;
UNARYEVID 5 < DCRVL(uedges) < 25 WEIGHT 0.5;
UNARYEVID 1.47 < DBRORT(uedges) < 1.67 WEIGHT 0.5;
UNARYEVID 0.04 < RELSIZE(uedges) < 0.15 WEIGHT 0.5;
UNARYEVID 140 < ABSSIZE(uedges) < 260 WEIGHT 0.5;
UNARYEVID 1.8 < SURECC(uedges) < 2.6 WEIGHT 0.5;
UNARYEVID 2.9 < SURSDA(uedgeb) < 3.1 WEIGHT 1.0;
UNARYEVID 1.45 < SURSDA(uedgeb) < 1.85 WEIGHT 1.0;
UNARYEVID 0.11 < RELSIZE(uedgeb) < 0.22 WEIGHT 0.5;
UNARYEVID 290 < ABSSIZE(uedgeb) < 570 WEIGHT 0.5;
UNARYEVID 3.6 < SURECC(uedgeb) < 5.2 WEIGHT 0.5;
UNARYEVID 1.47 < DBRORT(uedgeb) < 1.67 WEIGHT 0.5;
UNARYEVID 5 < DCRVL(uedgeb) < 15 WEIGHT 0.5;
UNARYEVID 38 < DCRVL(uedgeb) < 48 WEIGHT 0.5;
UNARYEVID 0.51 < RELSIZE(lside) < 0.65 WEIGHT 0.5;
UNARYEVID 460 < ABSSIZE(lside) < 910 WEIGHT 0.5;
UNARYEVID 2.3 < SURECC(lside) < 3.3 WEIGHT 0.5;
UNARYEVID 1.07 < DBRORT(lside) < 1.47 WEIGHT 0.5;
UNARYEVID 1.37 < DBRORT(lside) < 1.77 WEIGHT 0.5;
UNARYEVID 3.6 < DCRVL(lside) < 24 WEIGHT 0.5;
UNARYEVID 32.8 < DCRVL(lside) < 54 WEIGHT 0.5;
UNARYEVID 0.06 < DCURV(lside) < 0.12 WEIGHT 0.5;
UNARYEVID 1.8 < SURECC(lendb) < 2.9 WEIGHT 0.5;
UNARYEVID 70 < ABSSIZE(lendb) < 200 WEIGHT 0.5;
UNARYEVID 0.07 < RELSIZE(lendb) < 0.18 WEIGHT 0.5;
UNARYEVID 0.97 < DBRORT(lendb) < 2.17 WEIGHT 0.5;
UNARYEVID 4 < DCRVL(lendb) < 13 WEIGHT 0.5;
UNARYEVID 13 < DCRVL(lendb) < 27 WEIGHT 0.5;
UNARYEVID 0.07 < DCURV(lendb) < 0.14 WEIGHT 0.5;
UNARYEVID 33 < DCRVL(ledgea) < 55 WEIGHT 0.5;
UNARYEVID 3.6 < DCRVL(ledgea) < 13.6 WEIGHT 0.5;
UNARYEVID 3.6 < DCRVL(ledgeb) < 13.6 WEIGHT 0.5;
UNARYEVID 32 < DCRVL(ledgeb) < 54 WEIGHT 0.5;
UNARYEVID 0.26 < RELSIZE(ledge) < 0.38 WEIGHT 0.5;
UNARYEVID 230 < ABSSIZE(ledge) < 470 WEIGHT 0.5;
UNARYEVID 4.6 < SURECC(ledge) < 6.6 WEIGHT 0.5;
```

```
UNARYEVID 1.4 < DBRORT(ledge) < 1.8 WEIGHT 0.5;
UNARYEVID 0.20 < RELSIZE(handsides) < 0.28 WEIGHT 0.5;
UNARYEVID 56 < ABSSIZE(handsides) < 76 WEIGHT 0.5;
UNARYEVID 1 < SURECC(handsides) < 1.3 WEIGHT 0.5;
UNARYEVID 1.47 < DBRORT(handsides) < 1.67 WEIGHT 0.5;
UNARYEVID 2.7 < DCRVL(handsides) < 13.6 WEIGHT 0.5;
UNARYEVID 0.30 < RELSIZE(handsidel) < 0.38 WEIGHT 0.5;
UNARYEVID 80 < ABSSIZE(handsidel) < 110 WEIGHT 0.5;
UNARYEVID 1.2 < SURECC(handsidel) < 1.6 WEIGHT 0.5;
UNARYEVID 1.47 < DBRORT(handsidel) < 1.67 WEIGHT 0.5;
UNARYEVID 1 < DBPARO(handsidel) < 3 WEIGHT 0.3;
UNARYEVID 2.7 < DCRVL(handsidel) < 18.5 WEIGHT 0.5;
UNARYEVID 0.21 < DCURV(handsidel) < 0.25 WEIGHT 0.5;
UNARYEVID 0.21 < MAXSCURV(handend) < 0.25 WEIGHT 0.5;
UNARYEVID 0.32 < RELSIZE(handend) < 0.52 WEIGHT 0.5;
UNARYEVID 96 < ABSSIZE(handend) < 136 WEIGHT 0.5;
UNARYEVID 1 < SURECC(handend) < 1.2 WEIGHT 0.5;
UNARYEVID 1.47 < DBRORT(handend) < 1.67 WEIGHT 0.5;
UNARYEVID 3.6 < DCRVL(handend) < 18.5 WEIGHT 0.5;
UNARYEVID 0.21 < DCURV(handend) < 0.25 WEIGHT 0.5;
UNARYEVID 4.5 < SURSDA(robbodyside) < 4.9 WEIGHT 0.5;
UNARYEVID 2.5 < SURSDA(robbodyside) < 3.7 WEIGHT 0.5;
UNARYEVID 0.09 < MAXSCURV(robbodyside) < 0.14 WEIGHT 0.5;
UNARYEVID 0.9 < RELSIZE(robbodyside) < 1.1 WEIGHT 0.5;
UNARYEVID 1200 < ABSSIZE(robbodyside) < 1600 WEIGHT 0.5;
UNARYEVID 1.57 < SURECC(robbodyside) < 3.5 WEIGHT 0.5;
UNARYEVID 1.17 < DBRORT(robbodyside) < 1.97 WEIGHT 0.5;
UNARYEVID 1 < DBPARO(robbodyside) < 3 WEIGHT 0.3;
UNARYEVID 20 < DCRVL(robbodyside) < 36 WEIGHT 0.5;
UNARYEVID 40 < DCRVL(robbodyside) < 60 WEIGHT 0.5;
UNARYEVID -0.003 < DCURV(robbodyside) < 0.015 WEIGHT 0.5;
UNARYEVID 0.05 < DCURV(robbodyside) < 0.16 WEIGHT 0.5;
UNARYEVID 0.11 < RELSIZE(robshldend) < 0.40 WEIGHT 0.5;
UNARYEVID 156 < ABSSIZE(robshldend) < 248 WEIGHT 0.5;
UNARYEVID 0.9 < SURECC(robshldend) < 1.5 WEIGHT 0.5;
UNARYEVID 3.04 < DBRORT(robshldend) < 3.24 WEIGHT 0.5;
UNARYEVID 0 < DBPARO(robshldend) < 2 WEIGHT 0.3;
UNARYEVID 20.1 < DCRVL(robshldend) < 40 WEIGHT 0.5;
UNARYEVID 0.08 < DCURV(robshldend) < 0.15 WEIGHT 0.5;
UNARYEVID 0.105 < MAXSCURV(robshouldg) < 0.145 WEIGHT 0.5;
UNARYEVID -0.003 < MINSCURV(robshouldg) < 0.01 WEIGHT 0.5;
UNARYEVID 0.55 < RELSIZE(robshouldg) < 0.79 WEIGHT 0.5;
UNARYEVID 428 < ABSSIZE(robshouldg) < 828 WEIGHT 0.5;
UNARYEVID 1.5 < SURECC(robshouldg) < 3.5 WEIGHT 0.5;
UNARYEVID 1.4 < DBRORT(robshouldg) < 1.8 WEIGHT 0.5;
UNARYEVID 0.8 < DBRORT(robshouldg) < 1.1 WEIGHT 0.5;
```

```
UNARYEVID 0.9 < DBRORT(robshouldg) < 1.5 WEIGHT 0.5;
UNARYEVID 1 < DBPARO(robshouldg) < 3 WEIGHT 0.3;
UNARYEVID 5 < DCRVL(robshouldg) < 16 WEIGHT 0.5;
UNARYEVID 11 < DCRVL(robshouldg) < 21 WEIGHT 0.5;
UNARYEVID 18 < DCRVL(robshouldg) < 37 WEIGHT 0.5;
UNARYEVID 0.071 < DCURV(robshouldg) < 0.15 WEIGHT 0.5;
UNARYEVID -0.003 < DCURV(robshouldg) < 0.035 WEIGHT 0.5;
UNARYEVID 0.105 < MAXSCURV(robshoulds) < 0.145 WEIGHT 0.5;
UNARYEVID -0.003 < MINSCURV(robshoulds) < 0.01 WEIGHT 0.5;
UNARYEVID 0.9 < RELSIZE(robshoulds) < 1.1 WEIGHT 0.5;
UNARYEVID 60 < ABSSIZE(robshoulds) < 140 WEIGHT 0.5;
UNARYEVID 2 < SURECC(robshoulds) < 4 WEIGHT 0.5;
UNARYEVID 1.8 < DBRORT(robshoulds) < 2.6 WEIGHT 0.5;
UNARYEVID 1.5 < DBRORT(robshoulds) < 2.3 WEIGHT 0.5;
UNARYEVID -1 < DBPARO(robshoulds) < 1 WEIGHT 0.3;
UNARYEVID 6 < DCRVL(robshoulds) < 18 WEIGHT 0.5;
UNARYEVID 18 < DCRVL(robshoulds) < 30 WEIGHT 0.5;
UNARYEVID 0.03 < DCURV(robshoulds) < 0.131 WEIGHT 0.5;
ENDINV
```

The next section gives the geometric model for the specific surfaces. The syntax of the models is described in Chapter 7. The DEFAULT values are a position that can be used for drawing the models.

```
SURFACE uside DEFAULT ((0,0,1000),(0,0,0)) =
        PO/(0,0,0) BO/LINE
        PO/(19.6,0,0) BO/LINE
        PC/(61.8,7.4,0) BO/CURVE[7.65,0,0]
        PC/(61.8,22.4,0) BO/LINE
        PO/(19.6,29.8,0) BO/LINE
        PO/(0,29.8,0) BO/CURVE[-22.42,0,0]
        PLANE
        NORMAL AT (10,15,0) = (0,0,-1);
SURFACE uedges DEFAULT ((0,0,1000),(0,0,0)) =
        PO/(0,0,0) BO/LINE
        PO/(19.6,0,0) BO/LINE
        PO/(19.6,10,0) BO/LINE
        PO/(0,10,0) BO/LINE
        PLANE
        NORMAL AT (10,5,0) = (0,0,-1);
SURFACE uedgeb DEFAULT ((0,0,1000),(0,0,0)) =
        PO/(0,0,0) BO/LINE
        PO/(42.85,0,0) BO/LINE
        PO/(42.85,10,0) BCW/LINE
        PO/(0,10,0) BO/LINE
```

```
          PLANE
          NORMAL AT (21,5,0) = (0,0,-1);
SURFACE uends DEFAULT ((0,0,1000),(0,0,0)) =
          PO/(0,0,0) BCW/LINE
          PO/(10,0,0) BO/CURVE[0,0,-7.65]
          PO/(10,15,0) BCW/LINE
          PO/(0,15,0) BO/CURVE[0,0,-7.65]
          CYLINDER[(0,7.5,1.51),(10,7.5,1.51),7.65,7.65]
          NORMAL AT (5,7.5,-6.14) = (0,0,-1);
SURFACE uendb DEFAULT ((0,0,1000),(0,0,0)) =
          PO/(0,0,0) BO/LINE
          PO/(10,0,0) BO/CURVE[0,0,-22.42]
          PO/(10,29.8,0) BO/LINE
          PO/(0,29.8,0) BO/CURVE[0,0,-22.42]
          CYLINDER [(0,14.9,16.75),(10,14.9,16.75),22.42,22.42]
          NORMAL AT (5,15,-5.67) = (0,0,-1);
SURFACE lsidea DEFAULT ((0,0,1000),(0,0,0)) =
          PO/(0,0,0) BO/LINE
          PO/(44,0,0) BN/LINE
          PO/ (44,8.6,0) BN/LINE
          PO/(2,17,0) BN/CURVE[-10.96,1.29,0]
          PLANE
          NORMAL AT (22,6,0) = (0,0,-1);
SURFACE lsideb DEFAULT ((0,0,1000),(0,0,0)) =
          PO/(0,0,0) BO/LINE
          PO/(-44,0,0) BN/LINE
          PO/(-44,8.6,0) BO/LINE
          PO/(-2,17,0) BO/CURVE[10.96,1.29,0]
          PLANE
          NORMAL AT (-22,6,0) = (0,0,-1);
SURFACE ledgea DEFAULT ((0,0,1000),(0,0,0)) =
          PO/(0,0,0) BO/LINE
          PO/(44,0,0) BN/LINE
          PO/(44,8.6,0) BO/LINE
          PO/(0,8.6,0) BO/LINE
          PLANE
          NORMAL AT (22,4.3,0) = (0,0,-1);
SURFACE ledgeb DEFAULT ((0,0,1000),(0,0,0)) =
          PO/(0,0,0) BO/LINE
          PO/(42.8,0,0) BN/LINE
          PO/ (42.8,8.6,0) BO/LINE
          PO/ (0,8.6,0) BO/LINE
          PLANE
          NORMAL AT (22,4.3,0) = (0,0,-1);
SURFACE lendb DEFAULT ((0,0,1000),(0,0,0)) =
          PO/(0,0,0) BO/CURVE[0,0,-11.04]
```

```
          PO/(17,0,0) BO/LINE
          PO/(17,8.6,0) BO/CURVE[0,0,-11.04]
          PO/(0,8.6,0) BO/LINE
          CYLINDER [(8.5,0,7.04),(8.5,8.6,7.04),11.04,11.04]
          NORMAL AT (8.5,4.3,-4) = (0,0,-1);
SURFACE handsides DEFAULT ((0,0,1000),(0,0,0)) =
          PO/(0,0,0) BO/LINE
          PO/(7.7,0,0) BCW/LINE
          PO/(7.7,8.6,0) BO/LINE
          PO/(0,8.6,0) BO/LINE
          PLANE
          NORMAL AT (3.8,4.3,0) = (0,0,-1);
SURFACE handsidel DEFAULT ((0,0,1000),(0,0,0)) =
          PO/(0,0,0) BO/LINE
          PO/(0,8.6,0) BO/LINE
          PO/(7.7,8.6,0) BO/CURVE[3.04,3.04,0]
          PN/(12,4.3,0) BO/CURVE[3.04,-3.04,0]
          PO/(7.7,0,0) BO/LINE
          PLANE
          NORMAL AT (6,4.3,0) = (0,0,-1);
SURFACE handend DEFAULT ((0,0,1000),(0,0,0)) =
          PO/(0,0,0) BO/CURVE[0,-3.04,-3.04]
          PN/(0,4.3,-4.3) BO/CURVE[0,3.04,-3.04]
          PO/(0,8.6,0) BCW/LINE
          PO/(8.6,8.6,0) BO/CURVE[0,3.04,-3.04]
          PN/(8.6,4.3,-4.3) BO/CURVE[0,-3.04,-3.04]
          PO/(8.6,0,0) BCW/LINE
          CYLINDER [(0,4.3,0),(8.6,4.3,0),4.3,4.3]
          NORMAL AT (4.3,4.3,-4.3) = (0,0,-1);
SURFACE robbodyside DEFAULT ((0,0,1000),(0,0,0)) =
          PO/(-9,0,0) BO/CURVE[-6.364,0,-6.364]
          PN/(0,0,-9) BO/CURVE[6.364,0,-6.364]
          PO/(9,0,0) BN/LINE
          PO/(9,50,0) BO/CURVE[6.364,0,-6.364]
          PN/(0,50,-9) BO/CURVE[-6.364,0,-6.364]
          PO/(-9,50,0) BN/LINE
          CYLINDER [(0,0,0),(0,50,0),9,9]
          NORMAL AT (0,25,-9) = (0,0,-1);
SURFACE robshldend DEFAULT ((0,0,1000),(0,0,0)) =
          PN/(-8,0,0) BO/CURVE[-5.66,5.66,0]
          PN/(0,8,0) BO/CURVE[5.66,5.66,0]
          PN/(8,0,0) BO/CURVE[5.66,-5.66,0]
          PN/(0,-8,0) BO/CURVE[-5.66,-5.66,0]
          PLANE
          NORMAL AT (0,0,0) = (0,0,-1);
SURFACE robshoulds DEFAULT ((0,0,1000),(0,0,0)) =
```

```
          PO/(-8,0,0) BO/CURVE[-5.66,0,-5.66]
          PN/(0,0,-8) BO/CURVE[5.66,0,-5.66]
          PO/(8,0,0) BO/CURVE[0,-6.32,-6.32]
          PO/(0,8,-8) BO/CURVE[0,-6.32,-6.32]
          CYLINDER [(0,0,0),(0,1,0),8,8]
          NORMAL AT (0,4,-8) = (0,0,-1);
SURFACE robshould1 DEFAULT ((0,0,1000),(0,0,0)) =
          PO/(0,-8,0) BO/CURVE[0,-5.66,-5.66]
          PN/(0,0,-8) BO/CURVE[0,5.66,-5.66]
          PO/(0,8,0) BN/LINE
          PO/(29,8,0) BO/CURVE[0,5.66,-5.66]
          PN/(29,0,-8) BO/CURVE[0,-5.66,-5.66]
          PO/(29,-8,0) BN/LINE
          PO/(27,-8,0) BO/CURVE[0,-6.32,-6.32]
          PO/(19,0,-8) BO/CURVE[0,-6.32,-6.32]
          PO/(11,-8,0) BN/LINE
          CYLINDER [(0,0,0),(1,0,0),8,8]
          NORMAL AT (10,0,-8) = (0,0,-1);
SURFACE robshould2 DEFAULT ((0,0,1000),(0,0,0)) =
          PO/(0,-8,0) BO/CURVE[0,-5.66,-5.66]
          PN/(0,0,-8) BO/CURVE[0,5.66,-5.66]
          PO/(0,8,0) BN/LINE
          PO/(-29,8,0) BO/CURVE[0,5.66,-5.66]
          PN/(-29,0,-8) BO/CURVE[0,-5.66,-5.66]
          PO/(-29,-8,0) BN/LINE
          PO/(-27,-8,0) BO/CURVE[0,-6.32,-6.32]
          PO/(-19,0,-8) BO/CURVE[0,-6.32,-6.32]
          PO/(-11,-8,0) BN/LINE
          CYLINDER [(0,0,0),(-1,0,0),8,8]
          NORMAL AT (-10,0,-8) = (0,0,-1);
```

Then come the geometric models for the ASSEMBLYs:

```
ASSEMBLY robot DEFAULT ((0,0,1000),(0,0.7,4)) =
          robbody AT ((0,0,0),(0,0,0))
          link AT ((0,50,0),(0,0,0))
          FLEX ((0,0,0),(0,jnt1,3.14159));
ASSEMBLY link DEFAULT ((0,0,1000),(0,0.7,4)) =
          robshould AT ((0,0,0),(0,0,0))
          armasm AT ((0,8,-19),(0,0,0))
          FLEX ((0,0,0),(jnt2,0,0));
ASSEMBLY armasm DEFAULT ((0,0,1000),(0,0.7,4)) =
          upperarm AT ((0,0,0),(0,0,0))
          lowerarm AT ((43.5,0,0),(0,0,0))
          FLEX ((0,0,0),(jnt3,0,0));
```

```
ASSEMBLY upperarm DEFAULT ((0,0,1000),(0,0.7,4)) =
        uside AT ((-17,-14.9,-10),(0,0,0))
        uside AT ((-17,14.9,0),(0,3.14,1.5707))
        uendb AT ((-17,-14.9,0),(0,1.5707,3.14159))
        uends AT ((44.8,-7.5,-10),(0,1.5707,0))
        uedges AT ((-17,-14.9,0),(0,1.5707,4.7123))
        uedges AT ((-17,14.9,-10),(0,1.5707,1.5707))
        uedgeb AT ((2.6,-14.9,0),(0.173,1.5707,4.7123))
        uedgeb AT ((2.6,14.9,-10),(6.11,1.5707,1.5707));
ASSEMBLY lowerarm DEFAULT ((0,0,1000),(0,0.7,4)) =
        lsidea AT ((-9.4,-7.7,0),(0,0,0))
        lsideb AT ((-9.4,-7.7,8.6),(0,3.14,0))
        lendb AT ((-9.4,-7.7,0),(1.4536,1.5707,1.5707))
        ledgea AT ((-9.4,-7.7,8.6),(0,1.5707,4.7123))
        ledgeb AT ((-7.4,9.3,0),(6.083,1.5707,1.5707))
        hand AT ((34.6,-3.8,4.3),(0,0,0));
ASSEMBLY hand DEFAULT ((0,0,1000),(0,0.7,4)) =
        handsidel AT ((0,-4.3,-4.3),(0,0,0))
        handsidel AT ((0,4.3,4.3),(0,3.14,1.5707))
        handsides AT ((0,-4.3,4.3),(0,1.5707,4.71))
        handsides AT ((0,4.3,-4.3),(0,1.5707,1.5707))
        handend AT ((7.7,-4.3,-4.3),(0,1.57,0));
ASSEMBLY robbody DEFAULT ((0,0,1000),(0,0.7,4)) =
        robbodyside AT ((0,0,0),(0,0,0))
        robbodyside AT ((0,0,0),(0,3.14,0));
ASSEMBLY robshould DEFAULT ((0,0,1000),(0,0.7,4)) =
        robshldbd AT ((0,0,0),(0,0,0))
        robshldsobj AT ((0,0,0),(0,0,0));
ASSEMBLY robshldbd DEFAULT ((0,0,1000),(0,0.7,4)) =
        robshould1 AT ((0,8,-19),(0,1.5707,0))
        robshould2 AT ((0,8,-19),(0,1.5707,3.14159))
        robshldend AT ((0,8,10),(0,3.14,0));
ASSEMBLY robshldsobj DEFAULT ((0,0,1000),(0,0.7,4)) =
        robshoulds AT ((0,0,0),(0,1.5707,0))
        robshoulds AT ((0,0,0),(0,1.5707,3.14159));
ENDSTR
```

Lastly, there are the additional property constraints used by verification:

```
CONSTRAINT uside MAXSCURV(uside) < 0.05
CONSTRAINT uside ABSSIZE(uside) < 1900.0
CONSTRAINT uside ABSSIZE(uside) > 1050.0
CONSTRAINT uends ABSSIZE(uends) < 250.0
CONSTRAINT uendb ABSSIZE(uendb) < 430.0
CONSTRAINT uedges ABSSIZE(uedges) < 260.0
CONSTRAINT uedges SURECC(uedges) < 3.0
```

```
CONSTRAINT uedgeb ABSSIZE(uedgeb) < 570.0
CONSTRAINT lsidea ABSSIZE(lsidea) < 910.0
CONSTRAINT lsidea ABSSIZE(lsidea) > 300.0
CONSTRAINT lsideb ABSSIZE(lsideb) < 910.0
CONSTRAINT lsideb ABSSIZE(lsideb) > 300.0
CONSTRAINT lendb ABSSIZE(lendb) < 200.0
CONSTRAINT ledgea ABSSIZE(ledgea) < 470.0
CONSTRAINT ledgea ABSSIZE(ledgea) > 200.0
CONSTRAINT ledgeb ABSSIZE(ledgeb) < 470.0
CONSTRAINT ledgeb ABSSIZE(ledgeb) > 200.0
CONSTRAINT handsides ABSSIZE(handsides) < 76.0
CONSTRAINT handsidel ABSSIZE(handsidel) < 110.0
CONSTRAINT handend ABSSIZE(handend) < 136.0
CONSTRAINT robbodyside ABSSIZE(robbodyside) < 1600.0
CONSTRAINT robshldend ABSSIZE(robshldend) < 248.0
CONSTRAINT robshldend SURECC(robshldend) < 1.5
CONSTRAINT robshould1 ABSSIZE(robshould1) < 828.0
CONSTRAINT robshould2 ABSSIZE(robshould2) < 828.0
CONSTRAINT robshoulds ABSSIZE(robshoulds) < 130.0
CONSTRAINT robbodyside SURECC(robbodyside) > 2.0
CONSTRAINT robbodyside MAXSCURV(robbodyside) > 0.095
ENDCON
STOP
```

BIBLIOGRAPHY

The following abbreviations are used:

ANCAI - American National Conference on Artificial Intelligence
IJCAI - International Joint Conference on Artificial Intelligence
SRI - Stanford Research Institute

[**ABE83**] Abe, N., Itho, F., Tsuji, S., *Toward Generation of 3-Dimensional Models of Objects Using 2-Dimensional Figures and Explanations in Language*, Proceedings 8th IJCAI, pp1113-1115, 1983.

[**ACK85**] Ackley, D., Hinton, G., Sejnowski, T., *A Learning Algorithm for Boltzmann Machines*, Cognitive Science, Vol 9, pp147-169, 1985.

[**ADL75**] Adler, M., *Understanding Peanuts Cartoons*, Department of Artificial Intelligence Research Report 13, University of Edinburgh, 1975.

[**ADO86**] Adorni, G., Trucco, E., *A Quantitative Theory of Visual Perception: A Case Study*, in Cappellini and Marconi (eds), Advances in Image Processing and Pattern Recognition, pp 130-138, North Holland, Amsterdam, 1986.

[**AGI73**] Agin, G. J., Binford, T. O., *Computer Description of Curved Objects*, Proceedings 3rd IJCAI, pp629-640, 1973.

[**AGI79**] Agin, G. J., *Hierarchical Representation of Three-Dimensional Objects Using Verbal Models*, SRI Technical Note 182, 1979.

[**ALE83**] Alefeld, G., Herzberger, J., Introduction to Interval Computations, Academic Press, New York, 1983.

[**AMB75**] Ambler, A. P., Barrow, H. G., Brown, C. M., Burstall, R. M., Popplestone, R. J., *A Versatile System for Computer Controlled Assembly*, Artificial Intelligence, Vol. 6, pp129 - 156, 1975.

[**ARB79**] Arbib, M. A., *Local Organizing Processes and Motion Schemas in Visual Perception*, in Hayes, et al. (eds), Machine Intelligence 9, pp287-298, Ellis-Horwood, Chichester, 1979.

[**ASA84**] Asada, H., Brady, M., *The Curvature Primal Sketch*, Massachusetts Institute of Technology AI memo 758, 1984.

[**AYL88**] Aylett, J. C., Fisher, R. B., Fothergill, A. P., *Predictive Computer Vision for Robotic Assembly*, Journal of Intelligent and Robotic Systems, Vol. 1, pp185-201, 1988.

[**BAL81a**] Ballard, D. H., *Parameter Networks: Towards a Theory of Low-Level Vision*, Proceedings 7th IJCAI, pp1068-1078, 1981.

[**BAL81b**] Ballard, D. H., Sabbah, D., *On Shapes*, Proceedings 7th IJCAI, pp607-612, 1981.

[**BAL82**] Ballard, D. H., Brown, C. M., Computer Vision, Prentice-Hall, New Jersey, 1982.

[**BAL85**] Ballard, D. H., Tanaka, H., *Transformational Form Perception in 3D: Constraints, Algorithms, Implementations*, Proceedings 9th IJCAI, pp964-968, 1985.

[**BAR71**] Barrow, H. G., Popplestone, R. J., *Relational Descriptions in Picture Processing*, in Meltzer and Michie (eds), Machine Intelligence 6, pp377-396, Edinburgh University Press, Edinburgh, 1971.

[**BAR72**] Barrow, H. G., Ambler, A. P., Burstall, R. M., *Some Techniques for Recognizing Structures in Pictures*, in Watanabe (ed.) Frontiers of Pattern Recognition, pp1-29, Academic Press, New York, 1972.

[**BAR74**] Barrow, H. G., Burstall, R. M., *Subgraph Isomorphism, Matching Relational Structures and Maximal Cliques*, University of Edinburgh, Department of Artificial Intelligence, Working Paper 5, Nov 1974.

[**BAR76**] Barrow, H. G., Tenenbaum, J. M., *MSYS: a System for Reasoning About Scenes*, SRI Technical Note 121, 1976.

[**BAR78**] Barrow, H. G., Tenenbaum, J. M., *Recovering Intrinsic Scene Characteristics from Images*, in Hanson and Riseman (eds), Computer Vision Systems, pp3-26, Academic Press, New York, 1978.

[**BAR83**] Barnard, S. T., Pentland, A. P., *Three-Dimensional Shape from Line Drawing*, Proceedings 8th IJCAI, pp1062-1064, 1983.

[**BER83**] Berthod, M., *Global Optimization of a Consistent Labeling*, Proceedings 8th IJCAI, pp1065-1067, 1983.

[**BES85**] Besl, P. J., Jain, R. C., *Three Dimensional Object Recognition*, Association for Computing Machinery Computing Surveys, Vol 17, pp 75-145, 1985.

[**BES86**] Besl, P. J., *Surfaces in Early Range Image Understanding*, PhD Dissertation, Electrical Engineering and Computer Science Department (RSD-TR-10-86), University of Michigan, 1986.

[**BES88a**] Besl, P. J., *Range Imaging Sensors*, General Motors Research Publication GMR-6090, General Motors Research Laboratories, Warren, Michigan, 1988.

[**BES88b**] Besl, P. J., *Geometric Modelling and Computer Vision*, General Motors Research Publication GMR-6248, General Motors Research Laboratories, Warren, Michigan, 1988.

[**BIN71**] Binford, T. O., *Visual Perception by Computer*, IEEE Conference on Systems and Control, 1981.

[**BIN81**] Binford, T. O., *Inferring Surfaces from Images*, Artificial Intelligence, Vol. 17, pp205-244, 1981.

[**BIN82**] Binford, T. O., *Survey of Model-Based Image Analysis Systems*, International Journal of Robotics Research, Vol 1, pp18-64, 1982.

[**BIN87**] Binford, T. O., Levitt, T. S., Mann, W. B., *Bayesian Inference in Model-Based Machine Vision*, unpublished note, Computer Science, Stanford University, 1987.

[**BLA84**] Blake, A., *Reconstructing a Visible Surface*, Proceedings 3rd ANCAI, pp23-26, 1984.

[**BLA85**] Blake, A., *Specular Stereo*, Proceedings 9th IJCAI, pp 973-976, 1985.

[**BLE75**] Bledsoe, W. W., *A new method for proving certain Presburger formulas*, Proceedings 4th IJCAI, pp15-21, 1975.

[**BOI81**] Boissonnat, J. D., Faugeras, O. D., *Triangulation of 3D Objects*, Proceedings 7th IJCAI, pp658-660, 1981.

[**BOL80**] Bolles, R., *Locating Partially Visible Objects: The Local Feature Focus Method*, ANCAI 80 and SRI Technical Note 223, Aug 1980.

[**BOL83**] Bolles, R.C., Horaud, P., Hannah, M. J., *3DPO: a Three-Dimensional Part Orientation System*, Proceedings 8th IJCAI, pp1116-1120, 1983.

[**BOY87**] Boyer, K. L., Kak, A. C., *Color encoded structured light for rapid active ranging*, IEEE Transactions on Pattern Analysis and Machine Intelligence, Vol 9, pp 14-28, 1987.

[**BRA83a**] Brady, M., Yuille, A., *An Extremum Principle for Shape from Contour*, Proceedings 8th IJCAI, pp969-972, 1983.

[**BRA83b**] Brady, M., *Criteria for Representations of Shape*, in Beck, Hope and Rosenfeld (eds), Human and Machine Vision, Academic Press, London, 1983.

[**BRA84**] Brady, M., Ponce, J., Yuille, A., Asada, H., *Describing Surfaces*, Proceedings 2nd International Symp. on Robotics Research, 1984.

[**BRI70**] Brice, C. R., Fennema, C. L., *Scene Analysis Using Regions*, Artificial Intelligence, Vol. 1, pp205-226, 1970.

[**BRO81**] Brooks, R. A., *Symbolic Reasoning Among 3D Models and 2D Images*, Stanford AIM-343, STAN-CS-81-861, 1981.

[**CAI89**] Cai, L. D., Forthcoming PhD Thesis, Department of Artificial Intelligence, University of Edinburgh, 1989.

[**CAM84**] Cameron, S. A., *Modelling Solids in Motion*, PhD Thesis, Department of Artificial Intelligence, University of Edinburgh, 1984.

[**CER83**] Cernuschi-Frias, B., Bolle, R. M., Cooper, D. B., *A New Conceptually Attractive & Computationally Effective Approach to Shape from Shading*, Proceedings 8th IJCAI, pp966-968, 1983.

[**CHA79**] Chang, N. S., Fu, K. S., *Parallel Parsing of Tree Languages for Syntactic Pattern Recognition*, Pattern Recognition, Vol 11, page 213, 1979.

[**CHA82**] Chakravarty, I., *The use of characteristic views as a basis for recognition of three dimensional objects*, IPL-TR-034, Image Processing Laboratory, Rensselaer Polytechnic Institute, 1982.

[**CLO71**] Clowes, M. B., *On Seeing Things*, Artificial Intelligence, Vol. 2, pp79-116, 1971.

[**CLO80**] Clocksin, W., *The Effect of Motion Contrast on Surface Slant and Edge Detection*, Proceedings British Society for the Study of Artificial Intelligence and the Simulation of Behaviour Conference, 1980.

[**COL81**] Coleman, E. N., Jain, R., *Shape from Shading for Surfaces With Texture and Specularity*, Proceedings 7th IJCAI, pp652-657, 1981.

[**COW83**] Cowie, R. I. D., *The Viewer's Place in Theories of Vision*, Proceedings 8th IJCAI, pp952-958, 1983.

[**DAN82**] Dane, C., Bajcsy, R., *An Object-Centered Three Dimensional Model Builder*, Proceedings 6th International Conference on Pattern Recognition, pp348-350, 1982.

[**DAV87**] Davis, E., *Constraint Propagation with Interval Labels*, Artificial Intelligence, Vol 32, p281, 1987.

[**DRE81**] Dreschler, L., Nagel, H. H., *Volumetric Model and 3D-Trajectory of a Moving Car Derived from Monocular TV-frame Sequences of a Street Scene*, Proceedings 7th IJCAI, pp692-697, 1981.

[**DUD70**] Duda, R., Hart, P., *Experiments in Scene Analysis*, SRI Artificial Intelligence Group Technical note 20, Project 8259, Jan 1970.

[**DUD73**] Duda, R., Hart, P., Pattern Classification and Scene Analysis, John Wiley and Sons, New York, 1973.

[**DUR87**] Durrant-Whyte, H. F., *Uncertain geometry in robotics*, Proceedings IEEE Conference on Robotics and Automation, Vol. 2, p851, 1987.

[**FAH80**] Fahlman, S. E., *Design Sketch for a Million-Element NETL Machine*, Proceedings 1st ANCAI, pp249-252, 1980.

[**FAH81**] Fahlman, S. E., Touretzky, D. S., van Roggen, W., *Cancellation in a Parallel Semantic Network*, Proceedings 7th IJCAI, pp257-263, 1981.

[**FAL72**] Falk, G., *Interpretation of Imperfect Line Data as a Three-Dimensional Scene*, Artificial Intelligence, Vol 3, pp101-144, 1972.

[**FAN88**] Fan, T. J., Medioni, G., Nevatia, R., *Recognizing 3-D Objects Using Surface Descriptions*, Proceedings 2nd International Conference on Computer Vision, pp474-481, 1988.

[**FAU80**] Faugeras, O., *An Optimization Approach for Using Contextual Information in Computer Vision*, ANCAI-80, Aug 1980.

[**FAU83**] Faugeras, O. D., Hebert, M., *A 3-D Recognition and Positioning Algorithm Using Geometric Matching Between Primitive Surfaces*, Proceedings 8th IJCAI, pp996-1002, 1983.

[**FEL83**] Feldman, J. A., Ballard, D. H., *Computing With Connections*, in Beck, Hope and Rosenfeld (eds), Human and Machine Vision, Academic Press, London, pp 107-155, 1983.

[**FEL85**] Feldman, J. A., *Four Frames Suffice: a Provisional Model of Vision and Space*, The Behavioral and Brain Sciences, Vol 8, pp265-289, 1985.

[**FIS83**] Fisher, R. B., *Using Surfaces and Object Models to Recognize Partially Obscured Objects*, Proceedings 8th IJCAI, pp989-995.

[**FIS86a**] Fisher, R. B., *From Surfaces to Objects: Recognizing Objects Using Surface Information and Object Models*, PhD Thesis, University of Edinburgh, 1986.

[**FIS86b**] Fisher, R. B., *Recognizing Objects Using Surface Information and Object Models*, Proceedings 2nd IEE International Conference on Image Processing, London, pp 149-153, 1986.

[**FIS86c**] Fisher, R. B., *Identity Independent Object Segmentation in 2 1/2D Sketch Data*, Proceedings 1986 European Conference on Artificial Intelligence, pp148-153, July 1986.

[**FIS87a**] Fisher, R. B., *SMS: A Suggestive Modeling System For Object Recognition*, Image and Vision Computing, Vol 5, pp 98 - 104, 1987.

[**FIS87b**] Fisher, R. B., *Representing 3D Structures for Visual Recognition*, Artificial Intelligence Review, Vol. 1, pp 183-200, 1987.

[**FIS87c**] Fisher, R. B., *Model Invocation for Three Dimensional Scene Understanding*, Proceedings 10th IJCAI, pp805-807, 1987.

[**FIS87d**] Fisher, R. B., *Modeling Second-Order Volumetric Features*, Proceedings 3rd Alvey Vision Conference, pp79-86, Cambridge, 1987.

[**FIS88**] Fisher, R. B., Orr, M. J. L., *Solving Geometric Constraints in a Parallel Network*, Image and Vision Computing, Vol 6, 1988.

[**FRE77**] Freuder, E. C., *A Computer System for Visual Recognition Using Active Knowledge*, Proceeding 5th IJCAI, pp671-677, 1977.

[**GOA86**] Goad, C., *Fast 3-D Model Based Vision*, in Pentland (ed), From Pixels To Predicates, pp371-391. Ablex Publishing, New Jersey, 1986.

[**GRI81**] Grimson, W. E. L., From Images to Surfaces: a Computational Study of the Human Early Visual System, MIT Press, Cambridge, Massachusetts, 1981.

[**GRI84**] Grimson, W. E. L., Lozano-Perez, T., *Model-Based Recognition and Localization from Sparse Range or Tactile Data*, International Journal of Robotics Research, Vol. 3, pp3-35, 1984.

[**GRI87**] Grimson, W. E. L., *Recognition of Object Families Using Parameterized Models*, Proceedings 1st IEEE International Conference on Computer Vision, pp93-101, 1987.

[**GUZ67**] Guzman, A., *Decomposition of a Visual Scene Into Bodies*, Massachusetts Institute of Technology AI memo 139, 1967.

[GUZ68] Guzman, A., *Decomposition of a Visual Scene into Three-Dimensional Bodies*, Proceedings Fall Joint Computer Conference, pp291-304, 1968.

[HAN78a] Hanson, A., Riseman, E., *Segmentation of Natural Scenes*, in Hanson and Riseman (eds), Computer Vision Systems, Academic Press, New York, 1978.

[HAN78b] Hanson, A., Riseman, E., *VISIONS: a Computer System for Interpreting Scenes*, in Hanson and Riseman (eds), Computer Vision Systems, pp303-333, Academic Press, New York, 1978.

[HAN80] Hannah, M., *Bootstrap Stereo*, ANCAI-80, Aug 1980.

[HIL84] Hildreth, E. C., *Computations Underlying the Measurement of Visual Motion*, Artificial Intelligence, Vol 23, pp309-354, 1984.

[HIN76] Hinton, G., *Using Relaxation to Find a Puppet*, Proceedings British Society for the Study of Artificial Intelligence and the Simulation of Behaviour Conference, 1976.

[HIN81] Hinton, G., *A Parallel Computation that Assigns Canonical Object-based Frames of Reference*, Proceedings 7th IJCAI, pp683-685, 1981.

[HIN83] Hinton, G. E., Sejnowski, T. J., *Optimal Perceptual Inference*, Proceedings IEEE Computer and Pattern Recognition Conference, pp448-453, 1983.

[HIN85] Hinton, G. E., Lang, K. J., *Shape Recognition and Illusory Connections*, Proceedings 9th IJCAI, pp252-259, 1985.

[HOF87] Hoffman, R., Jain, A., *An Evidence-Based 3D Vision System For Range Images*, Proceedings 1st IEEE International Conference on Computer Vision, pp521-525, 1987.

[HOG84] Hogg, D. C., *Interpreting Images of a Known Moving Object*, PhD thesis, University of Sussex, 1984.

[HOP84] Hopfield, J. J., *Neurons With Graded Response Have Collective Computational Properties Like Those of Two-State Neurons*, Proceedings American National Academy of Science, Vol 83, pp3088-3092, 1984.

[HOR75] Horn, B., *Obtaining Shape from Shading Information*, in Winston (ed), The Psychology of Computer Vision, pp115-155, McGraw-Hill, New York, 1975.

[HOR81] Horn, B. K. P., Schunck, B. G., *Determining Optical Flow*, Artificial Intelligence, Vol 17, pp185-203, 1981.

[HUF71] Huffman, D. A., *Impossible Objects as Nonsense Sentences*, in Meltzer and Michie (eds), Machine Intelligence 6, Edinburgh University Press, Edinburgh, 1971.

[IKE81] Ikeuchi, K., *Recognition of 3D Objects Using the Extended Gaussian Image*, Proceedings 7th IJCAI, pp595-600, 1981.

[INO84] Inokuchi, S., Sato, K., Matsuda, F., *Range imaging system for 3D object recognition*, Proceedings 7th International Conference on Pattern Recognition, Montreal, pp806-808, 1984.

[JAR83] Jarvis, R. A., *A laser time-of-flight range scanner for robotic vision*, IEEE Transactions on Pattern Analysis and Machine Intelligence, Vol 5, pp122-139, 1983.

[KAK86] Kak, A. C., Boyer, K. L., Safranek, R. J., Yang, H. S., *Knowledge-Based Stereo and Structured-Light For 3D Robot Vision*, in Rosenfeld (ed), Techniques for 3-D Machine Perception, pp185-218, North Holland, Amsterdam, 1986.

[KAN79] Kanade, T., *A Theory of the Origami World*, Proceedings 6th IJCAI, pp454-456, 1979.

[KAN81] Kanade, T., Asada, H., *Non-contact Visual Three-Dimensional Ranging Devices*, Proceedings SPIE - International Society for Optical Engineering, pp48-53, April 1981.

[KEN83] Kender, J. R., *Environment Labelings in Low-Level Image Understanding*, Proceedings 8th IJCAI, pp1104-1107, 1983.

[KOE77] Koenderink, J. J., van Doorn, A. J., *How an ambulant observer can construct a model of the environment from the geometrical structure of the visual inflow*, in Hauske and Butenandt (eds), KYBERNETIK, pp224-247, 1977.

[KOE82] Koenderink, J. J., van Doorn, A. J., *The Shape of Smooth Objects and the Way Contours End*, Perception, Vol 11, pp129-137, 1982.

[KOS79] Koshikawa, K., *A Polarimetric Approach to Shape Understanding of Glossy Objects*, Proceedings 6th IJCAI, pp493-495, 1979.

[LON80] Longuet-Higgins, H. C., Prazdny, K., *The interpretation of a moving retinal image*, Proceedings of the Royal Society, Vol. B208, pp358-397, 1980.

[LOW84] Lowe, D. G., Binford, T. O., *Perceptual Organization as a Basis for Visual Recognition*, Proceedings ANCAI-84, pp255-260, 1984.

[LOW85] Lowe, D. G., *Visual Recognition from Spatial Correspondence and Perceptual Organization*, Proceedings 9th IJCAI, pp953-959, 1985.

[LUX83] Lux, A., Souvignier, V., *PVV - a Goal-Oriented System for Industrial Vision*, Proceedings 8th IJCAI, pp1121-1124, 1983.

[MAC73] Mackworth, A., *Interpreting Pictures of Polyhedral Scenes*, Artificial Intelligence, Vol 14, pp121-137, 1973.

[MAR78] Marr, D., Nishihara, H. K., *Representation and Recognition of the Spatial Organization of Three Dimensional Shapes*, Proceedings of the Royal Society, Vol. B200, pp 269-294, 1978.

[MAR82] Marr, D., Vision, pubs: W.H. Freeman and Co., San Francisco, 1982.

[MAY80] Mayhew, J., Frisby, J., *Computational and Psychophysical Studies Towards a Theory of Human Stereopsis*, Proceedings British Society for the Study of Artificial Intelligence and the Simulation of Behaviour Conference, July 1980.

[**MCI88**] McIvor, A. M., *An Analysis of Lowe's Model-based Vision System*, Proceedings 4th Alvey Vision Conference, pp73-78, 1988.

[**MIL68**] Miller, W. F., Shaw, A. C., *Linguistic Methods in Picture Processing - a Survey*, AFIPS Fall Joint Computer Conference, Vol 33, Part 1, p279, 1968.

[**MIN75**] Minsky, M. *A Framework for Representing Knowledge*, in Winston (ed), The Psychology of Computer Vision, pp 211-277, McGraw-Hill, New York, 1975.

[**MOA76**] Moayer, B., Fu, K. S., *A Tree System Approach for Fingerprint Pattern Recognition*, IEEE Transactions on Computers, Vol C-25, 1976.

[**MOR81**] Moravec, H. P., *Rover Visual Obstacle Avoidance*, 7th IJCAI, pp785-790, 1981.

[**NAG79**] Nagao, M., Matsuyama, T., Mori, H., *Structural Analysis of Complex Aerial Photographs*, Proceedings 6th IJCAI, pp610-616, 1979.

[**NAG83**] Nagel, H. H., *Constraints for The Estimation of Displacement Vector Fields from Image Sequences*, Proceedings 8th IJCAI, pp945-951, 1983.

[**NEV77**] Nevatia, R., Binford, T. O., *Description and Recognition of Curved Objects*, Artificial Intelligence, Vol. 8, pp77-98, 1977.

[**NIT77**] Nitzen, D., Brain, A. E., Duda, R. O., *The measurement and use of registered reflectance and range data in scene analysis*, Proceedings IEEE, Vol 65, pp206-220, 1977.

[**OHT79**] Ohta, Y., Kanade, T., Sakai, T., *A Production System for Region Analysis*, Proceedings 6th IJCAI, Aug 1979.

[**OHT81**] Ohta, Y., Maenobu, K., Sakai, T., *Obtaining Surface Orientation from Texels Under Perspective Projection*, Proceedings 7th IJCAI, pp746-751, 1981.

[**OHT86**] Ohta, Y., Watanabe, M, Ikeda, K., *Improving depth map by right-angled trinocular stereo*, Proceedings 1986 International Conference on Pattern Recognition, Paris, pp 519-521, 1986.

[**ORR87**] Orr, M. J. L., Fisher, R. B., *Geometric Reasoning for Computer Vision*, Image and Vision Computing, Vol 5, pp233-238, August 1987.

[**OSH81**] Oshima, M., Shirai, Y., *Object Recognition Using Three-Dimensional Information*, Proceedings 7th IJCAI, pp601-606, 1981.

[**PAE87**] Paechter, B., *A New Look At Model Invocation With Special Regard To Supertype Hierarchies*, MSc Dissertation, Department of Artificial Intelligence, University of Edinburgh, 1987.

[**PEN82**] Pentland, A. P., *Local Computation of Shape*, Proceedings European Conference on Artificial Intelligence, pp199-204, 1982.

[**PEN83**] Pentland, A. P., *Fractal-Based Description*, Proceedings 8th IJCAI, pp973-981, 1983.

[**PEN88**] Pentland, A. P., *The Parts of Perception*, in Brown (ed), Advances in Computer Vision, Vol 2, Lawrence Erlbaum Associates, New Jersey, 1988.

[**PIP82**] Pipitone, F. J., *A Ranging Camera and Algorithms for 3D Object Recognition*, PhD thesis, Department of Electrical Engineering, Rutgers University, 1982.

[**POP75**] Popplestone, R. J., Brown, C. M., Ambler, A. P., Crawford, G. F., *Forming Models of Plane-And-Cylinder Faceted Bodies from Light Stripes*, Proceedings 4th IJCAI, pp 664-668, 1975.

[**POR87**] Porrill, J., Pollard, J., Pridmore, T., Bowen, J. B., Mayhew, J. E. W., Frisby, J. P., *TINA: The Sheffield AIVRU Vision System*, Proceedings 10th IJCAI, pp 1138-1145, 1987.

[**POT83**] Potmesil, M., *Generating Models of Solid Objects by Matching 3D Surface Segments*, Proceedings 8th IJCAI, pp1089-1093, 1983.

[**PRA79**] Prazdny, K., *Motion and Structure from Optical Flow*, Proceedings 6th IJCAI, pp702-704, 1979.

[**REQ77**] Requicha, A. A. G., Voelcker, H. B., *Constructive Solid Geometry*, University of Rochester, Production Automation Project memo TM-25, 1977.

[**RIE83**] Rieger J. H., Lawton, D. T., *Sensor Motion and Relative Depth from Difference Fields of Optic Flows*, Proceedings 8th IJCAI, pp1027-1031, 1983.

[**ROB65**] Roberts, L. G., *Machine Perception of Three-Dimensional Solids*, Tippett, J. T. (ed.), Optical and Electro-Optical Information Processing, MIT Press, Ch. 9, Cambridge, Massachusetts, p159-197, 1965.

[**ROS72**] Rosenfeld, A., Milgram, D. L., *Web Automata and Web Grammars*, Meltzer et al. (eds), Machine Intelligence 7, Edinburgh University Press, Edinburgh, 1972.

[**ROS78**] Rosenfeld, A., *Iterative Methods in Image Analysis*, Pattern Recognition, Vol 10, page 181, 1978.

[**ROS87**] Rosenfeld, A., *Recognizing Unexpected Objects: A Proposed Approach*, Proceedings DARPA Image Understanding Workshop, pp620-627, 1987.

[**SAM87**] Sampson, R. E., *3D range sensor via phase shift detection*, IEEE Computer, Vol 20, pp23-24, 1987.

[**SCH75**] Schank, R. C., Abelson, R. P., *Scripts, Plans and Knowledge*, Proceedings 4th IJCAI, pp 151-157, 1975.

[**SEL60**] Selfridge, O. G., Neisser, V., *Pattern Recognition by Machine*, Scientific American, Vol. 203, pp60-68, 1960.

[**SHA80**] Shapiro, L., Moriarty, J., Mulgaonkar, P., Haralick, R., *Sticks, Plates, and Blobs: a Three-Dimensional Object Representation for Scene Analysis*, ANCAI-80, Aug 1980.

[**SHI71**] Shirai, Y., Suwa, M., *Recognition of Polyhedrons with a Range-Finder*, Proceedings 2nd IJCAI, pp80-87, 1971.

[**SHI75**] Shirai, Y., *Analyzing Intensity Arrays Using Knowledge About Scenes*, Winston (ed), The Psychology of Computer Vision, pp93-113, Ch 3, McGraw-Hill, New York, 1975.

[**SHI78**] Shirai, Y., *Recognition of Real-World Objects Using Edge Cue*, in Hanson and Riseman (eds), Computer Vision Systems, pp353-362, Academic Press, New York, 1978.

[**SHN79**] Shneier, M., *A Compact Relational Structure Representation*, Proceedings 6th IJCAI, pp 818-826, 1979.

[**SHO77**] Shostak, R. E., *On the SUP-INF method for proving Presburger formulas*, Journal of the Association for Computing Machinery, Vol 24, pp529-543, 1977.

[**STE79**] Stevens, K. A., *Representing and Analyzing Surface Orientation*, in Winston and Brown (eds), Artificial Intelligence: An MIT Perspective, Vol 2, p101-125, MIT Press, Cambridge, Massachusetts, 1979.

[**STE81**] Stevens, K. A. *The Visual Interpretation of Surface Contours*, in Brady (ed), Computer Vision, pp 47-73, North Holland Publishing Company, Amsterdam, 1981.

[**STE83**] Stevens, K. A., *The Line of Curvature Constraint and The Interpretation of 3D Shape from Parallel Surface Contours*, Proceedings 8th IJCAI, pp1057-1061, 1983.

[**SUG79**] Sugihara, K., *Automatic Construction of Junction Dictionaries and Their Exploitation of the Analysis of Range Data*, Proceedings 6th IJCAI, pp 859-864, 1979.

[**TEN73**] Tenenbaum, J., *On Locating Objects by Their Distinguishing Features in Multi-Sensory Images*, SRI Tech Note 84 project 1187, Sept 1973.

[**TEN74**] Tenenbaum, J., Garvey, T., Weyl, S., Wolf, H., *An Interactive Facility for Scene Analysis Research*, SRI report 87, project 1187, Jan 1974.

[**TER83**] Terzopoulos, D., *The Role of Constraints and Discontinuities in Visible-Surface Reconstructions*, Proceedings 8th IJCAI, pp1073-1077, 1983.

[**TER87**] Terzopoulos, D., Witkin, A., Kass, M., *Symmetry-Seeking Models for 3D Object Reconstruction*, Proceedings 1st IEEE International Conference on Computer Vision, pp 269-276, 1987.

[**THO83**] Thorpe, C., Shafer, S., *Correspondence in Line Drawings of Multiple Views of Objects*, Proceedings 8th IJCAI, pp959-965, 1983.

[**TUR74**] Turner, K. J., *Computer Perception of Curved Objects Using a Television Camera*, PhD thesis, University of Edinburgh, 1974.

[**WAL75**] Waltz, D., *Understanding Line Drawings of Scenes with Shadows*, Winston, The Psychology of Computer Vision, pp19-91, McGraw-Hill, New York, 1975.

[**WES82**] Westphal, H., *Photometric Stereo Considering Diffuse Illumination*, Proceedings 6th International Conference on Pattern Recognition, pp310-312, 1982.

[**WIT80**] Witkin, A., *A Statistical Technique for Recovering Surface Orientation from Texture in Natural Imagery*, ANCAI-80, Aug 1980.

[**WIT83a**] Witkin, A. P., *Scale-Space Filtering*, Proceedings 8th IJCAI, pp1019-1022, 1983.

[**WIT83b**] Witkin, A. P., Tenenbaum, J. M., *What Is Perceptual Organization For?*, Proceedings 8th IJCAI, pp1023-1026, 1983.

[**WOO79**] Woodham, R., *Analyzing Curved Surfaces Using Reflectance Map Techniques*, in Winston and Brown (eds), Artificial Intelligence: An MIT Perspective, Vol 2, p161-182, MIT Press, Cambridge, Massachusetts, 1979.

[**YAC79**] Yachida, M., Ikeda, M., Tsuji, S., *A Knowledge Directed Line Finder for Analysis of Complex Scenes*, Proceedings 6th IJCAI, pp984-991, 1979.

[**YIN81**] Yin, B. L., *A Program Which Recognizes Overlapping Objects*, Department of Artificial Intelligence, Univerrsity of Edinburgh, Working Paper 93, 1981.

[**YIN84**] Yin, B. L., *Combining Vision Verification with a High Level Robot Programming Language*, PhD thesis, University of Edinburgh, 1984.

[**YOR81**] York, B. W., Hanson, A. R., Riseman, E. M., *3D Object Representation and Matching with B-Splines and Surface Patches*, Proceedings 7th IJCAI, pp648-651, 1981.

[**ZUC77**] Zucker, S., Hummel, R., Rosenfeld, A., *An Application of Relaxation Labeling to Line and Curve Enhancement*, IEEE Transactions on Computers, Vol. C-26, April 1977.

INDEX